IMAGES
of America

ELK GROVE VILLAGE

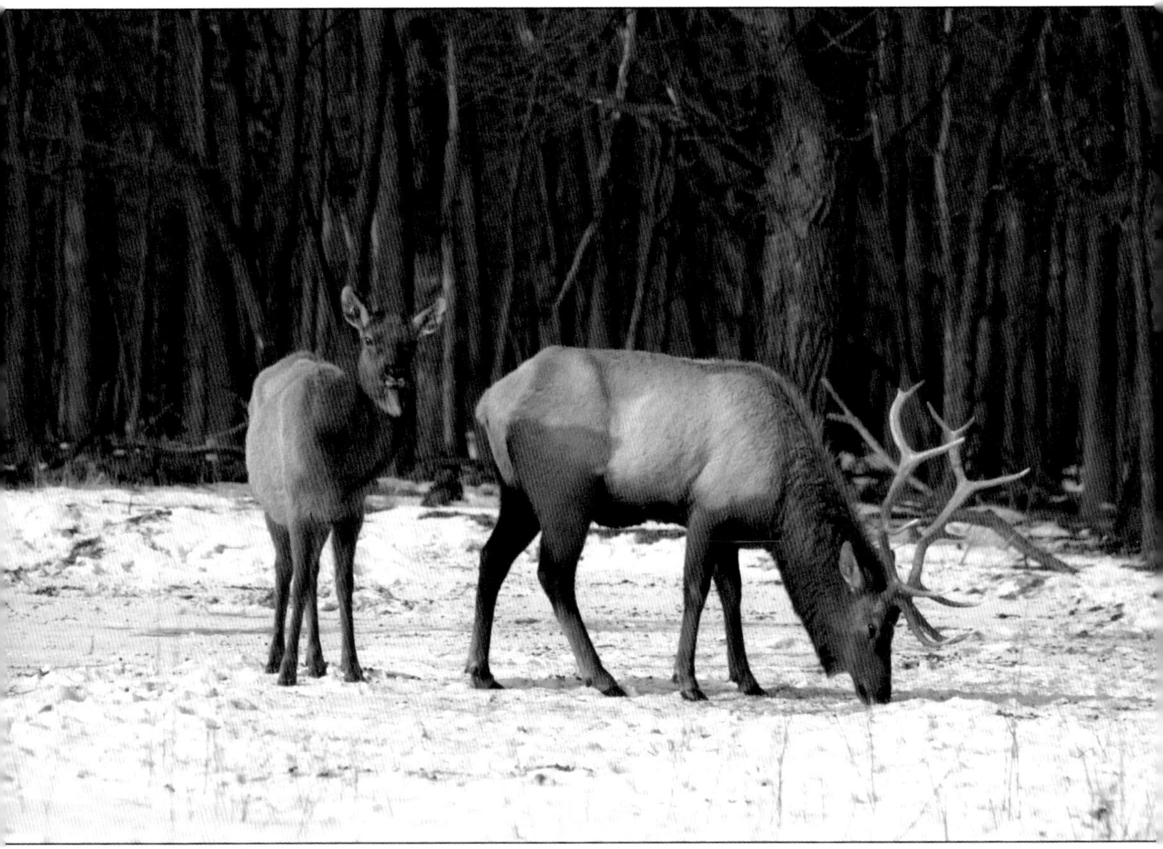

Elk roamed the area where Elk Grove Village exists today. After the land was settled, the elk disappeared. Because the family of William Busse wanted the animals back where they once roamed, they purchased elk from Wyoming and put them on their property. Today they are kept safe in an area of the forest preserve by the corner of Arlington Heights and Higgins Roads.

On the cover: Please see above. (Kelly Behnke.)

IMAGES
of America

ELK GROVE VILLAGE

Nancy Colby and Kelly Behnke

ARCADIA
PUBLISHING

Copyright © 2008 by Nancy Colby and Kelly Behnke
ISBN 978-0-7385-6165-3

Published by Arcadia Publishing
Charleston SC, Chicago IL, Portsmouth NH, San Francisco CA

Printed in the United States of America

Library of Congress Catalog Card Number: 2008929315

For all general information contact Arcadia Publishing at:
Telephone 843-853-2070
Fax 843-853-0044
E-mail sales@arcadiapublishing.com
For customer service and orders:
Toll-Free 1-888-313-2665

Visit us on the Internet at www.arcadiapublishing.com

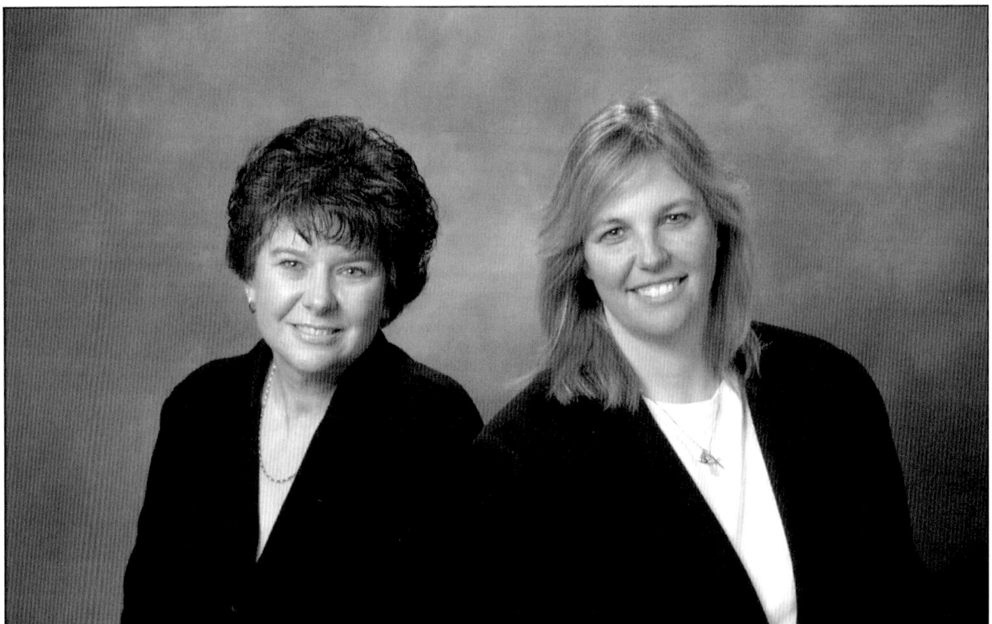

Coauthors Nancy Colby and Kelly Behnke have both been very interested in preserving history through their love of genealogy. Readers are invited to sit down and enjoy a touch of history along with a glimpse of the exceptional community today.

CONTENTS

ACKNOWLEDGMENTS

None of this would have been possible without the help of the following people and organizations, whose contributions we gratefully appreciate and acknowledge.

First and absolutely foremost, we would especially like to thank Emil Schiavo, who has made a significant contribution to the success of this book. We are grateful beyond words for the use of all of his photographs. We would have needed a couple more months just to take all of the pictures.

Several institutions were also of great help during the course of this project, including Sandy Denninger, Farmhouse Museum curator for the Elk Grove Historical Society (EGHS), for making available the use of the community's historical images; Donna Carl Dahl, director of archives, for making available the historical images found at the Alexian Brothers Historical Museum (ABHM); we graciously thank village clerk Ann (Renie) Walsh, executive secretary to the mayor Pat Droschak, and deputy village manager Matt Roan, whose help, support, and guidance provided unlimited access to the village's archive collection. Unless otherwise indicated, all images are courtesy of Nancy Colby, Kelly Behnke, and other residents.

To all those who took time, effort, and energy to gather pictures and educate us over and over again, your contributions greatly helped in the making of this book.

We extend special thanks to our families for all their support and encouragement. Your understanding during the hours that were spent away from the family while we were researching was truly appreciated.

INTRODUCTION

Elk Grove Village covers 12 square miles northwest of Chicago in Cook and DuPage Counties. It has a population of over 36,000, with more then 3,600 businesses and enterprises employing over 90,000 people and still expanding. Elk Grove Village strives to blend family-friendly neighborhoods. Over the last 51 years, the village has rapidly developed into one of the most dynamic communities in the suburban area surrounding Chicago. An excellent system of air, rail, and highway facilities are close at hand to provide strategic connections for area businesses as well as traveling ease for commuters. Nearby waterway harbors on Lake Michigan furnish economical, year-long barge service for industrial shipping. The village incorporated features such as underground utilities, curving child-safe streets, and a variety of available model homes.

Located 22 miles from Chicago and only minutes from O'Hare International Airport, Elk Grove Village has received several top awards, including Best Hometown and Fabulous Place, from *Chicago* magazine in 2006. The quality of schools, health care, recreational facilities, and housing costs were among the criteria for communities to be listed as one of the nation's *50 Fabulous Places to Raise Your Family*, a guide book for those considering moving or relocating. Residents know that Elk Grove Village is the exceptional community with traditional values; it is nice to know that other people recognize it.

Relocate-America named Elk Grove Village as one of the top 100 places to live in the United States. The village has also received five Governor's Hometown awards, recognition by the American Public Works Association for best projects, a Soles and Spokes bicycling award, economic development awards, innovation awards, and countless other recognitions. *U.S. News and World Report* recognized Elk Grove High School as one of the top 96 high schools in the nation.

What makes this town a great place to live are its dedicated officials, top-notch schools, beautiful parks, safe streets, easy commute, and the cultural whirl of downtown Chicago. Yes, Elk Grove Village has all of this to offer and more. None of this comes as a surprise to the residents of the village.

As a lifelong resident of Elk Grove Village, Mayor Craig Johnson has a strong commitment to his community. This philosophy continues today. He has never missed a village board meeting, even when he was ill. Leadership was also a trait instilled in Johnson. His father was a Cub Scout leader for him, just like Johnson was to his own children. Coaching came naturally to him as well. He loves to teach children how to be their best through sports, Scouts, or just by leading through example. He considers working with children the best part of his mayoral job. Johnson's determination is his greatest strength and asset. He works tirelessly and endlessly to achieve a goal that will benefit the community. A motto that village trustee Jim Petri says, "Politicians always do what is popular. Statesmen do what is right." Johnson thrives on doing what is right.

Busse Woods, a designated nature preserve since 1964, is a part of one of the largest public recreational areas in the state of Illinois. Elk Grove Village residents are lucky to have this nature preserve right in their backyard. Recreational activities include fishing, boating, picnicking, walking, rollerblading and biking on the many trails, as well as bird watching. It also happens to be the home of a herd of about 10 elk.

In pioneer times, elk roamed the area where the village exists today. Before 1922, the elk disappeared with the settling of the land. The family of William Busse purchased elk from someone in Jackson Hole, Wyoming, for the price of $1,250. The Busses wanted these animals back in the area that they originated. The elk were then put on property owned by the Busse family. Today the elk live in an area by Arlington Heights and Higgins Roads. Due to maintenance costs, the herd is kept at around 10 animals.

Included among the village's most charming resources are its many beautiful parks. The Elk Grove Park District, named one of the 25 best parks and recreation agencies in the United States, maintains over 450 acres of land. Elk Grove Village represents an exciting blend of all the best ingredients—thriving businesses, superb schools, a state-of-the-art hospital, peaceful neighborhoods, and a way of life that is dynamic, profitable, and immensely agreeable.

One of the brightest stars in the town's showcase of attractions is its residential neighborhoods. These tranquil and pleasant neighborhoods are abundantly lined with leafy shade trees and blanketed with neatly trimmed lawns. In various sections of town, lakes dimple the earth and provide opportunities for fishing and sailing.

One of the town's unique attractions that is highly showcased is its residential amenities. From an indoor carousel to a water park centrally located within a residential section of town, residents do not have to travel far to spend a fun-filled day.

Other areas that attract families are the local businesses. There are always many families, kids, and teams gathering at the local ice-cream spot. Still very reasonably priced, a family can find entertainment or celebrate a birthday at the local theater. These are just two of the many places families can go for entertainment.

Opportunities are abundant for all residents of Elk Grove Village if one is interested in sports. Boys and girls, young and old, can find many different teams, leagues, or just something instructional if they want to play any sports game. Two common ways youth's play is by signing up for a park district program or by joining or trying out for a junior high or high school team. Adult residents can participate in park district programs.

Prior to 1966, Elk Grove Village oversaw the community's parks and recreation program. In 1966, a referendum was passed creating a special district to manage the community's parks, creating the Elk Grove Park District. Today the park district maintains over 450 acres. Thirty-nine parks, three Olympic-size pools, and 11 tennis courts are just a few of the amenities. Residents enjoy sports like baseball, basketball, dance, golf, tennis, wallyball, racquetball, swimming, in-line hockey, and soccer to name a few.

Students in the local junior highs and high schools enjoy sports like water polo, volleyball, bocce ball, cross-country, basketball, in-line hockey, and football. Students must follow the six pillars of character while playing these sports. The pillars include trustworthiness, respect, responsibility, fairness, caring, and citizenship. By following the six pillars of character, students learn how to lose gracefully or to pursue victory with honor.

Incorporated in October 2000, Elk Grove Village Italian Sister Cities bonded the community with the city of Termini Imerese in Sicily, Italy. The bond was formed after a visit by village trustee Pat Feichter, visiting on another matter, who noted the similarities between the two communities. From the enthusiastic talks with the mayor of Termini Imerese and his staff, a bond of warm friendship has extended in both directions across the ocean, involving the chamber of commerce, Rotary Club and Lion's Club, schools, business, and hospitals. The process was then set in motion to officially establish a sister city relationship.

Elk Grove Village and Termini Imerese are located near major international transportation facilities, O'Hare International Airport and a major Mediterranean seaport. Both cities are located in major metropolitan areas, centered on the large cities of Chicago and Palermo. Each town is an industry-rich suburb of a larger city and has similar populations of approximately 33,000. Most important, they share the same ideas regarding what a community should be.

Elk Grove residents share the desire to experience and appreciate the many traditions, values, and beliefs within the Italian culture and to expand and improve both cities by generating an atmosphere in which exchange and cooperation in a long-term municipal partnership is stimulated. People will realize that both populations are more alike than different, and there is much to gain from the exchange of ideas and cultures.

Elk Grove Village Italian Sister Cities strives to create and strengthen cultural exchanges by blending both the Italian and American heritages, stimulating international trade and economic development, and expanding the exchange of information and technology, medicine, environment, social services, and education between the two cities. By promoting international recognition of people, Sister Cities is influential and educational for adults and children, making the organization beneficial to everyone involved.

Paul P. Harris formed the world's first service club, the Rotary Club of Chicago, on February 23, 1905. Harris was an attorney who wished to capture in a professional club the same friendly spirit he felt in the small towns of his youth. The Rotary name derived from the early practice of rotating meetings among members' offices.

As Rotary grew, its mission expanded beyond club members' professional and social interests. Rotarians began pooling their resources and contributing their talents to help serve communities in need. The organization's dedication to this ideal is best expressed in its motto: Service above Self. As it approached the 21st century, Rotary worked to meet society's changing needs, expanding its service efforts to address such pressing issues as environmental degradation, illiteracy, world hunger, and children at risk.

The Rotary Club in Elk Grove was chartered on November 23, 1970, and has operated continuously since that time. Recent membership includes 30 members. The Rotary Club supports many local organizations in a variety of ways, including direct financial support, assistance with projects and programs, and serving on various boards and committees. Each year, the Rotary Club offers thousands of dollars in scholarships to students that reside in the village as well as supporting various programs and activities at the schools.

The Rotary Club conceived and operates Rotary Fest, the only community-wide festival in the village, with entertainment, carnival rides, games, as well as a parade and fireworks hosted by the village. The Rotary also sponsors RibFest, a sanctioned barbecue competition. These are the primary means that the Rotary Club uses to fund its charitable activities.

The Rotary Club of Elk Grove, Rotary International, and the Rotary Foundation also take active roles in trying to alleviate suffering and improve lives in communities throughout the world. Rotary as an organization has led the drive to eradicate polio worldwide. Rotary has bridged areas to allow immunization teams to inoculate all people.

In 1962, the Peony Pageant hosted the finals of the Miss Illinois contest. The Peony Parade has been replaced with the Elk Grove Village Hometown Parade. Instead of peonies, the theme of the parade is changed each year.

In 2006, Elk Grove Village celebrated 50 years of excellence. The whole community took part in the yearlong celebration that included activities and festivities to honor the village's history and continued growth. The first three months of the year included a 50th anniversary Elk Grove Village trivia night, a formal Mardi Gras dinner dance, and children and senior events, such as the Sweetheart Dance. In the spring, the Interfaith Council presented Pro Football Hall of Fame member Michael Singletary. Residents attended a health awareness walk, a health fair, as well as other health education activities. The June events included a parade and a 1950s sock hop.

There was much anticipation during the month of July, when a lucky resident won the Hometown Home Giveaway. This home was built and donated by Centex Corporation. Anyone could buy a raffle ticket for $50 for their chance to win this fully furnished home. Ten finalists were selected to pick a key in hopes that the key opened the door to the new house. REO Speedwagon performed for the residents of Elk Grove Village after the winner of the furnished home was announced. The residents enjoyed the free concert, free ice cream, and free brownies that were given to all in attendance. Residents also enjoyed internationally recognized event Tour of Elk Grove International Cycling Classic bike race, a pioneer days celebration, a fifth remembrance of September 11, 2001, a government open house, educational activities, another dinner dance, and lastly ending with a New Year's Eve family fun day.

A new bronze elk monument statue titled *Royalty* was also dedicated to the exceptional community and now proudly stands in front of the village hall. The community of Elk Grove Village has shown pride and unity for the last 50 years and will continue to earn its exceptional community title.

The town's founders probably did not dream just how successful this planned community would turn out to be. The farms are gone; the prairies have given way to homes, there are areas of industry where businesses thrive, and there are commercial areas for shopping.

Take a closer look at Elk Grove Village and discover why so many individuals and firms find this to be the exceptional community.

One

The Exceptional Community

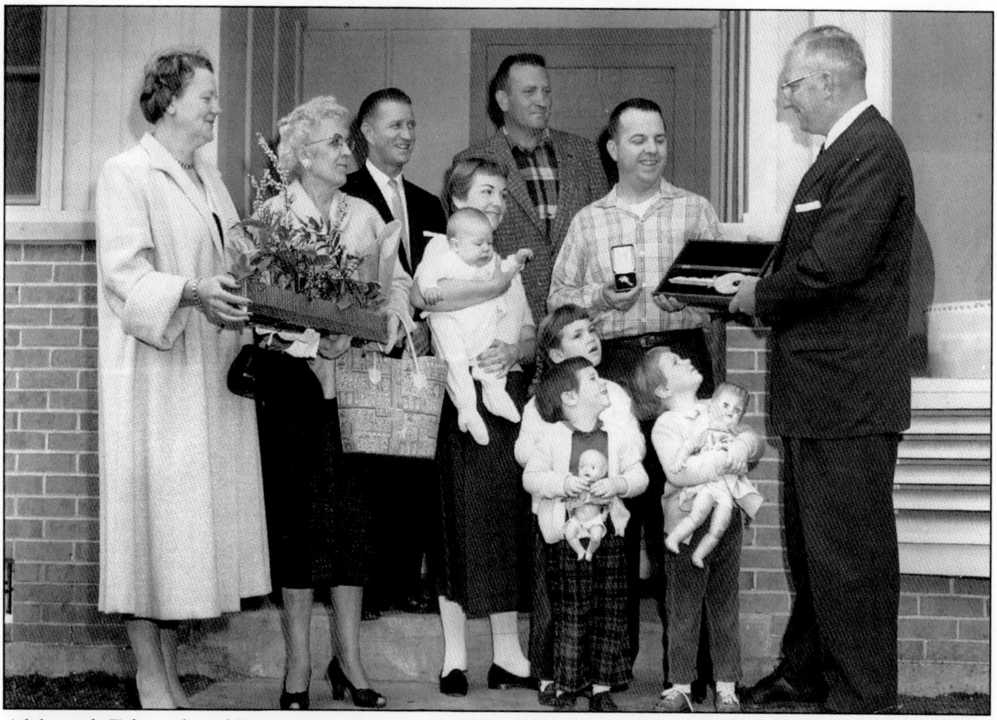

Although Edward and Emma Youngquist were the first to buy a home in Elk Grove, their preferred home location resulted in a later occupancy. Francis (holding the small key) and Barbara Walsh (holding the baby) are presented a gold key in October 1957 by village president Charles "Chic" Hodlmair and his wife, Ruth, because they were the first family to move into their home in the village. (EGHS.)

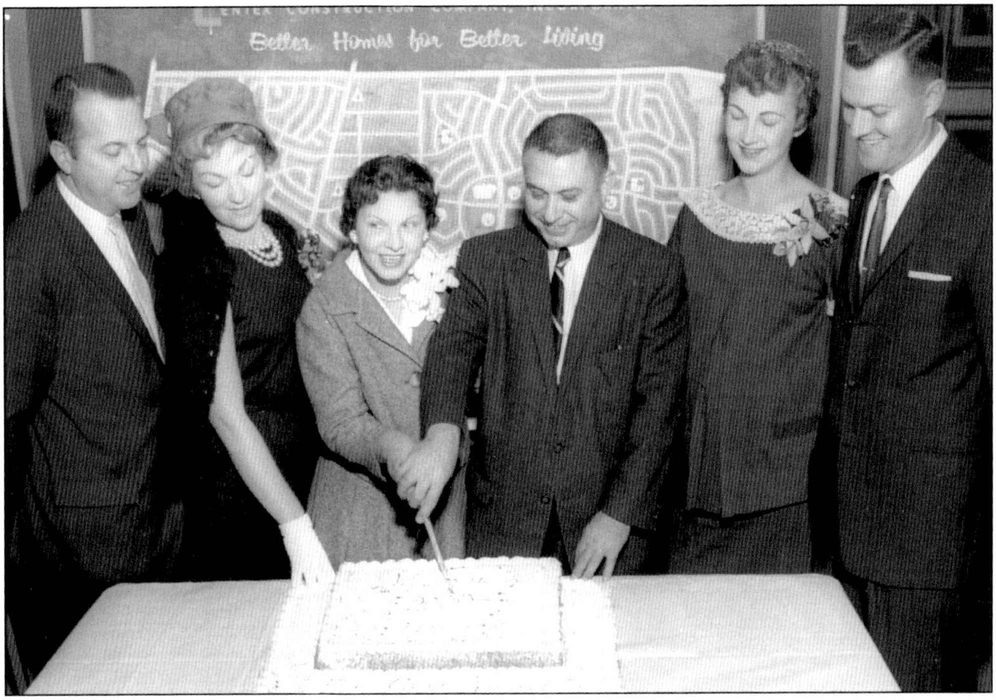

Buying a home in the planned community was cause for a celebration. Cutting the cake is the 2,000th family to purchase a home in Elk Grove. To their left is Francis and Barbara Walsh, the first family to move into Elk Grove. The couple on the right is unidentified. (EGHS.)

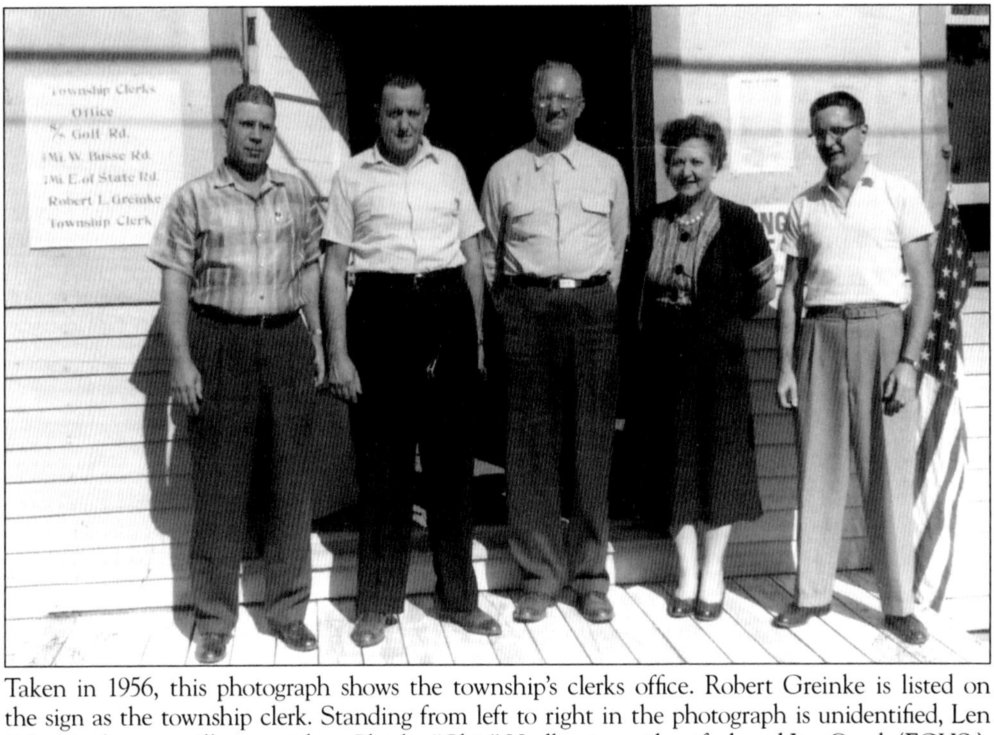

Taken in 1956, this photograph shows the township's clerks office. Robert Greinke is listed on the sign as the township clerk. Standing from left to right in the photograph is unidentified, Len Scharringhausen, village president Charles "Chic" Hodlmair, unidentified, and Jim Carol. (EGHS.)

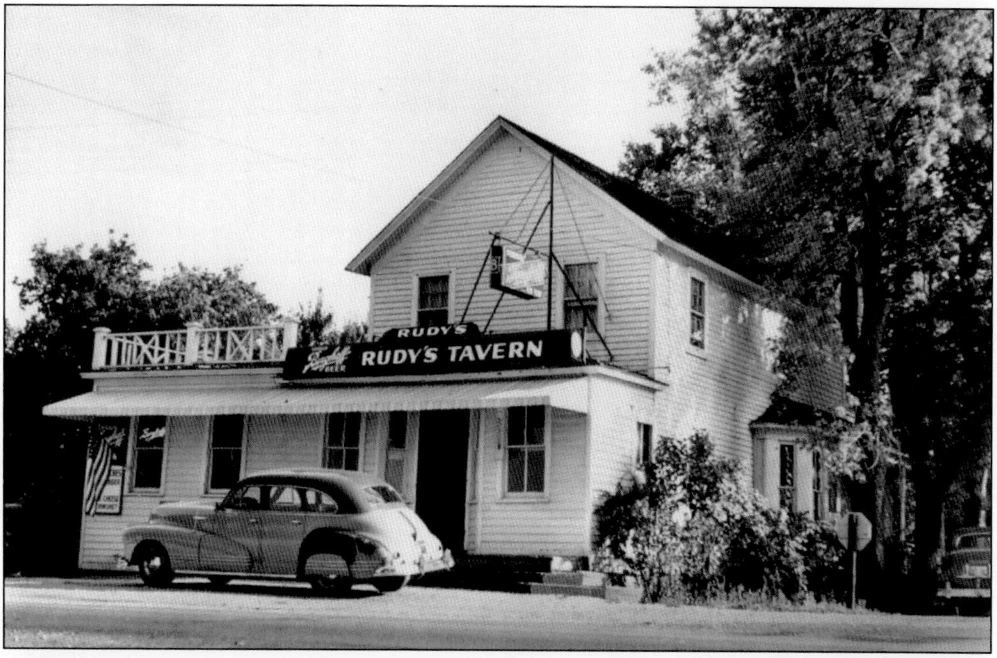

Located at the corner of State Street (Arlington Heights Road) and Higgins Road, Rudy's Tavern was a gathering place for many people heading to the Arlington Race Track. In 1956, Rudy's became a community center and the first post office for the village. The picture above was taken in 1952. (EGHS.)

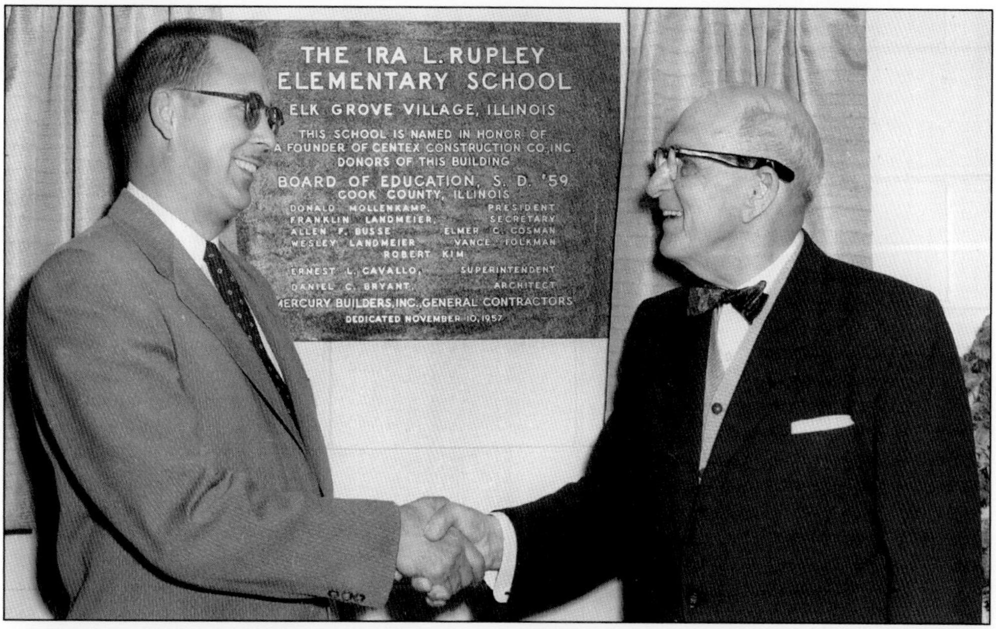

Two schools opened in 1957 to meet the educational needs of the village; Ridge School, located at Ridge and Delphia Avenues, and Rupley School, located at Oakton Street and Ridgewood Road. Donald L. Mollenkamp (left), president of Elk Grove School District 59, accepts a new $175,000 elementary school building from Ira L. Rupley (right), executive vice president of Centex Corporation on November 10, 1957. (EGHS.)

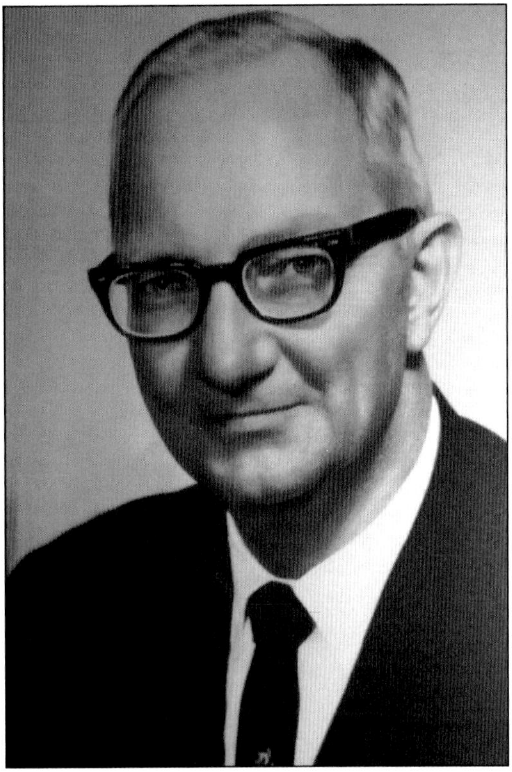

Charles "Chic" Hodlmair was the village's first president from 1956 to 1961. He had a vision of an ideal community. Sketching his idea on a napkin and presenting it to Centex Corporation, his vision "included a town that was one third residential, one third industrial, and one third parks and schools," recalls his son Scott. His ideals and beliefs are what is known today as an exceptional community. He died in 1986.

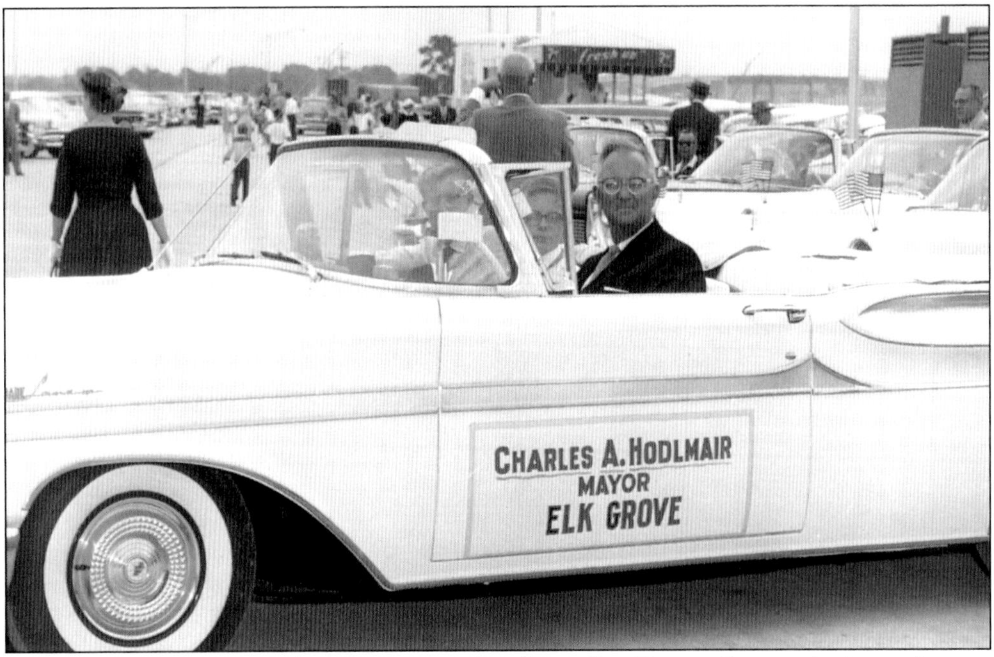

In 1954, Hodlmair was a realtor for Ben F. Eidamiller in Des Plaines. Because he knew the area that became Elk Grove, he was selected to implement the idea of a planned community. In 1956, he became the first village president, using board members homes for meetings. He is seen here during a village parade. (EGHS.)

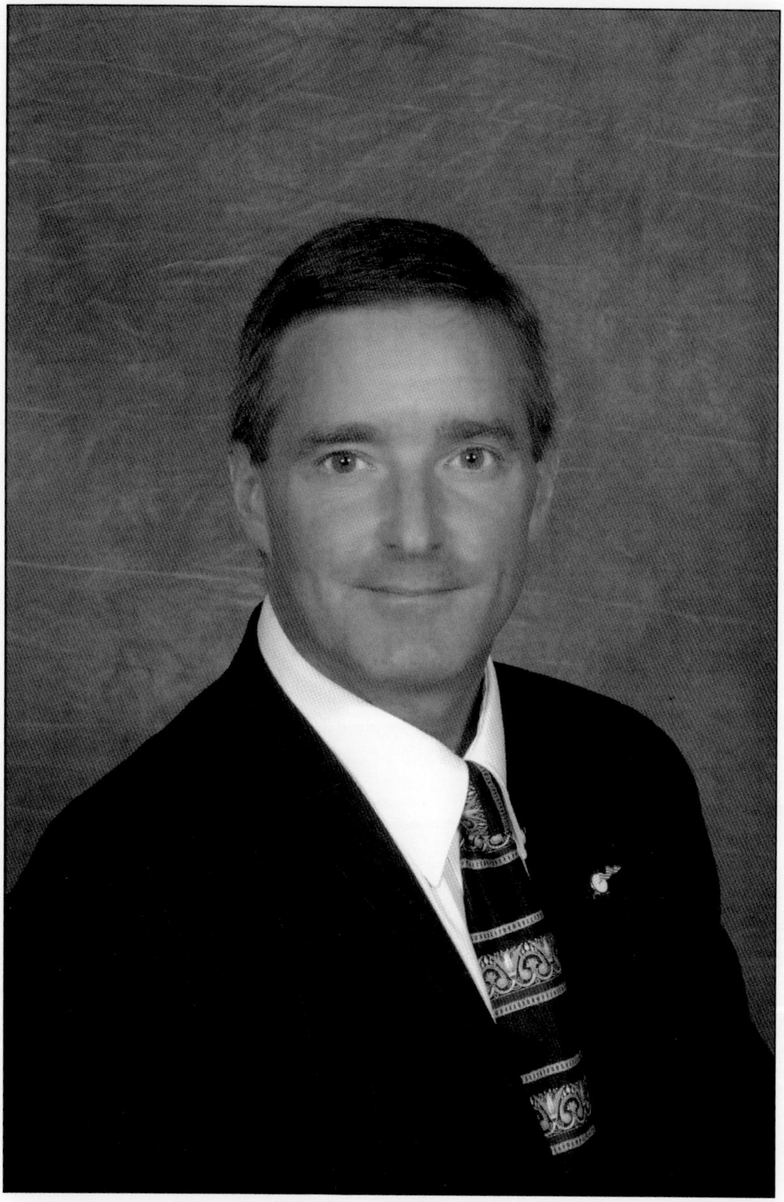

Craig Johnson was born and raised in Elk Grove Village. His family was one of the first 350 families to move into Elk Grove Village. His parents started an insurance business, Johnson Insurance Company, in 1958. Today Johnson owns the business with his brother-in-law Billy Beaupre. Johnson Insurance is the oldest business in Elk Grove Village, thriving for 50 consecutive years. Johnson ran for village board in 1993 and won. In 1997, he became the mayor of Elk Grove Village. His accomplishments are too numerous to mention. Some more important accomplishments include protecting the community borders so the village does not lose property to the city of Chicago, keeping the tax base intact, bringing a sense of community to Elk Grove Village with residential enhancements, beginning an annual tree-lighting ceremony, and implementing the Alexian Brothers Tour of Elk Grove Village bike race. Johnson's roots are deep in Elk Grove Village, and he has a strong commitment to his community. His story is one example of many why Elk Grove Village is an exceptional place to live and raise a family.

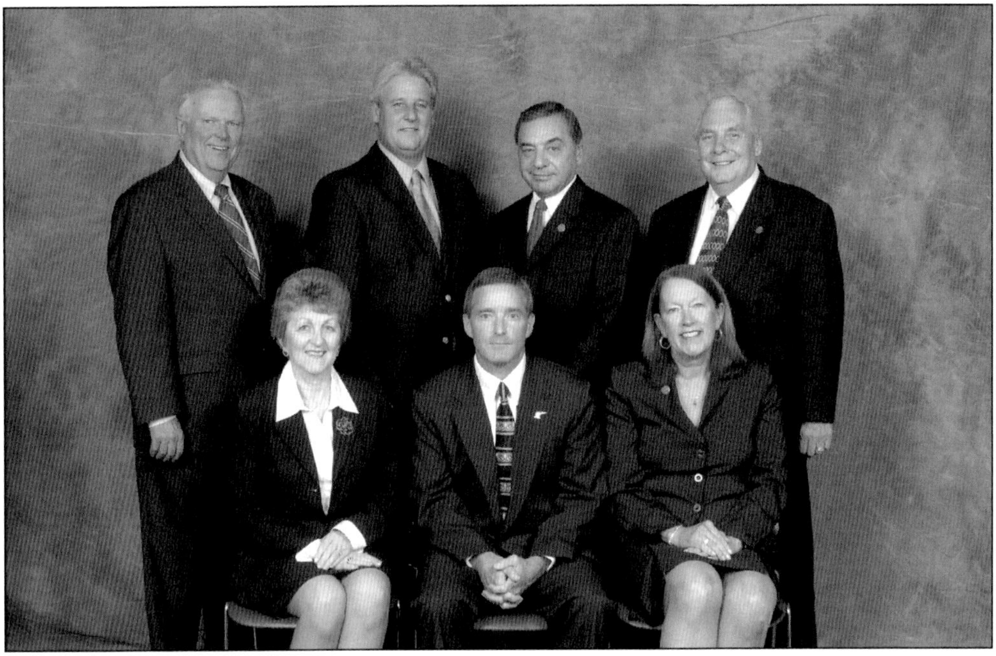

Combined, village trustees have over 99 years of service to the community. Pictured from left to right are (first row) Nancy Cznarik (1989), Mayor Craig Johnson (1993), and Chris Prochno (1997); (second row) Pat Feichter (1997), Jeff Franke (2007), Sam Lissner (1995), and Jim Petri (1979). The dates signify the years the trustees began their service.

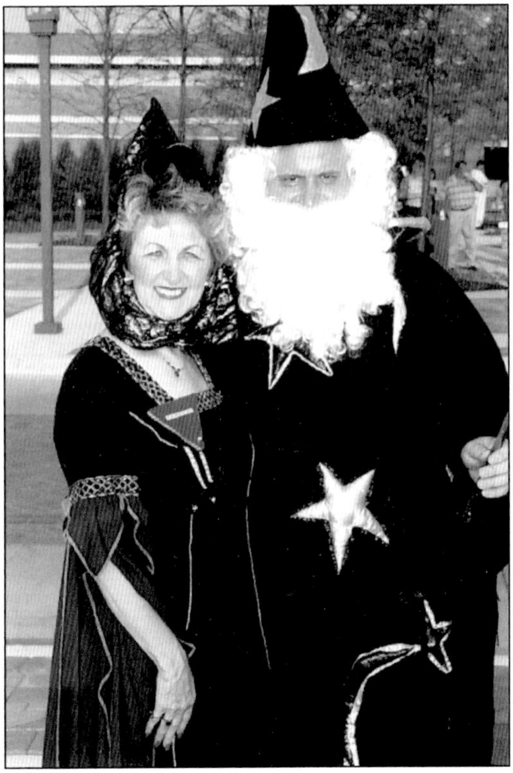

"Camelot of the Northwest Suburbs" was the theme of the grand opening to the Elk Grove Village Green on September 12, 1998. Prior to the renovation, the area was known as Grove Mall. The Elk Grove Village Green is the open area behind town center where the fountain and many bronze statues are located. Nancy Cznarik kicked off the evening as a lady in waiting, and her husband Frank was Merlin the Magician.

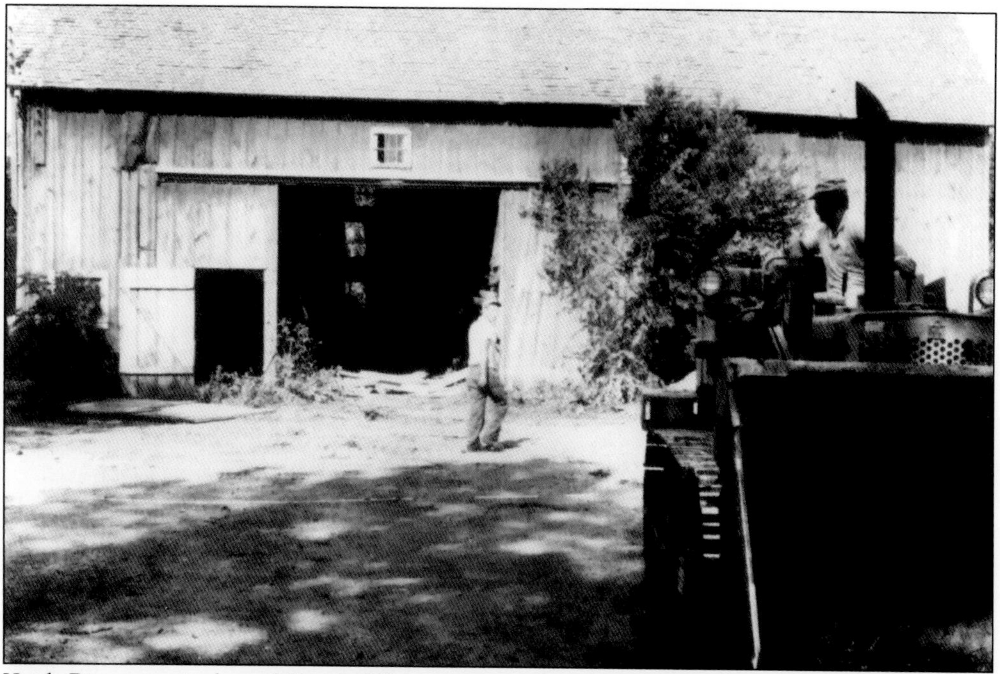

Keith Biene, son-in-law of Carrie Ollman, sits on the tractor preparing to tear down the barn in 1962. An unidentified representative from the Biene Excavating Company overseas the demolition of the structure. Having been empty for a year or two, the Biene Excavating Company paved the way to a new future by removing the dilapidated existing barn on the property that became St. Alexius Hospital. Brother Gregory Isenhart, pictured below on the right, watches patiently as one era ends and a new vision begins. The groundbreaking for the hospital was held on December 14, 1963, and was blessed by the Most Reverend Aloysius J. Wycislo, D.D., auxiliary bishop of Chicago. Isenhart was responsible for the building of the patient tower of St. Alexius. (Alexian Brothers Medical Center.)

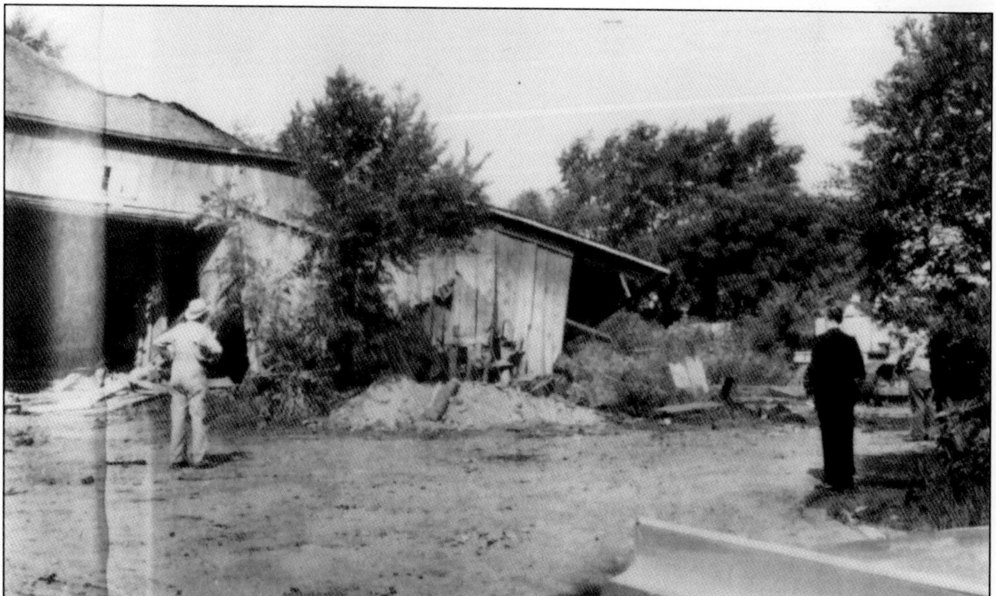

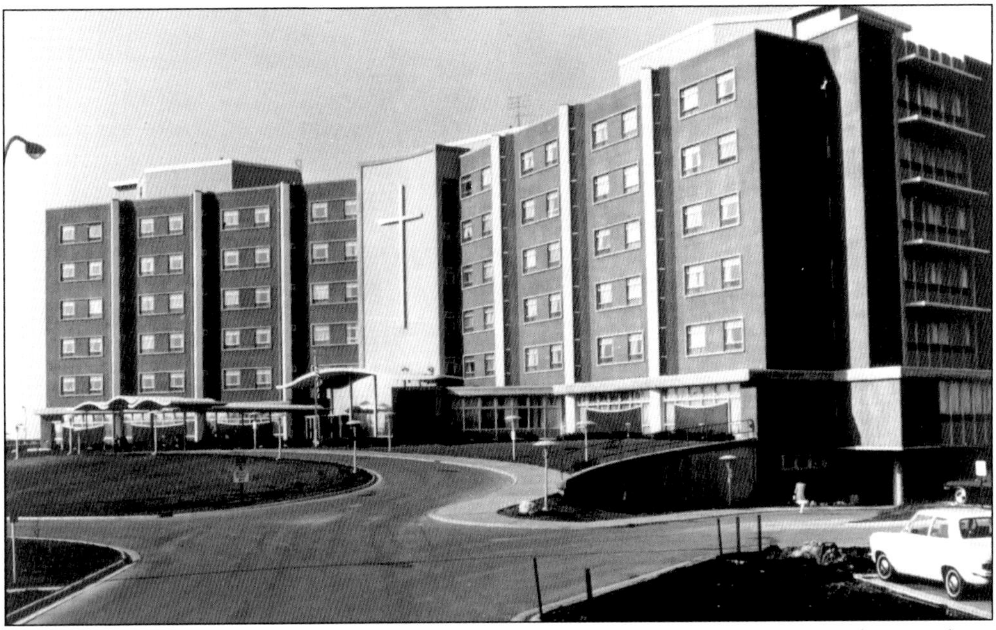

Constructed in 1966, St. Alexius Hospital opened its doors May 14, 1966, and was a busy hospital caring for residents throughout the northwest suburbs. Brother Gregory Isenhart was the hospital's first administrator. Centex Corporation donated five acres of the 30 acres of land that eventually house the hospital. In 1971, the hospital saw a need to expand with the growing population. (Alexian Brothers Medical Center.)

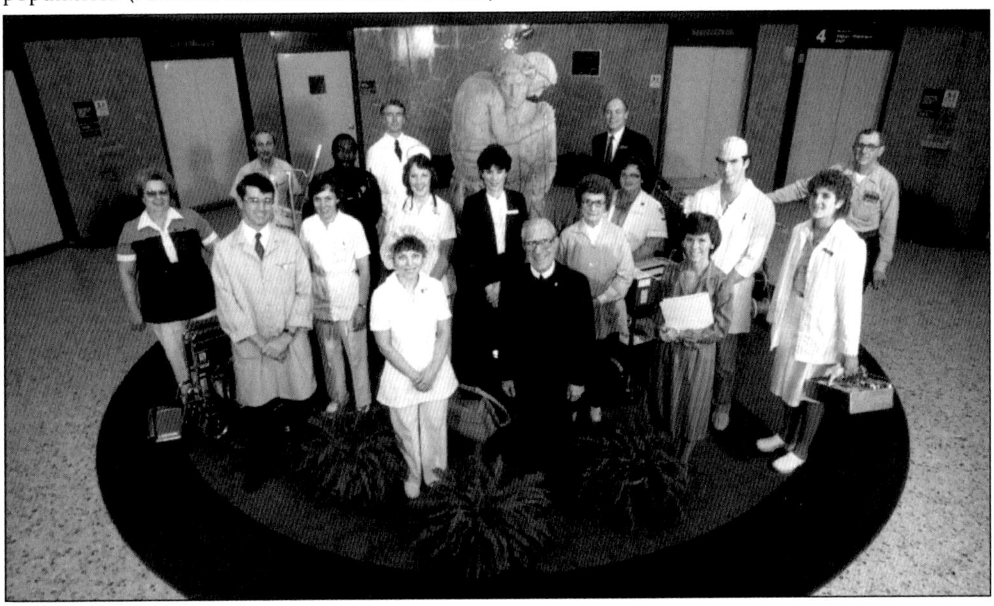

Pictured here in 1983, the staff, physicians, and volunteers of Alexian Brothers Medical Center stand with Brother Louis Roncoli, C.F.A., to illustrate the teamwork that is necessary to operate a quality health-care facility. In the background is the statue that was presented in 1878 to the Alexian Brothers in Chicago by the Alexian Brothers in Germany. Originally, this statue was known as St. John of God, but today the statue is known as Jesus the Healer. (Alexian Brothers Medical Center.)

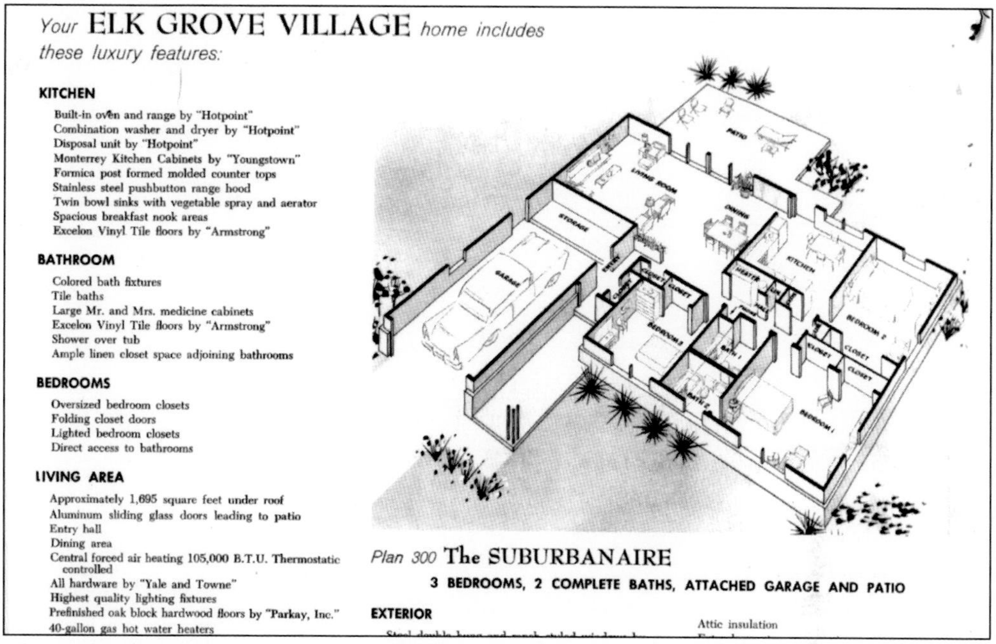

Chicagoland's smartest new suburb, Elk Grove Village, was a planned community, and those involved remained open for the evolving change in the marketplace. One change occurred when the Fox Run Golf Course was developed. Originally, there were no plans for such an amenity, but the demand became apparent. In 1989, Centex Corporation built the last house in the development. Pictured is the floor plan for the Suburbanaire luxury model home. Some of the luxury features included knickknack shelves and planter boxes in the living area. All these amenities and more afforded a buyer this 1,695-square-foot house for the moderate asking price of $19,950 to live in the beautiful picturesque suburb. Today as well as in the early years of the community, "a home in Elk Grove Village is still your smartest investment." (EGHS.)

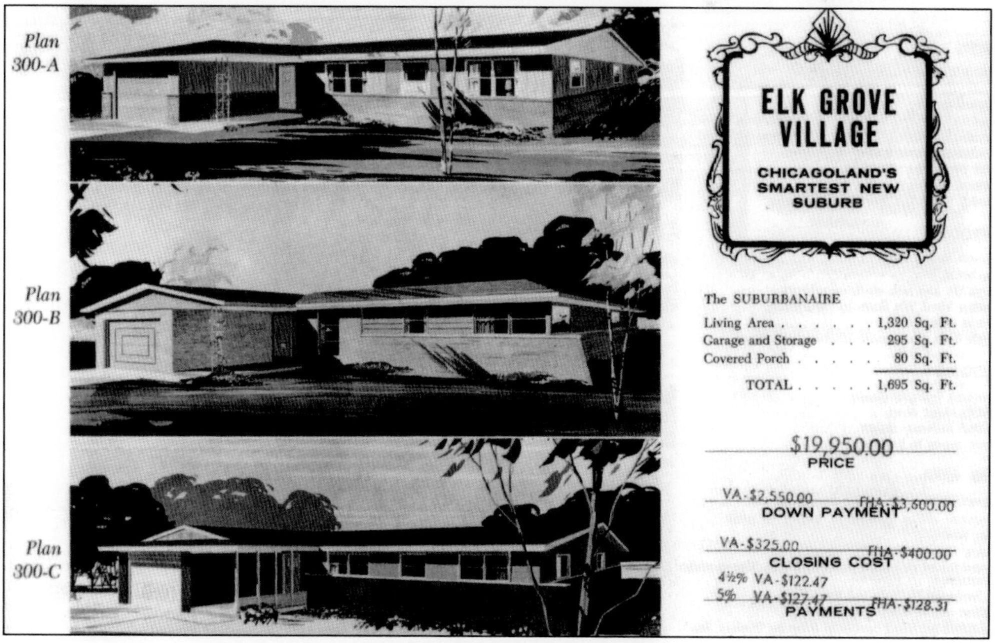

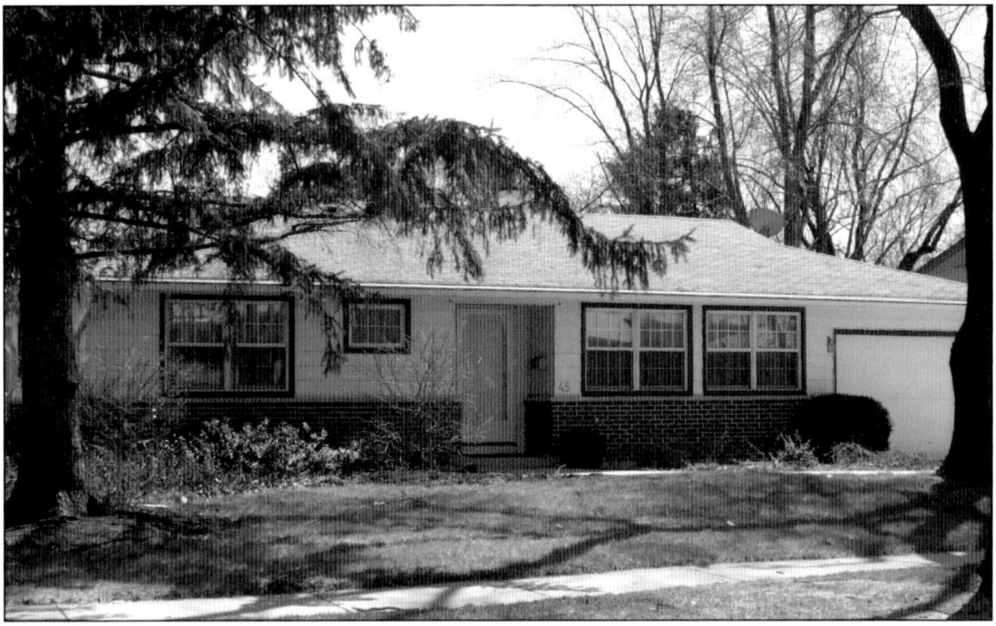

The building of the first homes in the planned community was a job given to Centex Corporation of Dallas. After the builders were identified, publicity of the new homes became prolific. To heighten the interest and excitement even more, a 10-foot wall was constructed to hide the models being built. The first house built is located at 45 Forest Lane. Houses were priced in the moderate range of $15,000 to $20,000.

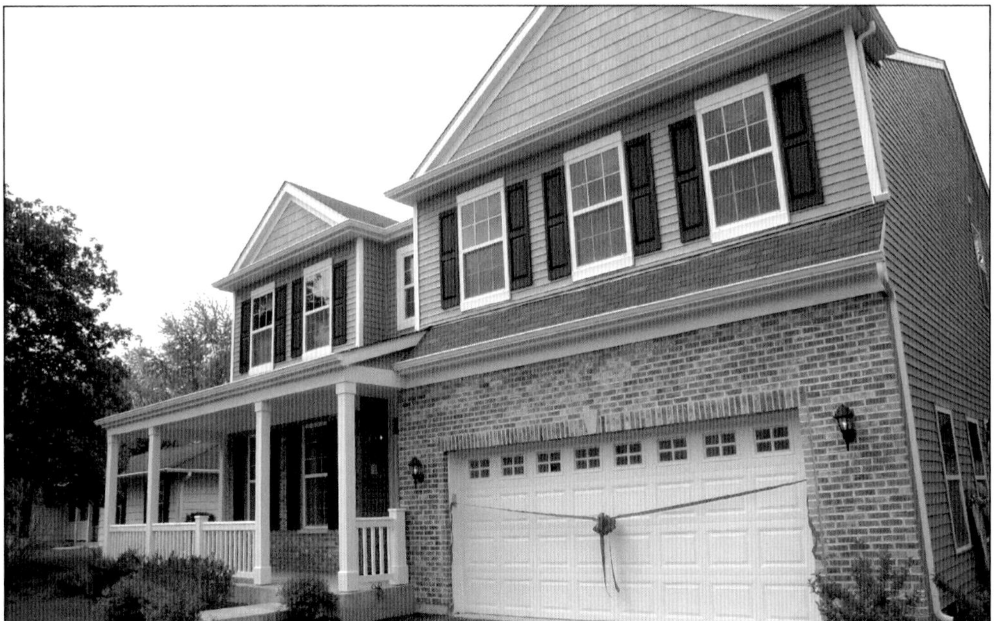

Centex Corporation had the honor of building the last house constructed in the village. Located at 1099 Cheltenham Road, a $500,000 home was given to a lucky winner of the Hometown Home Giveaway in July 2006. Longtime residents Emil and Barbara Schiavo won the newly built, fully furnished home.

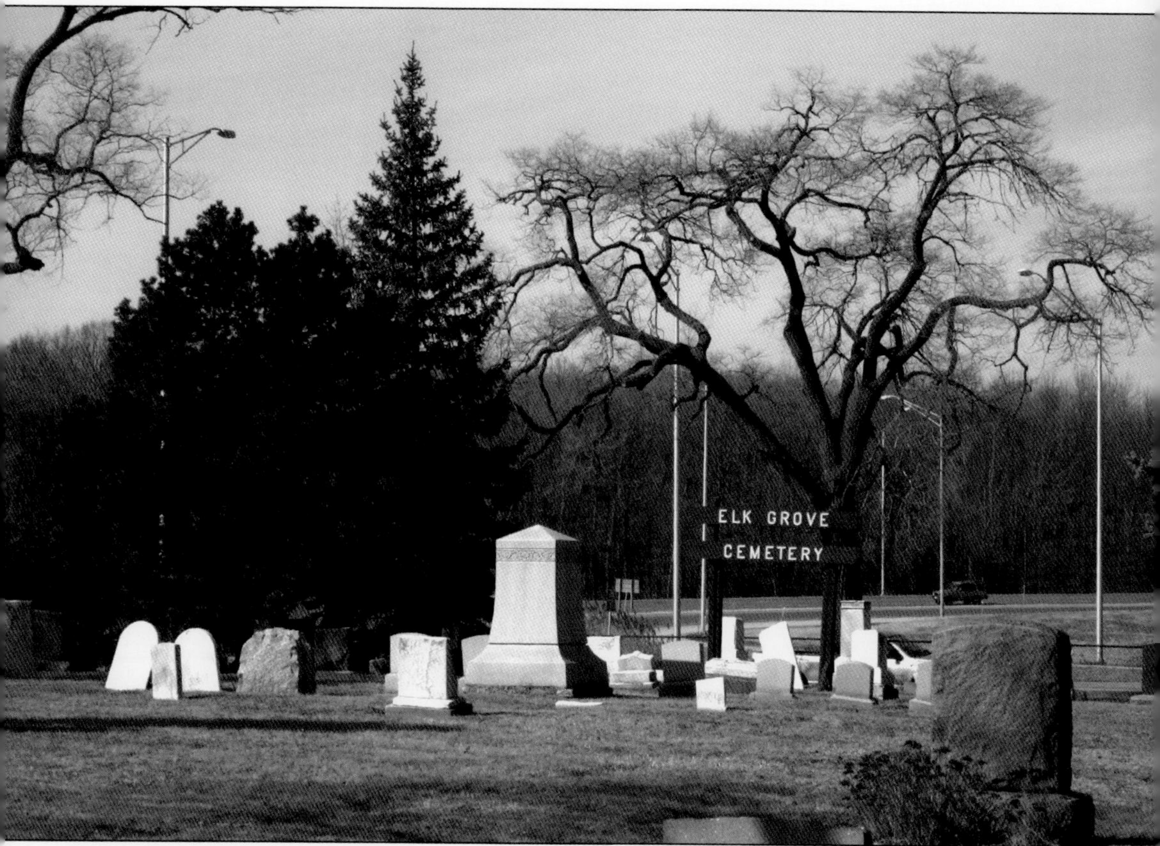

Hard-to-find Elk Grove Cemetery is a small cemetery located under the off ramp for Interstate 90 on Arlington Heights Road. It is believed that the cemetery was established when Dr. Fred T. Miner offered to bury the body of Edwin Draper, an infant less than two years old who died on July 1, 1837, on a little knoll on his farm. Three more Draper children are also buried on this same little knoll. Miner deeded the land to the Congregational Church, which came later to be known as the Elk Grove Cemetery. Visiting the cemetery, the markers depict a lot of the earlier settlers and their families. Because many children are buried there, one can guess the tragic tale of infant mortality in the pioneer days.

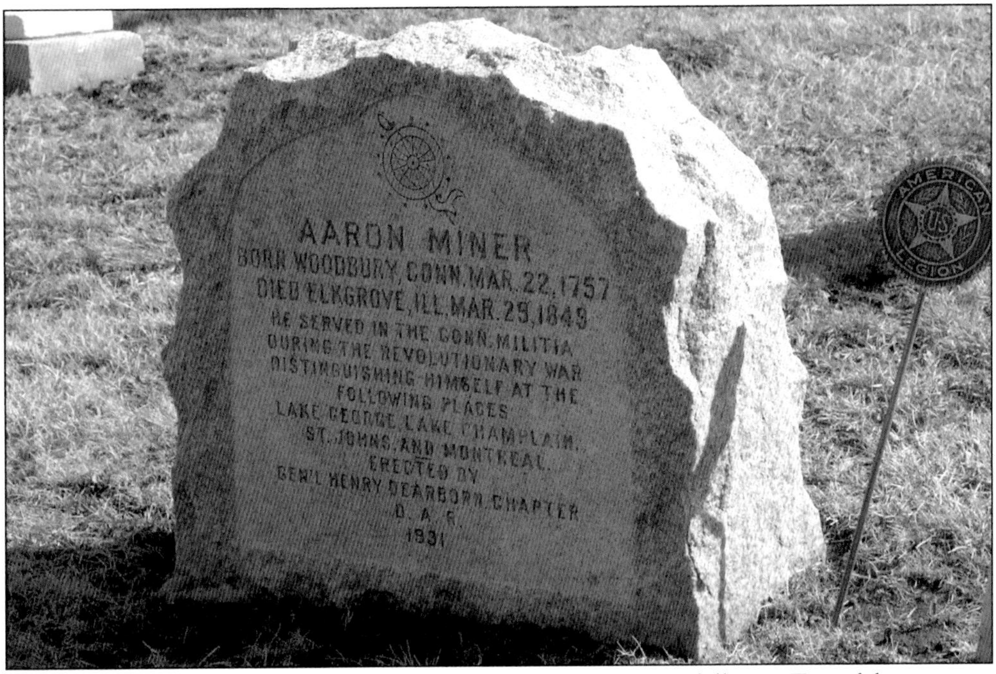

A total of five Revolutionary War veterans are buried in the state of Illinois. Two of the veterans are buried in the Elk Grove Cemetery. They are Aaron Miner and Eli Skinner. Miner was one of the first pioneers to settle in what is now Elk Grove Village. He was born on March 22, 1757, and died on March 29, 1849. He served in the Connecticut militia. In 1775 at age 15, Skinner became a fifer, a person who plays a flutelike instrument in a military band, because he was too young to enlist in the war. In the early 1830s, he moved with his family to a house on State Road (now named Arlington Heights Road) and Algonquin Road.

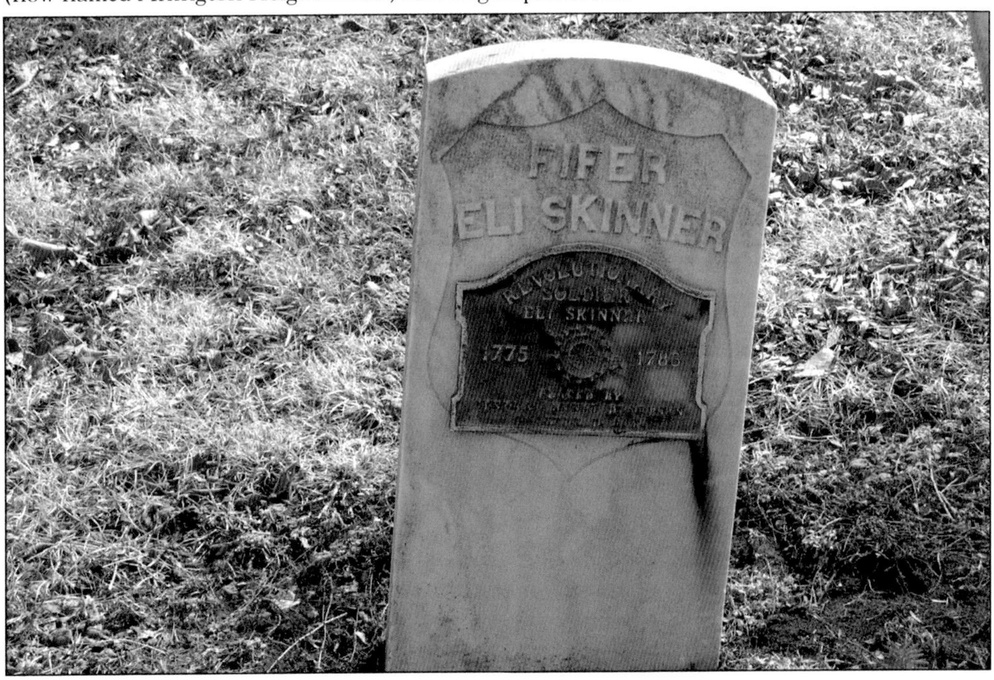

Part of the residential enhancement program was the 44-foot-tall redbrick clock tower on Wellington Avenue between the village hall and the library. This was considered the "final piece" to the Elk Grove Town Center–Village Green project. Wellington Avenue had to be narrowed from 33 feet to 25 feet in order to accommodate the tower plaza.

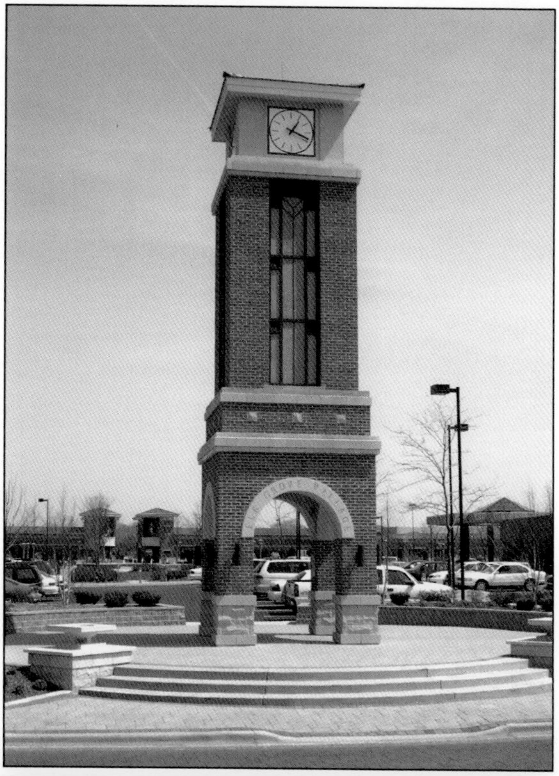

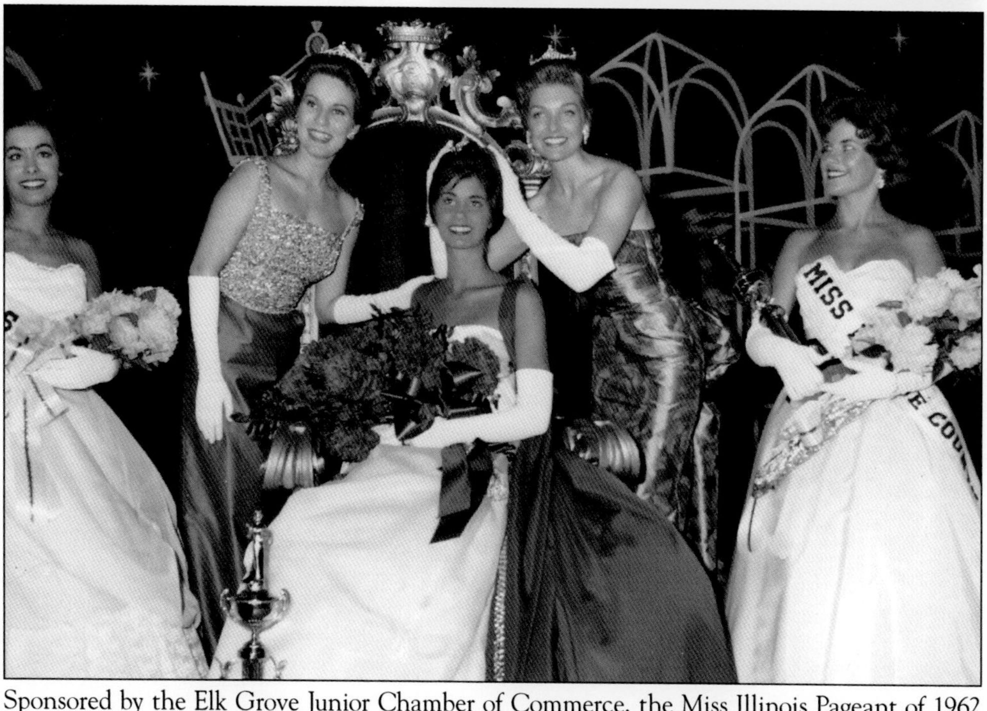

Sponsored by the Elk Grove Junior Chamber of Commerce, the Miss Illinois Pageant of 1962 was held June 27–30 in Elk Grove Village. The winner of the pageant was Pam Gilbert of Carbondale. Crowning her is the 1961 Miss Illinois winner, Jacqueline Kaye Bingert. (EGHS.)

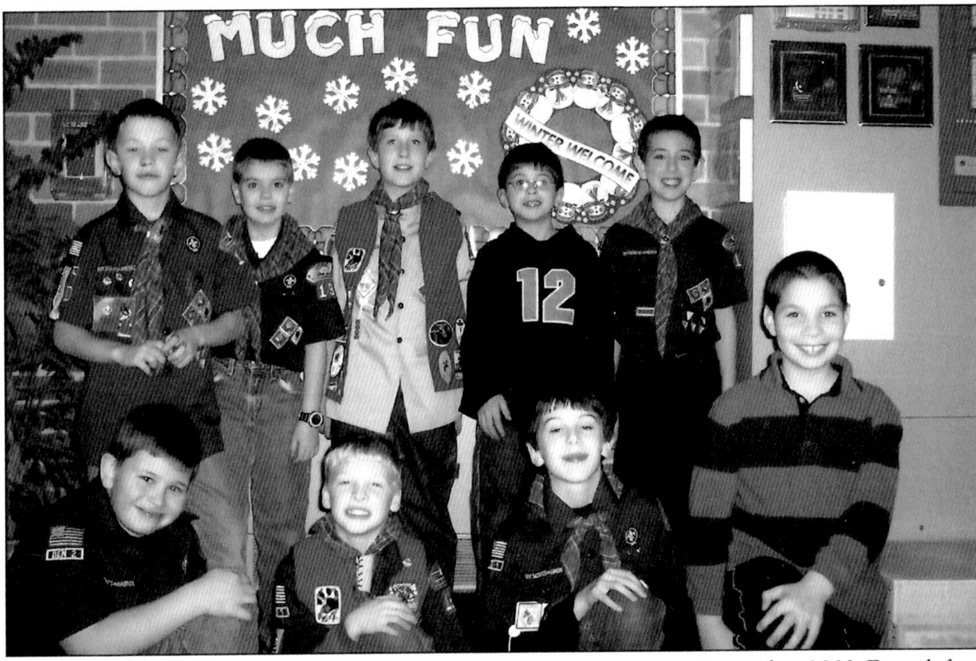

The Cobras, Cub Scout pack 199, enjoy their holiday celebration in December 2003. From left to right are (first row) John Ackerman, T. J. Kiszka, Ryan Chittenden, and Michael Baert; (second row) Harrison Fleck, Danny Loftus, Evan Barr, Tommy Clarizio, and Stephen Baert. Cub Scouts get together several times a month to participate in community service and family events.

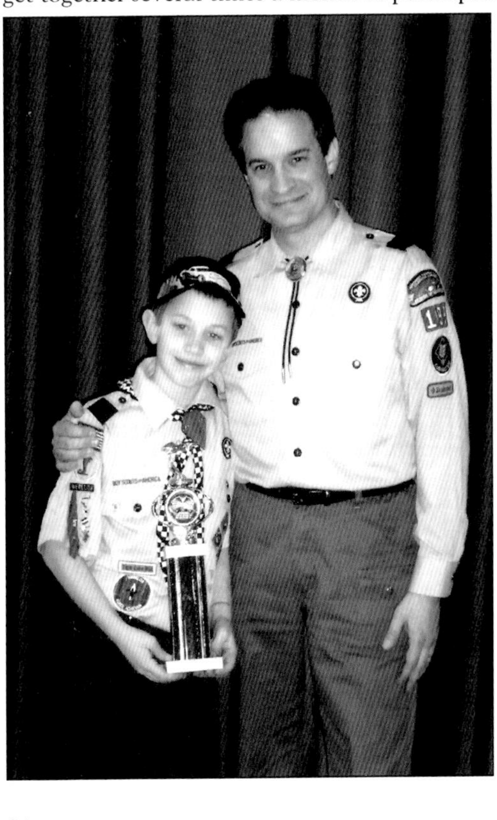

Harrison Fleck, on the left, proudly holds his first-place trophy, with his dad, Scout master Steven Fleck, in 2005. The Pinewood Derby Race is an annual event in Cub Scouts, usually held in the beginning of each calendar year. It is one of the highlights of Cub Scouts, as most boys enjoy making their cars with the help of a parent or guardian.

At a cake auction fund-raiser for their Cub Scout pack, Webelos Steven Zary and Wolf Anthony Zary proudly display their patriotic Uncle Sam's hat cake. Scouting for boys starts as early as first grade. Cub Scouts is for boys age 7 through 10, Boy Scouts are for ages 10 through 18, and then young men can be in the venturing program through 21 years old.

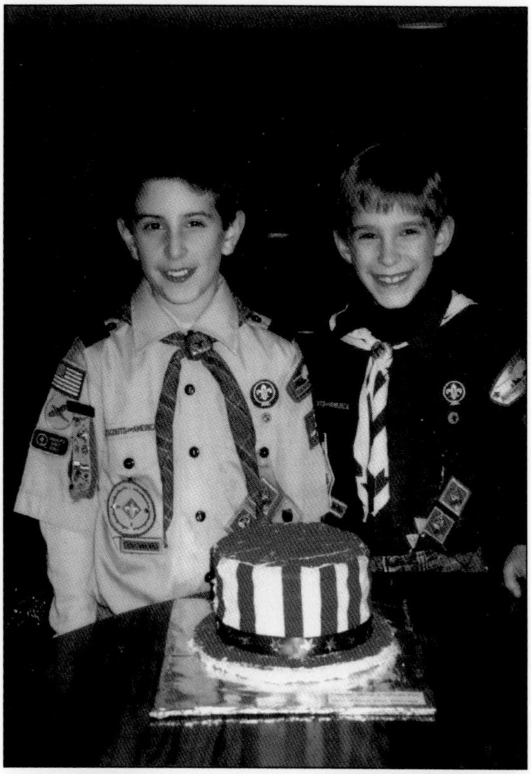

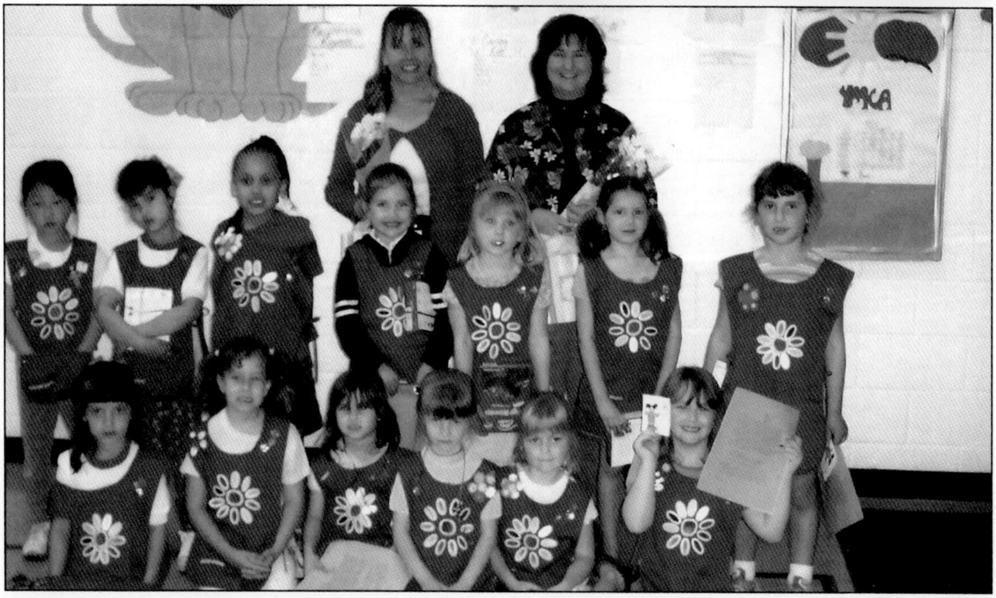

Here are Daisy Girl Scouts before they begin their bridging ceremony at Adolph Link Elementary School in the spring of 2004. Bridging is when a girl moves up to the next level in Scouts. From left to right are (first row) Ellee Fillmore, Sandra Gerhardt, Baily Hornstein, Meredith Fleck, Katie Klingsporn, and Katie Rodefer; (second row) Jennifer Bolek, Sydney Olson, Keyera Shaw, Nicole Hennings, Stephanie Stanislawski, Jennifer Shive, and Amanda Locascio; (third row) leaders Nancy Hennings and Sharon Olson.

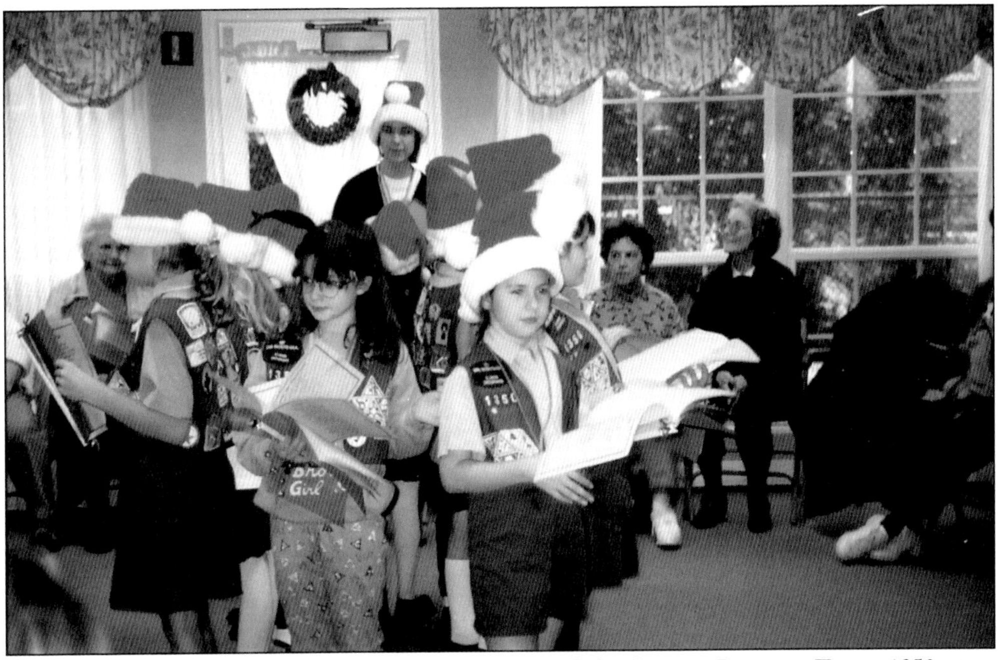

Jaclyn Ford and Katrina Sipolt, with their Queen of the Rosary Brownie Troop 1350, sing Christmas Carols at a residential nursing home. Girl Scouting begins at age five at the Daisy level and continues with Brownies, Juniors, then Cadets. Elk Grove Village is a part of the fourth-largest Girl Scout council in the United States.

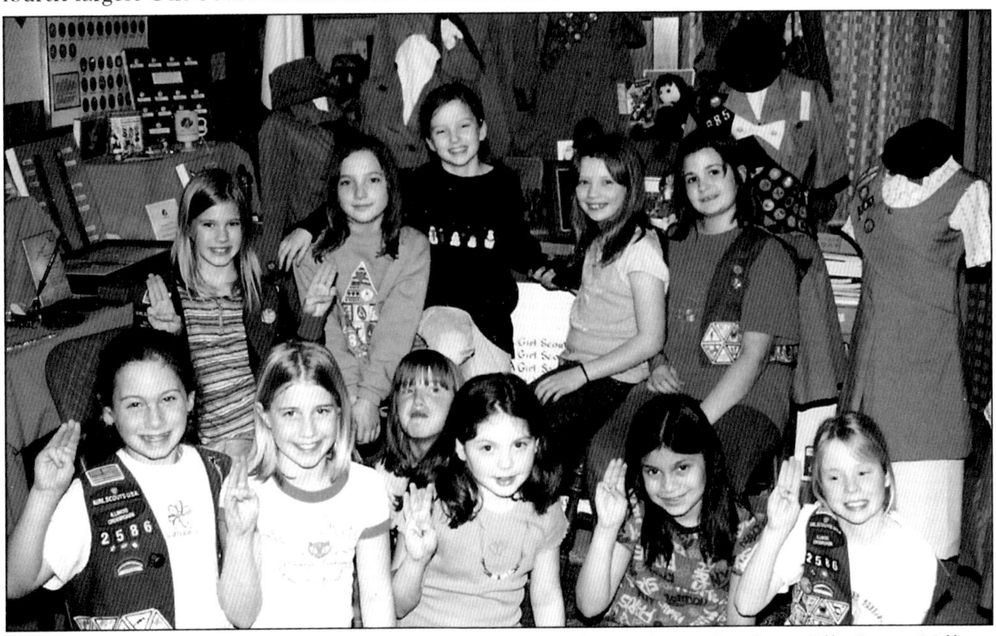

The history of Girl Scouting is something anybody can learn about thanks to Elk Grove Village resident Peggy Rogers. Turning one room of her house into a Girl Scout Museum called the Daisy Chain, Rogers has taught hundreds of girls how Girl Scouting has evolved to what it is today. Brownie Troop 2586 visits the museum where they can see uniforms, pins, and handbooks from many decades.

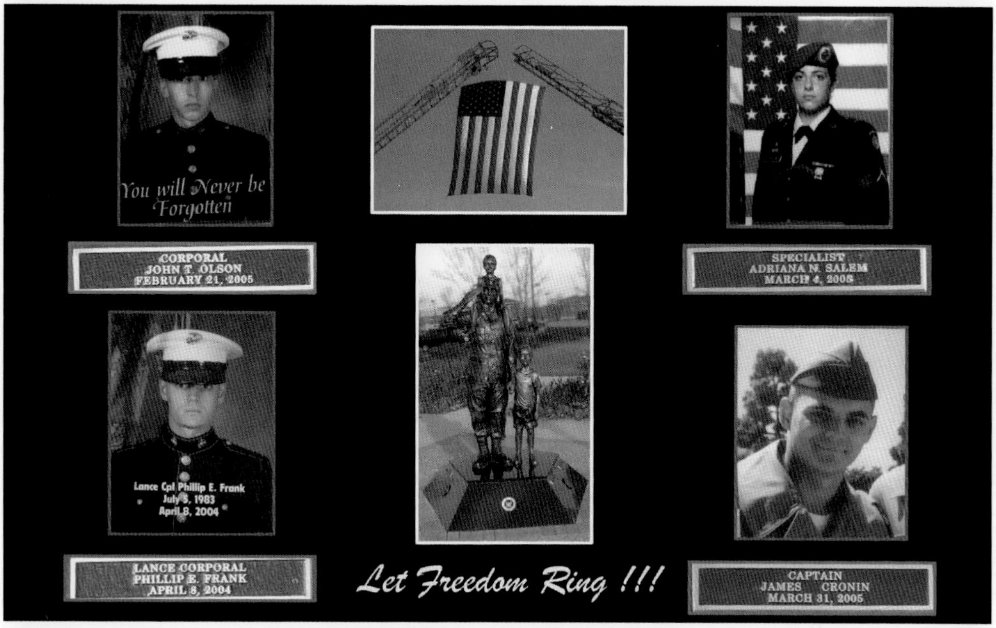

Between April 2004 and March 2005, Elk Grove Village lost four residents who served the country. A bronze memorial statue was placed near the Elk Grove Village Green "in dedication to those that serve. In respect for those that gave the ultimate sacrifice." The statue, titled *Let Freedom Ring,* was dedicated on Veteran's Day, November 11, 2005, to all former and current military personnel in honor of their service to the country.

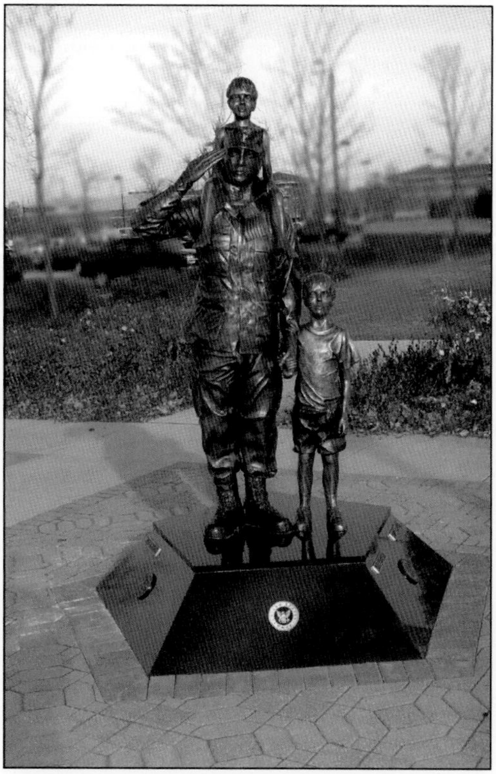

The *Let Freedom Ring* statue honors five branches of military services. Names of the fallen soldiers were placed above their branches' respective emblems. Fallen soldiers include Cpl. John Olson, Lance Cpl. Phillip E. Frank, Specialist Adriana N. Salem, and Capt. James Cronin. The sculpture was designed by James Haire of Westchester, Illinois. It depicts a member of the military with young children, representing a dual theme of military service and family.

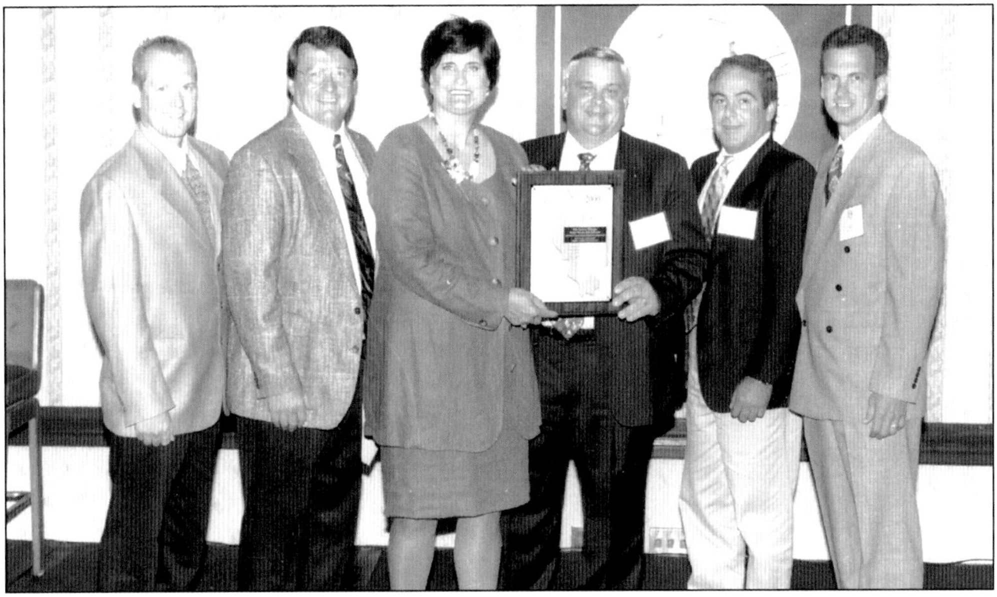

In 2000, Chief Steve Schmidt was presented with the Governor's Hometown award for Smart Parents, Safe Kids. From left to right are officer Chuck Walsh, officer Paul Syverson, unidentified state representative, Chief Steve Schmidt, Deputy Chief Larry Hammar, and Sgt. Dave Naumann. The village received first place in the category of senior involvement with its Police and Seniors Together program. The program unites seniors in the community with friends and police for assistance when faced with abuse.

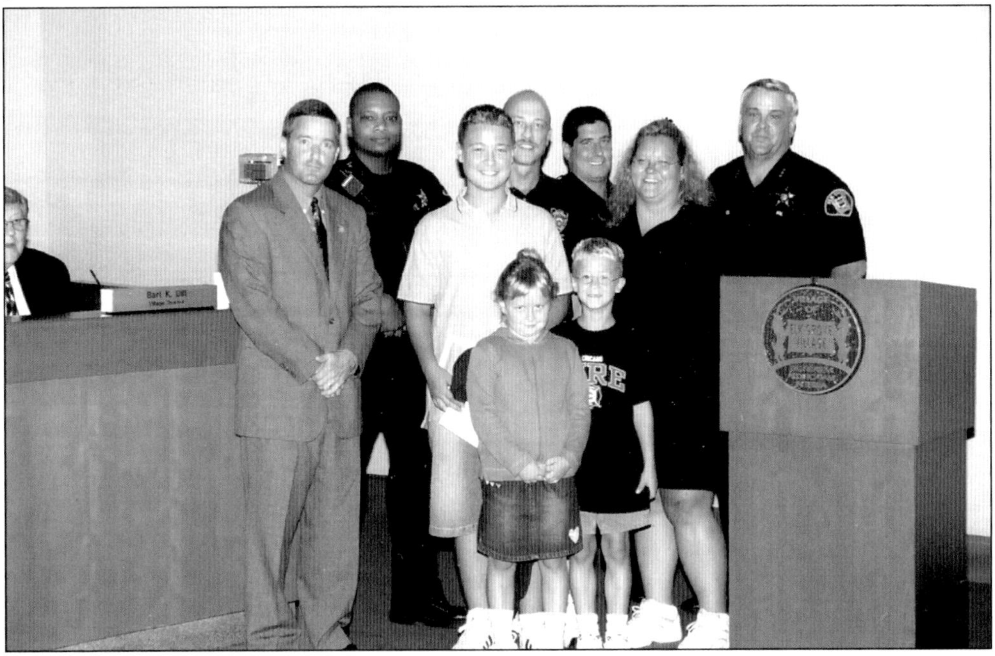

Mayor Craig Johnson and police representatives Chief Steve Schmidt, Sgt. Keith Briggs, and officer John Williams present Character Counts awards to all recipients. Televised village hall meetings are typically the place where Johnson formerly presents award recipients because it showcases their accomplishments in front of the community.

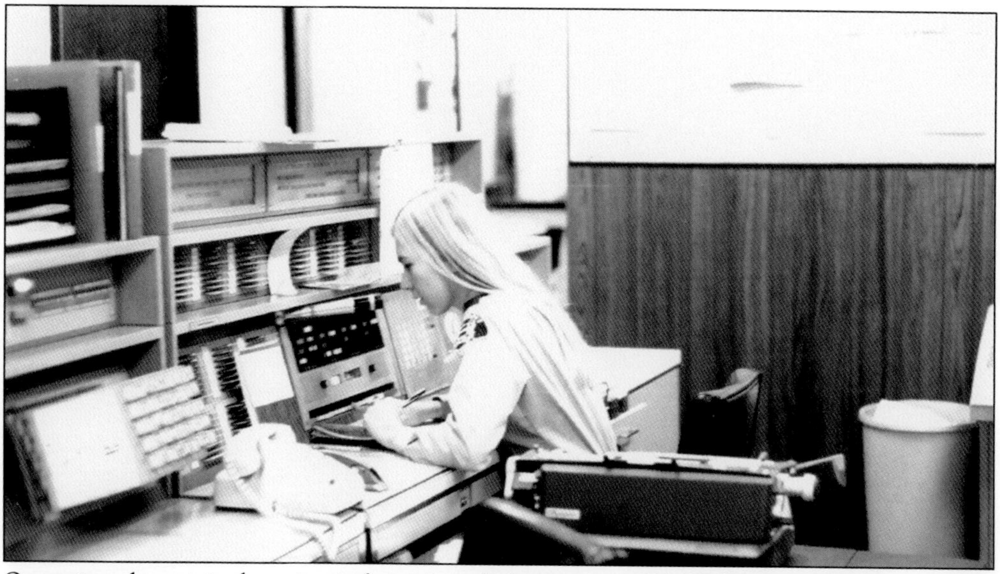

Operating the original station information desk center at 901 Wellington Avenue, an early 1970s community service officer listens to a dispatch and radios an officer at the scene. Over the years, technology has changed the way information is displayed and relayed to the proper departmental officials.

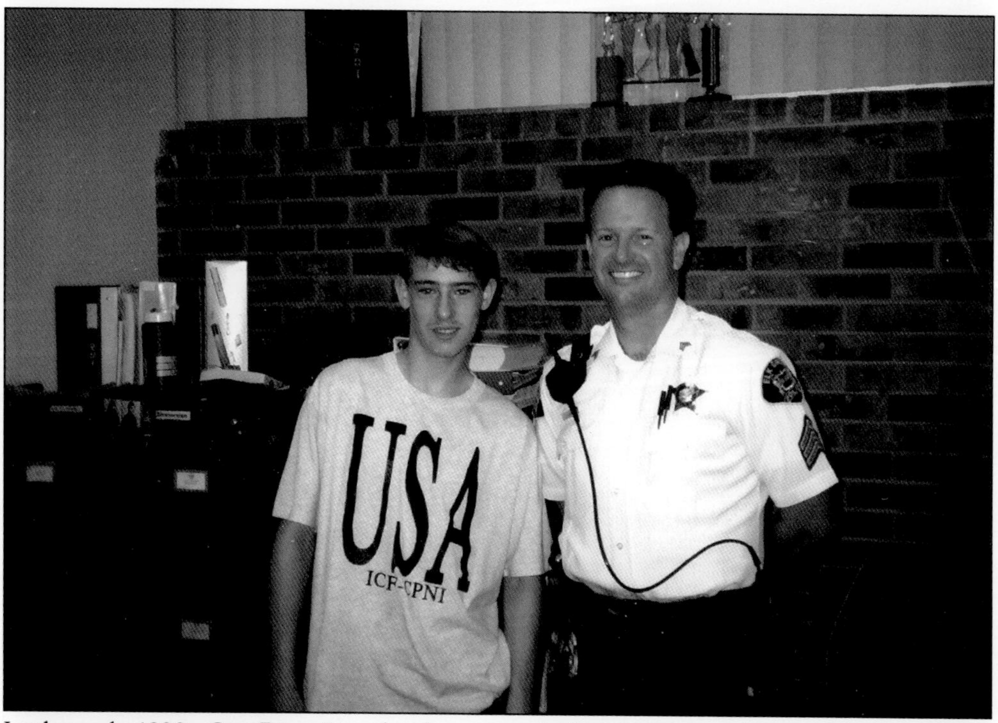

In the early 1990s, Sgt. Dion Zinnel welcomes an Irish exchange student visiting the village. Learning about other country's governments, laws, and security as well as cultures and traditions is important to the understanding that communities are different but their goals are very much the same.

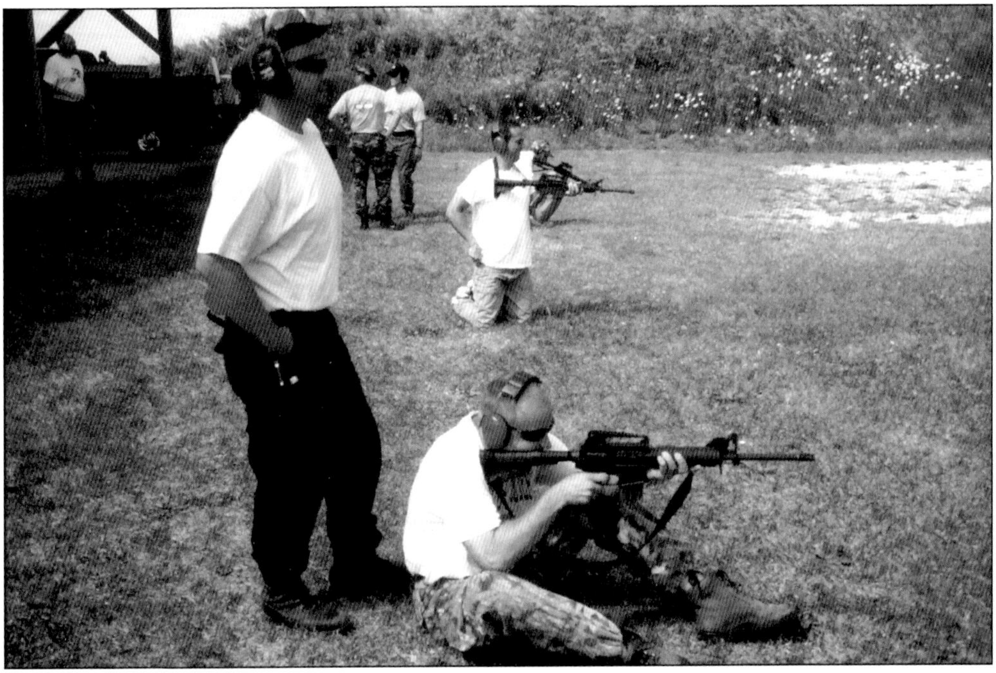

Range official Jeff Andrzejewski provides direction to Deputy Chief Dion Zinnel during a carbine rifle training session in Marsailles. Carbine training is accomplished on an annual basis at this military site. Officer Call Sabo is in the background also applying shooting skills.

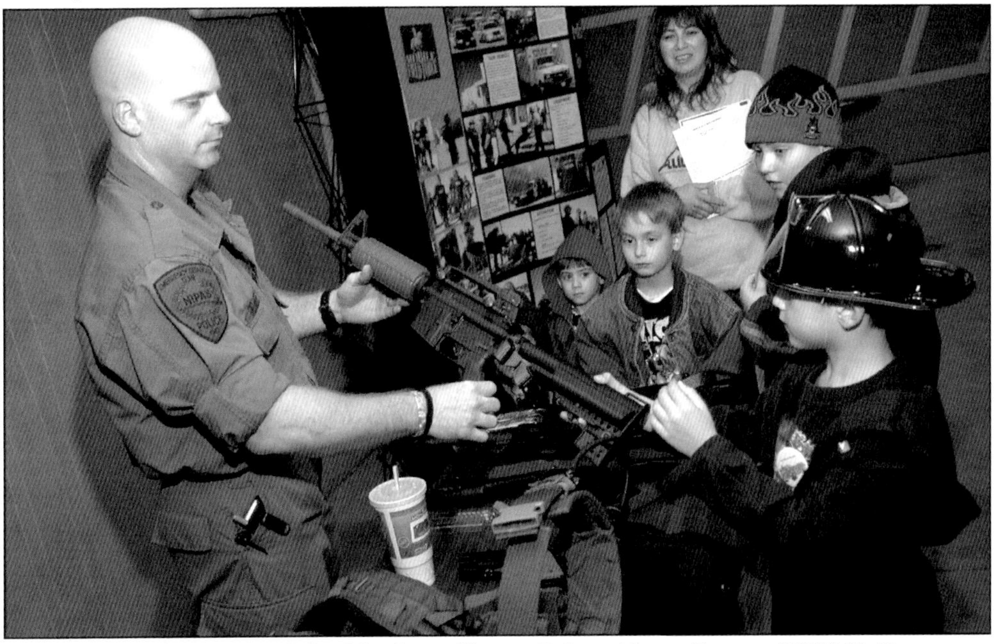

Officer Richard Gigante of the Northern Illinois Police Alarm System (NIPAS) Emergency Services team provides a special weapons demonstration of a carbine gun training to some curious boys at the Elk Grove Village open house. This gun fires simunitions, which is similar to shooting paint-ball, allowing officers to train with nonlethal ammunition. Proper gun respect, handling, and safety education is highly stressed to children and adults to decrease accidental gun injuries.

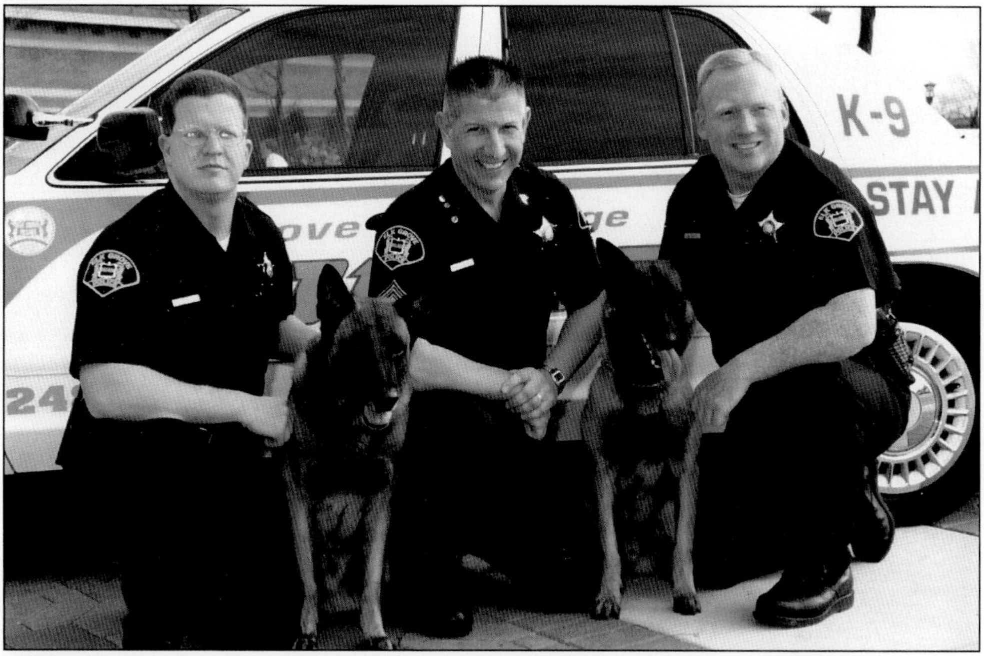

Pictured is the Elk Grove Village K-9 Unit, including officer Matt Fiorito (left) and his canine partner, Mike; Sgt. Mark Waclawski; and officer John Bazukas (right) and his canine partner, Sjowy. Canines are a vital part of the force because their keen sense helps in the discovery of drugs. Police canines are trained to capture and contain criminals until the proper authorities take over.

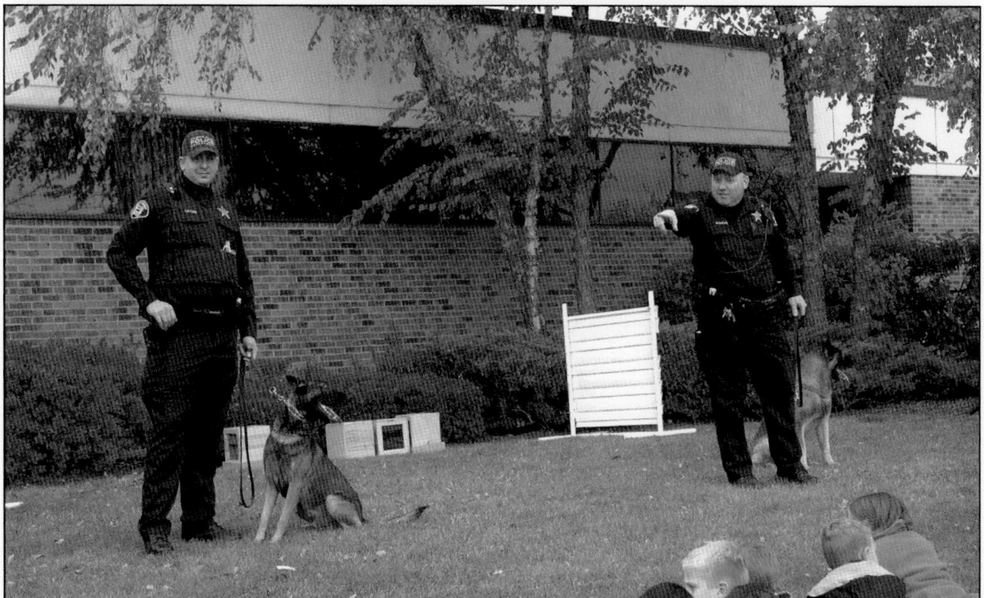

Canine officers Rick Meyers (left) with his canine partner, Vasco, and Bazukas with Sjowy are providing a canine demonstration at the village hall open house. Canines are trained for drug searches, tracking, and handler protection. The dog lives with the handler both on and off duty. Sjowy retired in 2007 after several years of dedicated service. Bazukas now cares for him as a family pet.

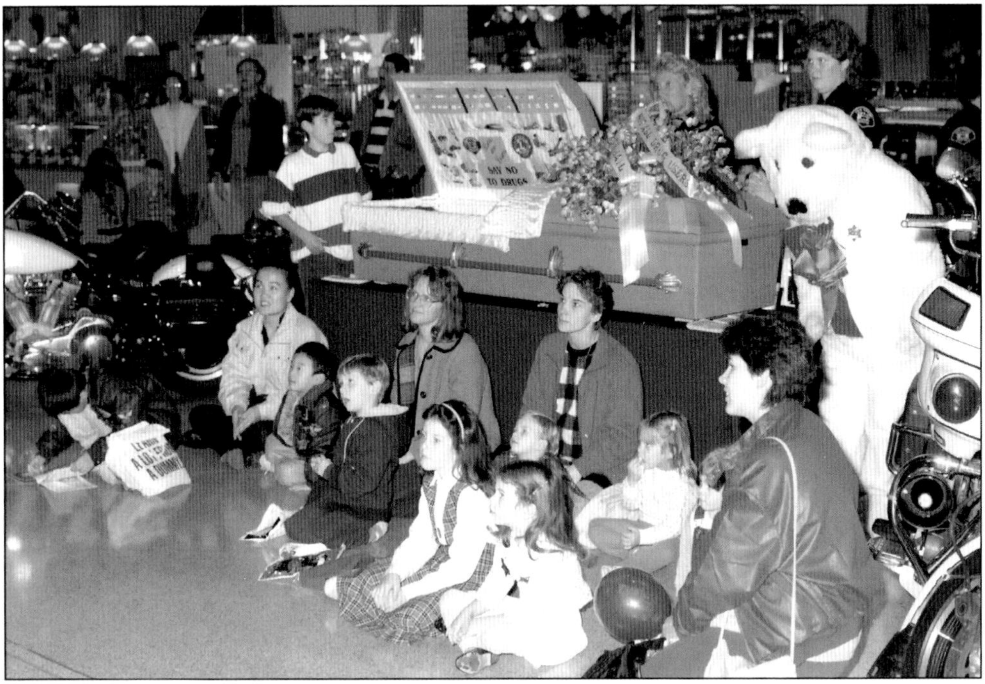

Early 1980s law enforcement shopping mall displays were used as a means to educate the public in police procedures, equipment, drug education, and awareness. The casket was an eye-catching, innovative way to express the dangerous path that drugs can take to destroy lives.

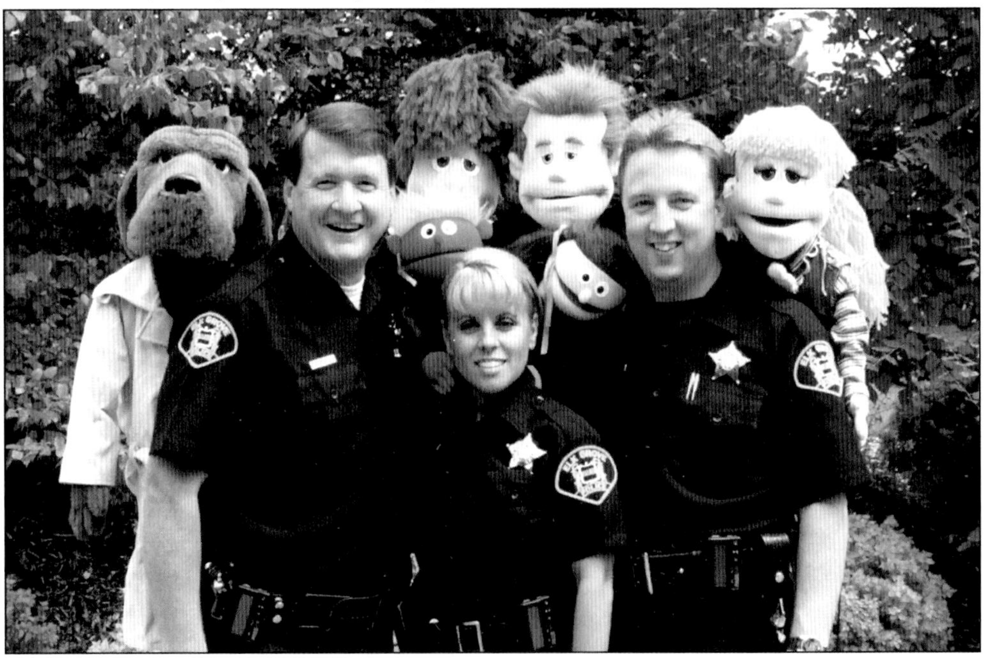

The 1990s Crime Prevention Unit, from left to right, are Paul Syverson, Deb Ruszkowski, and Tom Froelich. They are joined by their best puppet friends, which were used in crime-prevention displays for over 10 years. Children and adults alike were captivated by the puppet performances. Children were more focused on learning when the teaching was presented in a fun and exciting way.

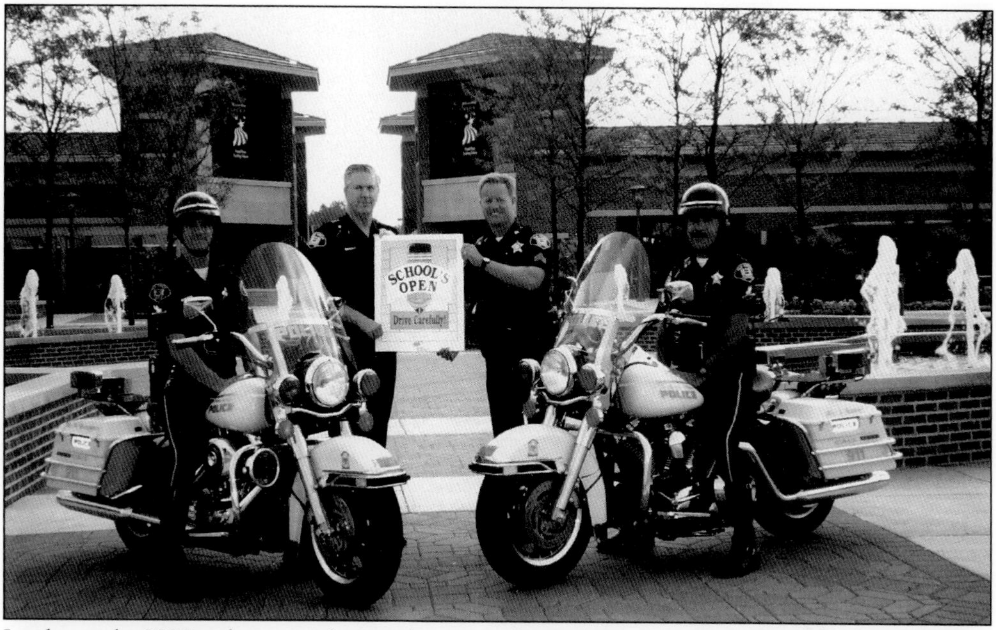

In the early 2000s, the annual special notice about alerting traffic awareness and "School's Open" was displayed throughout the community. Holding the sign is Comdr. Jack Romme (left) and Sgt. Dion Zinnel (right). On motorcycles are traffic officers Myles Greenberg (left) and John Suarez. The photograph was taken by the village fountain, which leads to the Elk Grove town center located at Biesterfield and Arlington Heights Roads.

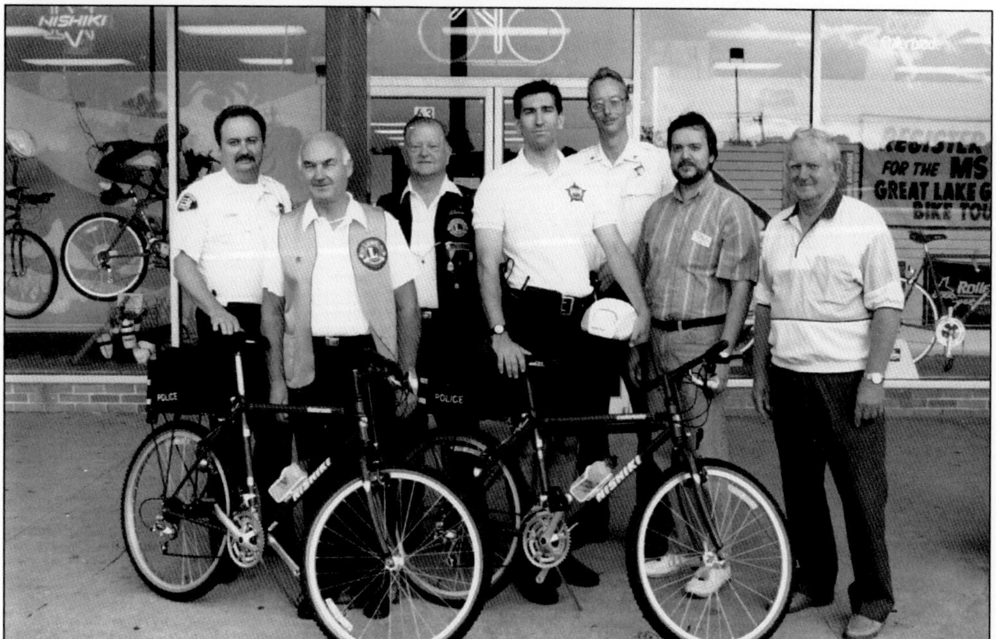

Late-1980s Elk Grove police accept donated police bikes from Elk Grove Lion's club representatives. The bikes were obtained from the Village Cycle and Sports shop located in the Elk Grove Woods Plaza on the corner of Higgins and Arlington Heights Roads. Village Cycle and Sport has been serving the community since 1982.

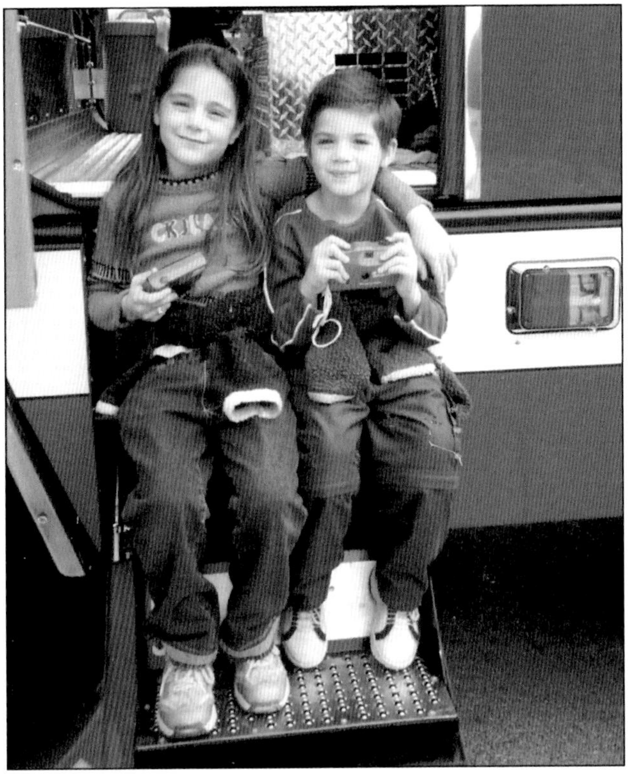

One popular education program is the Fire Safety House. The Fire Safety House is a 28-foot mobile home featuring real-life hazards, including heat and smoke. Hazards are simulated in a safe and self-contained environment. The Fire Safety House not only visits every elementary school within the village each spring but can also be seen during Fire Prevention Week at the open house. Here are Mikala and Peter Piazza at an open house in 2003.

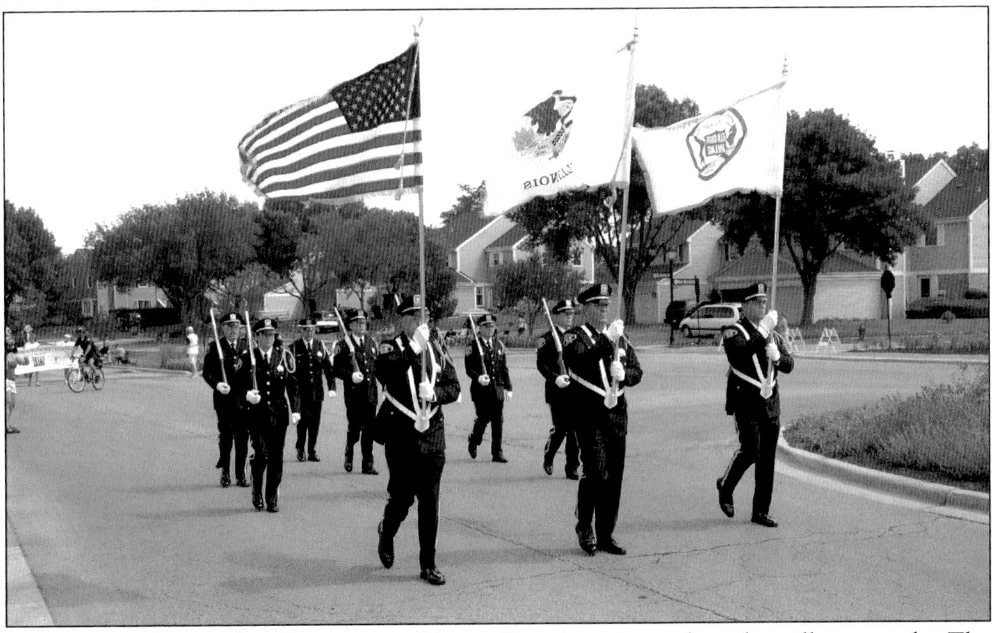

Elk Grove Village Police Department Honor Guard is pictured at the village parade. The honor guard was formed in the early 2000s and is made up of officers from both patrol and investigations. They appear at various functions, including the Memorial Day services at the park district, graduation ceremonies at the police academy, the annual hometown parade, and other police conferences in the suburbs.

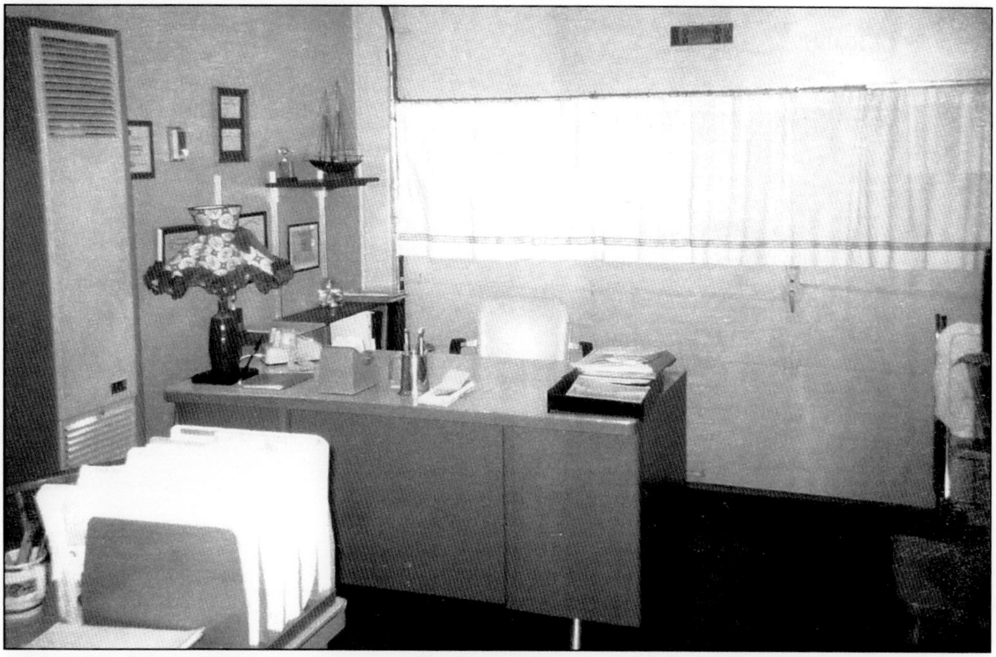

Founded in Chicago in 1955, George and Barbara Johnson opened up Johnson Insurance Agency. In January 1958, the Johnson family moved their business into a one-car garage. George became the first and only village insurance commissioner, an unpaid advisory role. Little did anyone know that the agency would become the longest-running business in the village.

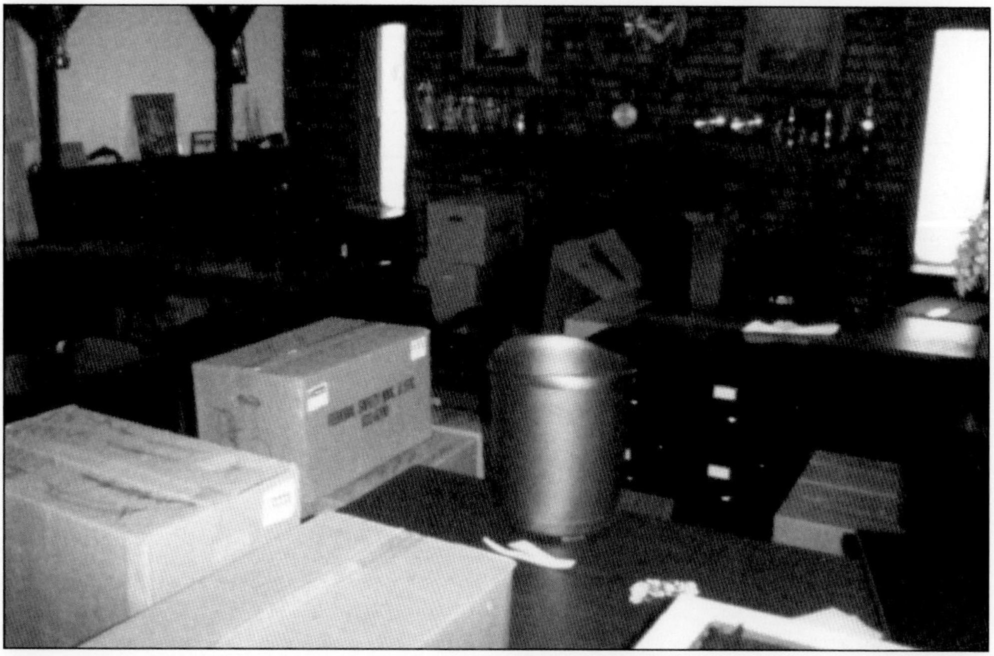

What was once a two-car garage is now home to the ever-expanding insurance company. Mayor Craig Johnson, son of George and Barbara, remembers the hometown feel when customers walked up to his father to pay their bill while he was mowing the lawn. Craig ended his teaching career in 1983 and followed in his father's footsteps to carry on the family business.

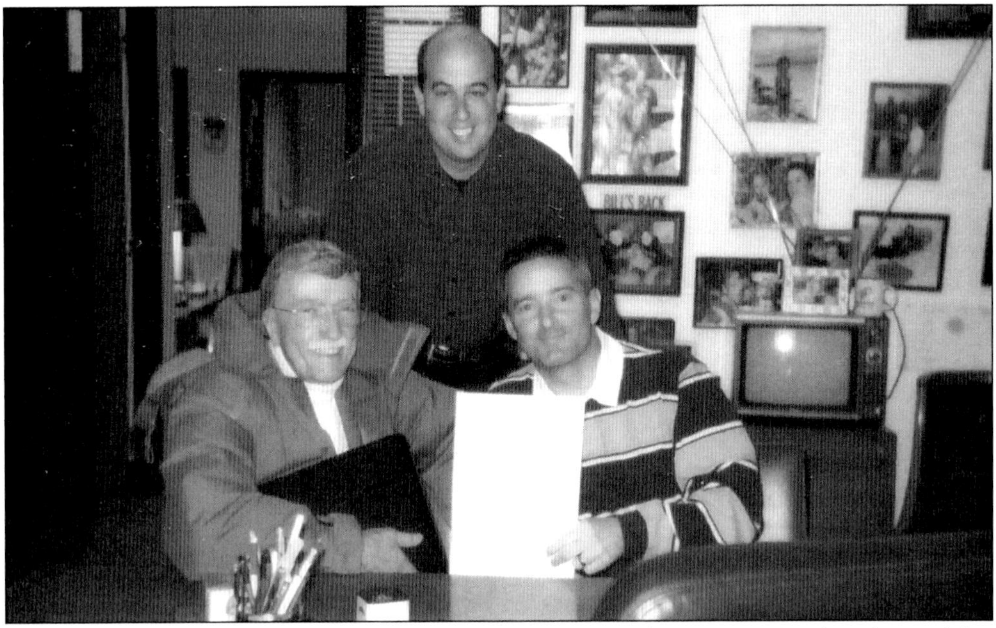

A turning point in Craig Johnson's life began on December 14, 2005, when he and his brother-in-law and longtime resident Billy Beaupre became partners. George Johnson (left), with son Craig (right) and Beaupre (standing), signs over the ownership of Johnson Insurance Agency, now located in the American Chartered Bank building, as pictured above. George officially retired after 50 years of service.

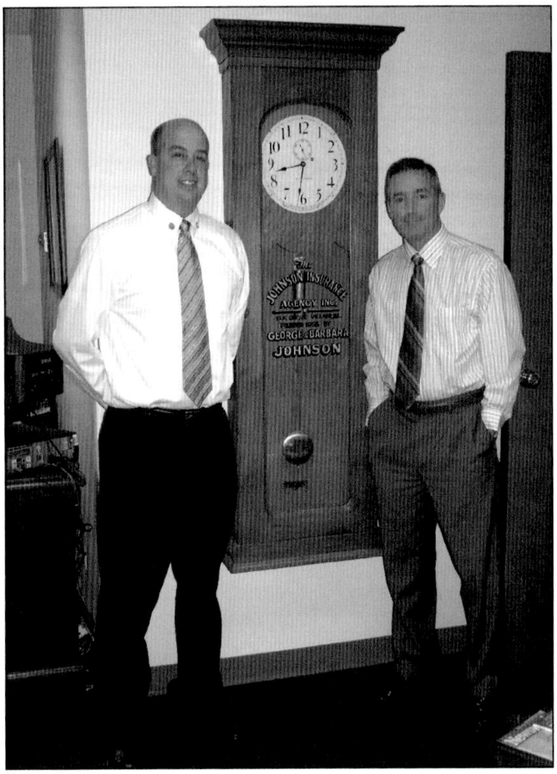

As a constant reminder of his family heritage, George's 1855 antique clock brings an old-time feel to the family-based office. George's father, an antique dealer, painstakingly reconstructed the clock and presented it to him as a gift. Proudly standing on the left is co-owner Beaupre with Craig on the right in 2008.

Over the years, the insurance agency progressively grew from a one-car garage to a more spacious two-car garage to the current office located at 450 East Higgins Road, Suite 200. Family owned and operated, the business still has a hometown feel because of the family's deep roots within the community.

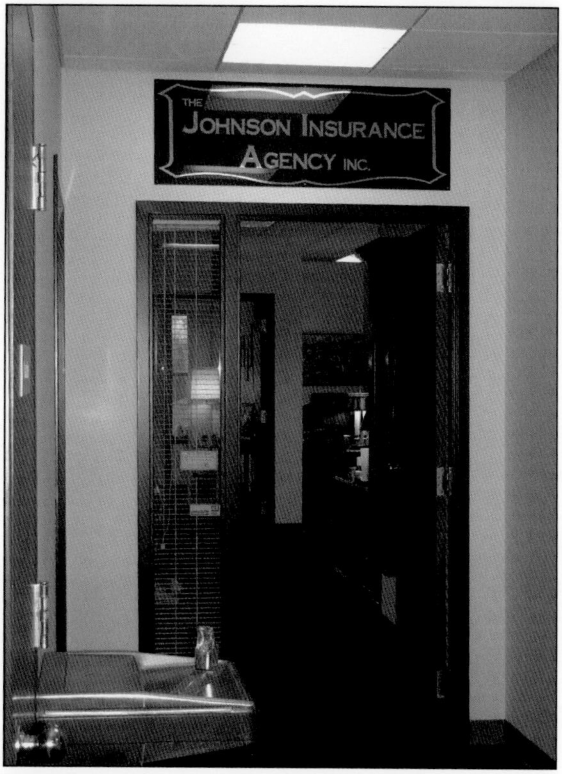

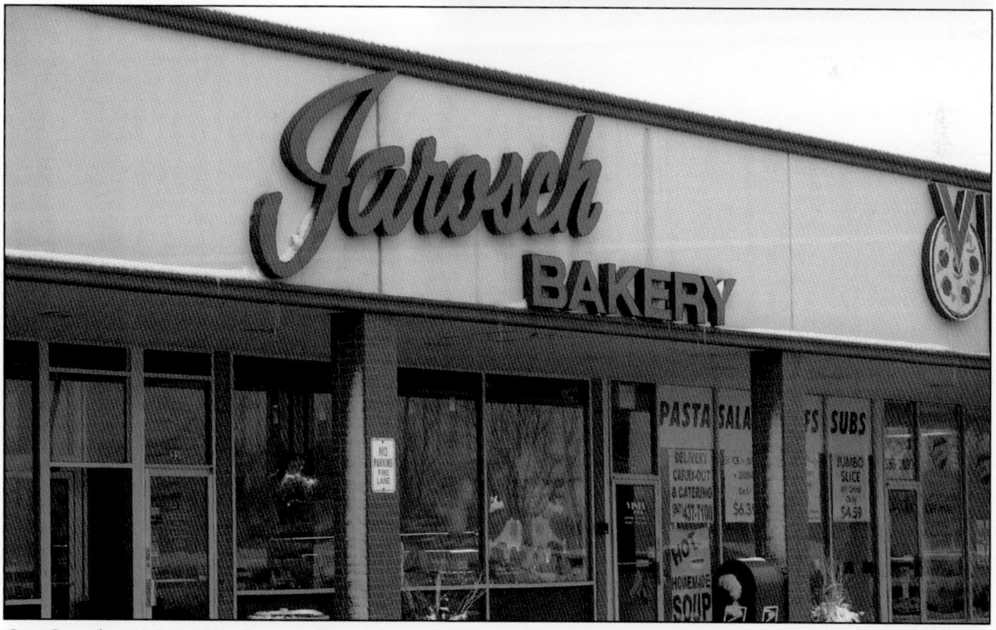

On October 15, 1959, George Jarosch and his son Herbert opened the Jarosch Bakery doors. It was one of seven stores in the Elk Grove Park and Shop Mall. Currently, Ken and Kathy Jarosch run the bakery. They are the third generation of the Jarosch family to run the family business, rich with family tradition. Jarosch Bakery is the oldest business remaining in the same location in the village.

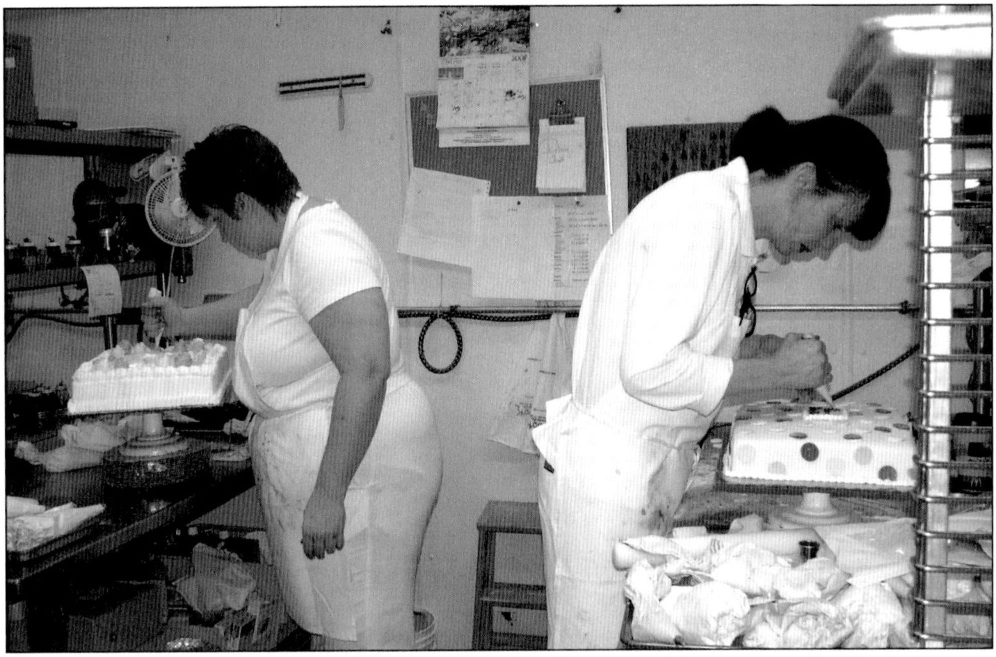

Start with a ton of sugar, a ton of flour, 400 pounds of butter, and 500 eggs, and add a dedication to producing quality products and providing a high level of customer service. Cakes, pastries, breads, and other goodies are baked daily, as Barbara Russel (left) and head decorator Marianne Domino can testify to.

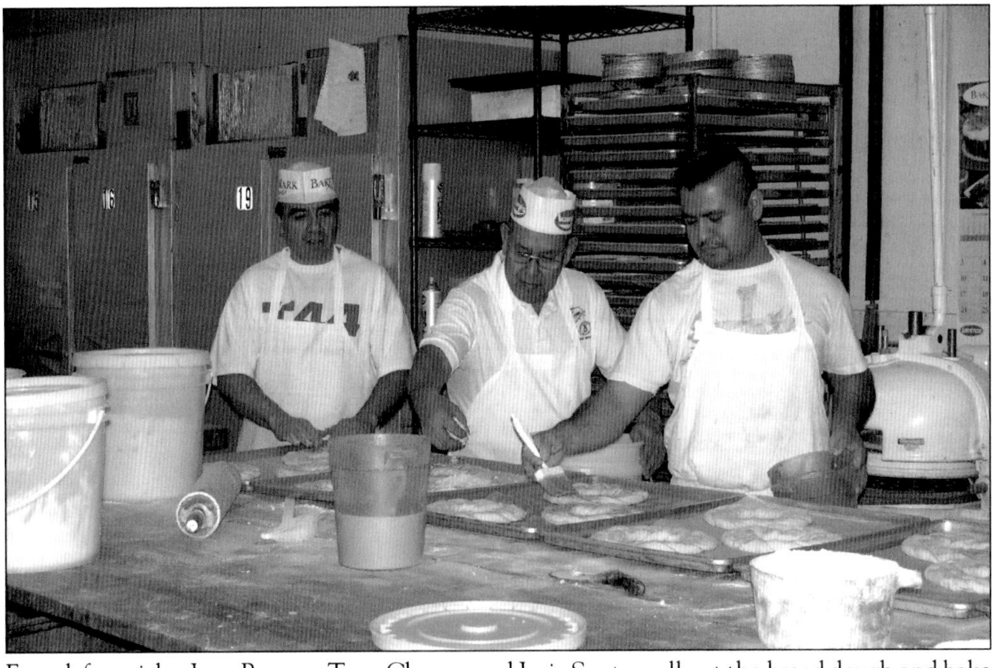

From left to right, Juan Roman, Tony Chavez, and Josie Santos roll out the bread dough and bake pastries with pride. The original personnel complement consisted of George Jarosch, Herbert Jarosch, and two bakers, plus two women and two high school girls in the early days. Today the bakery employs a staff of over 50 to keep up with the demand.

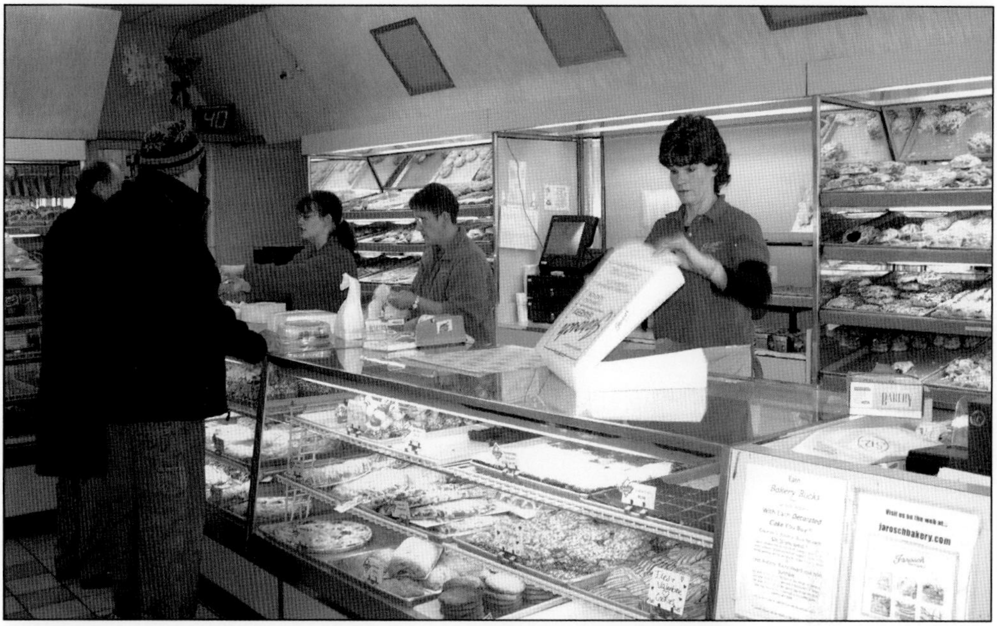

If one needs some delicious pastries, cakes, cookies, or just a loaf of bread from Jarosch Bakery, they should take a number. For almost 50 years, people have been lining up inside the bakery to buy their favorite items. Alicia Phillips, Jackie Crouse, Marie Modlisz, and Leslee Coleman are just four of the many friendly employees who will gather and package customer's everyday or holiday pastry needs.

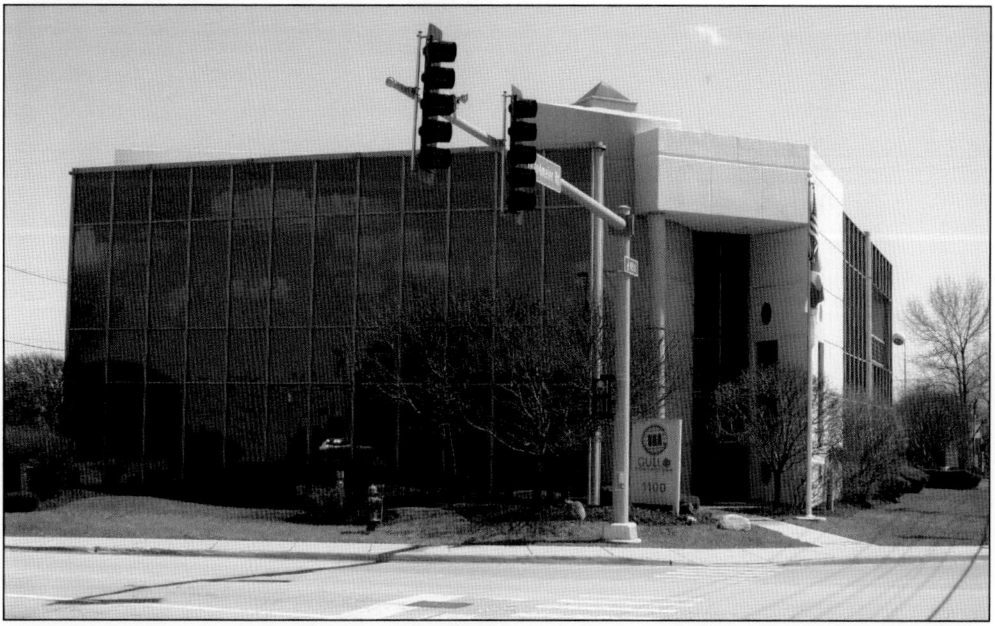

Coming to America at age 18, Giovanni Gullo, president of Gullo International, had many obstacles to overcome. Having no money and not speaking English, Gullo was able to learn English in six months. Starting his own industrial painting company in 1972, his desires and ambition led him to owning his own development company. The Gullo family continues to give back to the community that has embraced them.

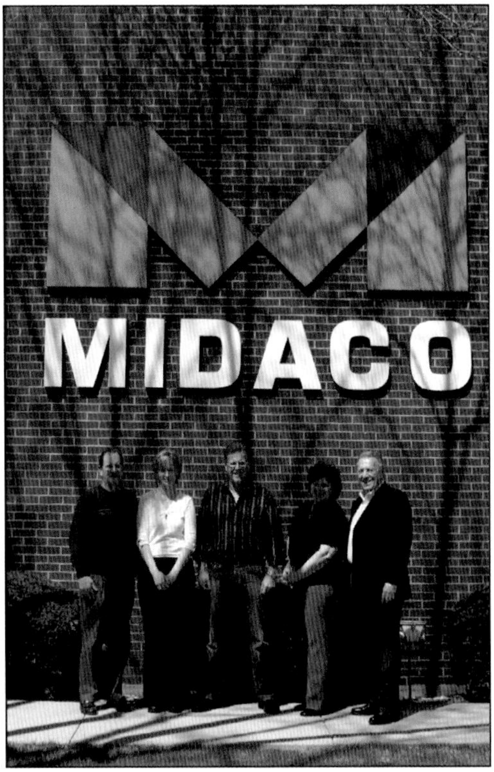

Established in 1969 by Michael Cayley Sr., Midaco Corporation started as a job shop and now sells a complete line of products worldwide. Located in the Business Park at 2000 East Touhy Avenue, Midaco employs 45 people. With a combined total of 159 service years, from left to right, are Mac Keith, Pam Werfel, Mike Cayley Jr., Mary Baran, and Cayley Sr. Cayley Sr. is also the founder of Happy Memories, a charitable organization that has served Elk Grove Village residents and the surrounding areas for 20 years by providing them with a Christmas meal and presents for children. Retired police sergeant Ken Krzywicki, along with employees and other business volunteers, are very involved, donating a lot of time. One hundred percent of the donations go directly to the community. Below, a family enjoys sharing a moment with Santa played by Cayley Jr.

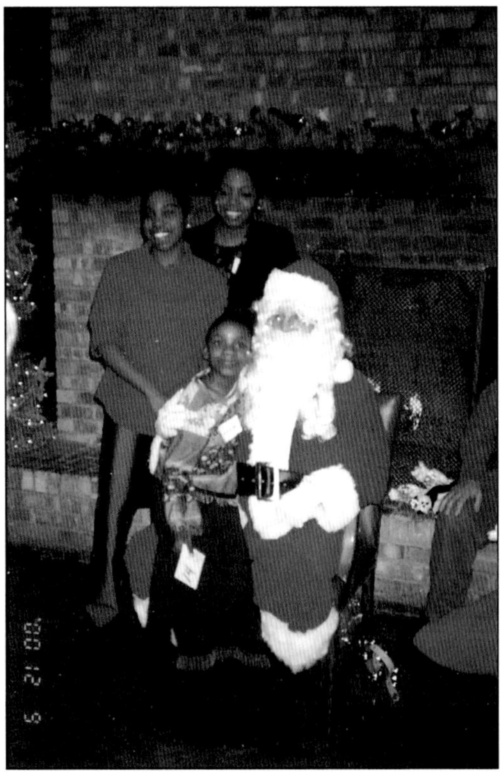

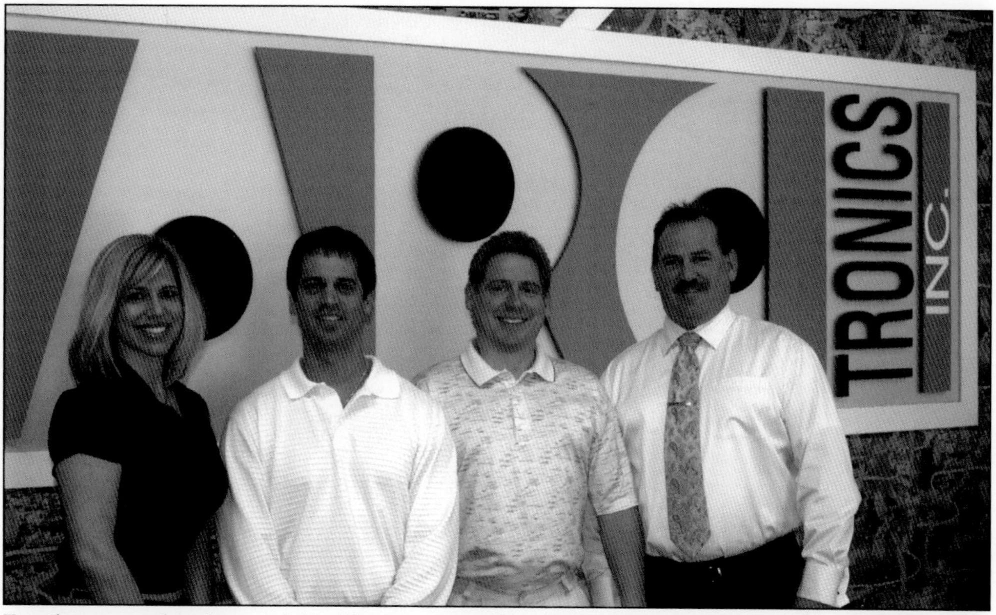

Family operated and owned Arc-Tronics opened in 1972 in Business Park. Owner and president Conrad Goeringer employs 175 people at 1150 Pagni Drive. His children, Marla Goeringer, Matthew Goeringer, Mark Goeringer, and Michael Goeringer help their father with the operation of the company. Conrad and his company also support Happy Memories. Many businesses in the industrial park area give back to the community in many ways.

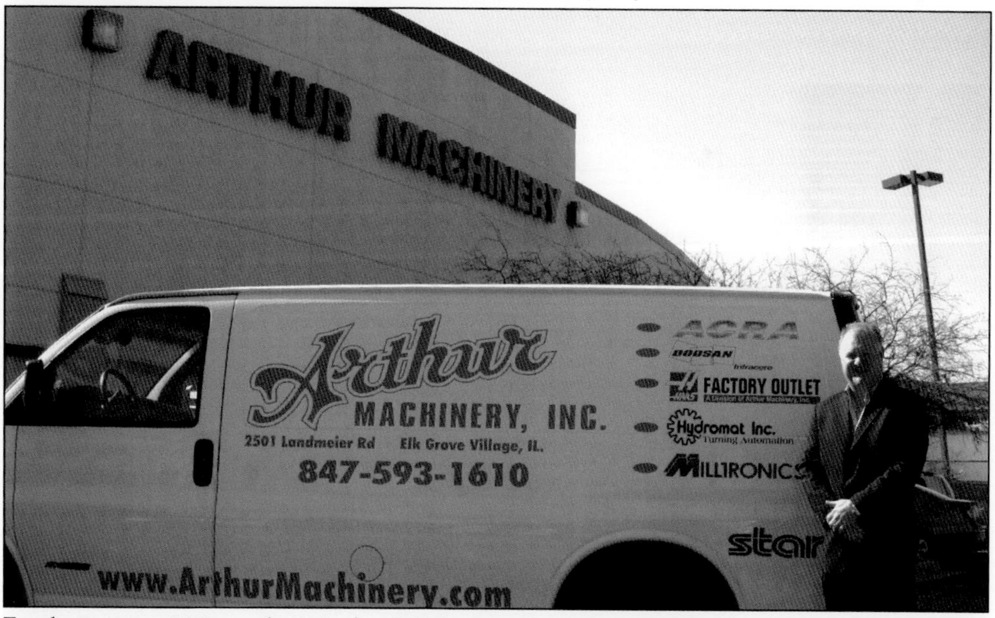

Employing over 100 people is Arthur Machinery. Opening in 1983, founder Bob Arthur shares ownership with his son Chad (pictured above). Although the company specializes in CNC and manual machine tools, Chad is continually expanding his company by partnering with other village businessmen like Xavier Kaufmann, who is celebrating 52 years in the field. Chad is president of the Nuts, Bolts, and Thingamajigs Foundation, helping to create the next generation of artisans, inventors, engineers, and repairmen.

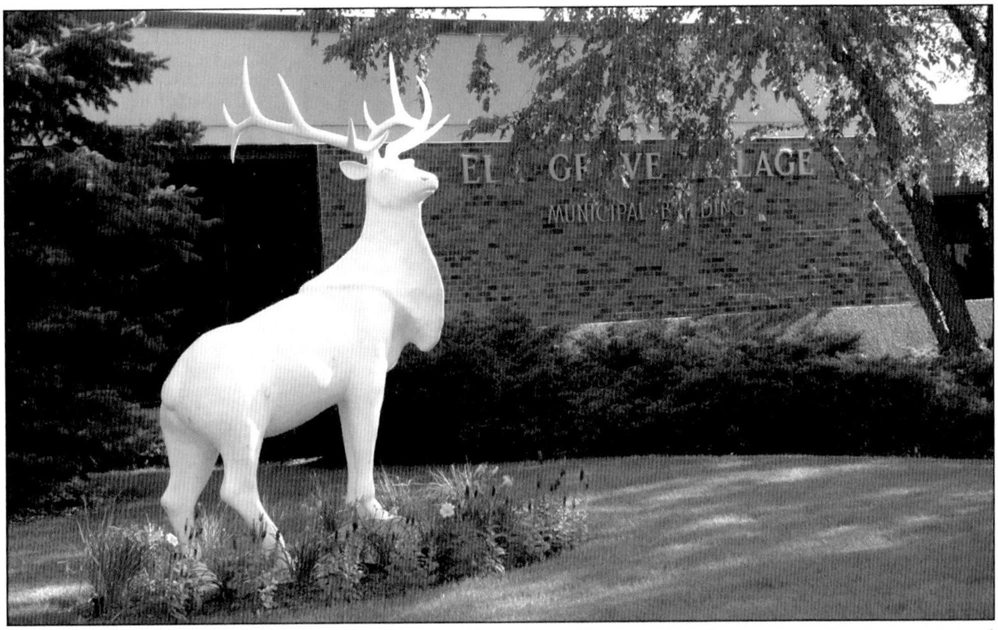

In November 1989, a likeness of a life-size fiberglass elk was added to the village's municipal complex lawn at Biesterfield Road and Wellington Avenue. It stood nine feet tall and weighed 1,000 pounds. Arlington Heights resident Fran Volz received $5,000 for his sculpted creation. Due to deterioration, the elk was damaged when trying to relocate it during the municipal construction in 2006.

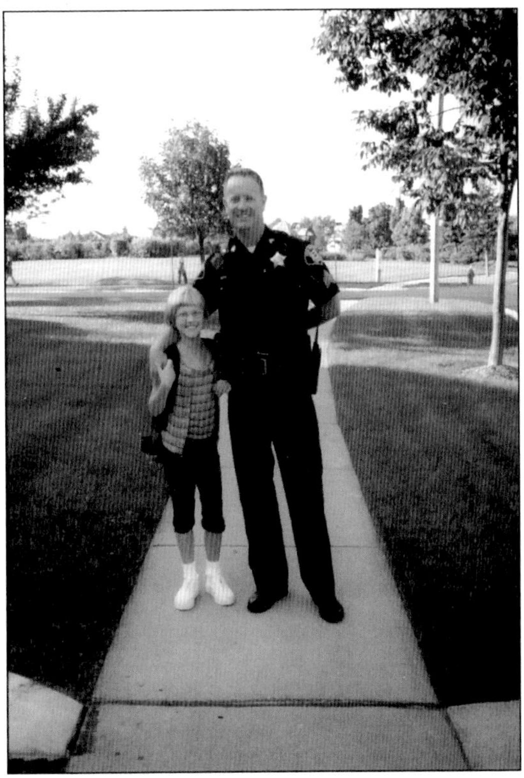

Resident Dion Zinnel, with his daughter Diana, is excited about the first day of school. Diana will take the bus to Frederick Nerge School, one of the 22 elementary schools in district 54 that serve Elk Grove Village and neighboring communities. Elk Grove District 59 also serves residents in Elk Grove Village and neighboring communities with its 11 elementary schools.

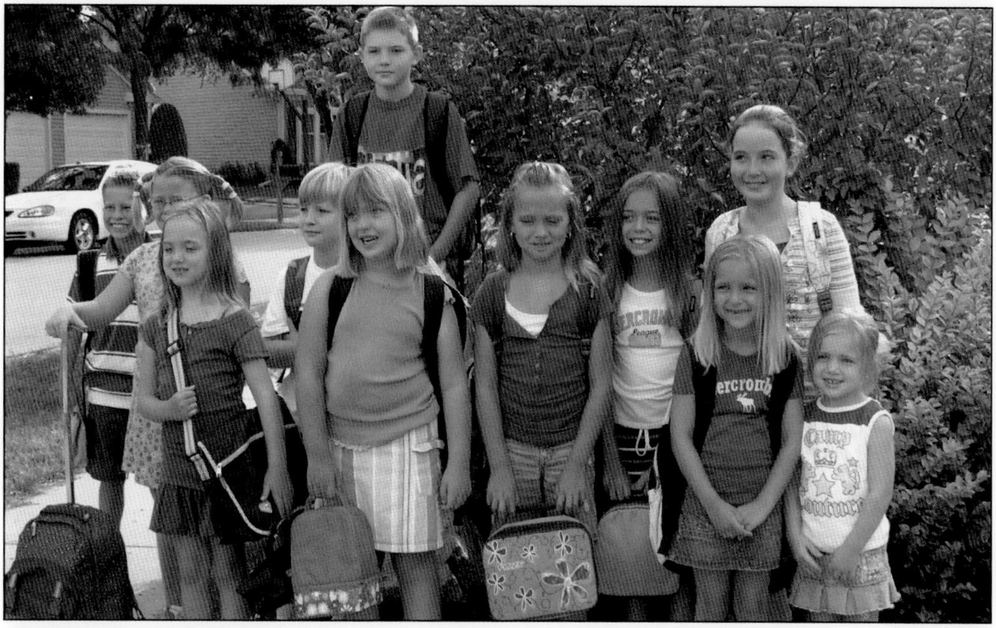

Waiting for the bus, Frederick Nerge School kids anxiously line up for a picture on the first day of school. From left to right are (first row) Scotty Ruzanski, Lisa Prazma, Jessica Ryan, Michael Prazma, Emma Rabe, Jamie Ryan, Taylor Ryan, Mikayla Ruzanski, and Juliana Minini; (second row) Jordan Colby and Sarah Tozer. Nerge is one of 22 elementary schools in Schaumburg District 54.

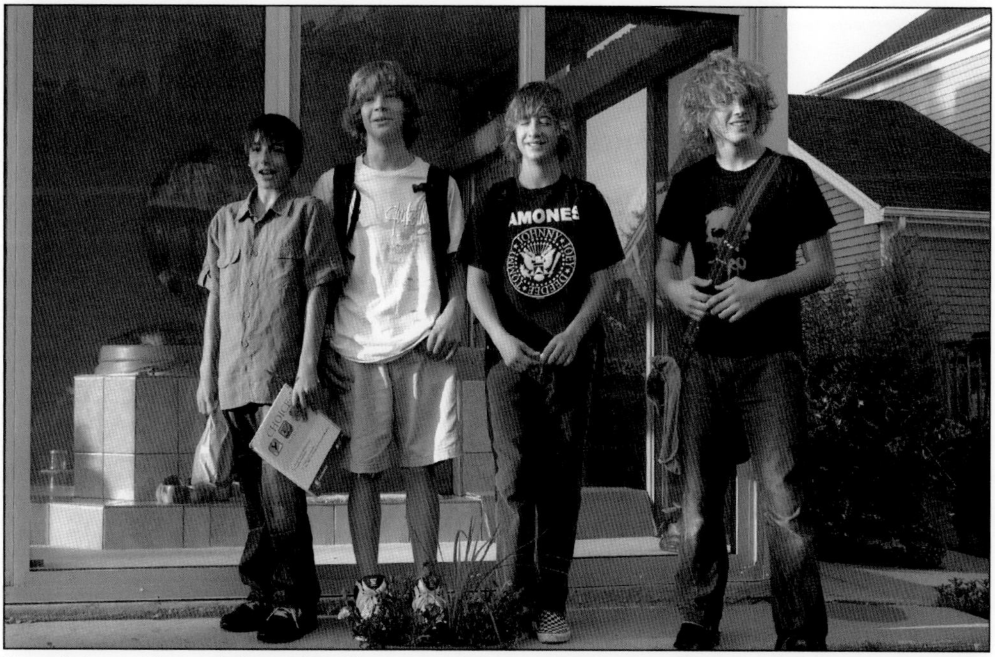

From left to right, eighth graders Shawn Buckel, Ryan Colby, Kyle Kingsmill, and Kyle Charmelo happily pose for a mom's first-day-of-school picture before walking to Margaret Mead Junior High. Elk Grove students attend schools in Schaumburg District 54, while others attend Elk Grove District 59 schools.

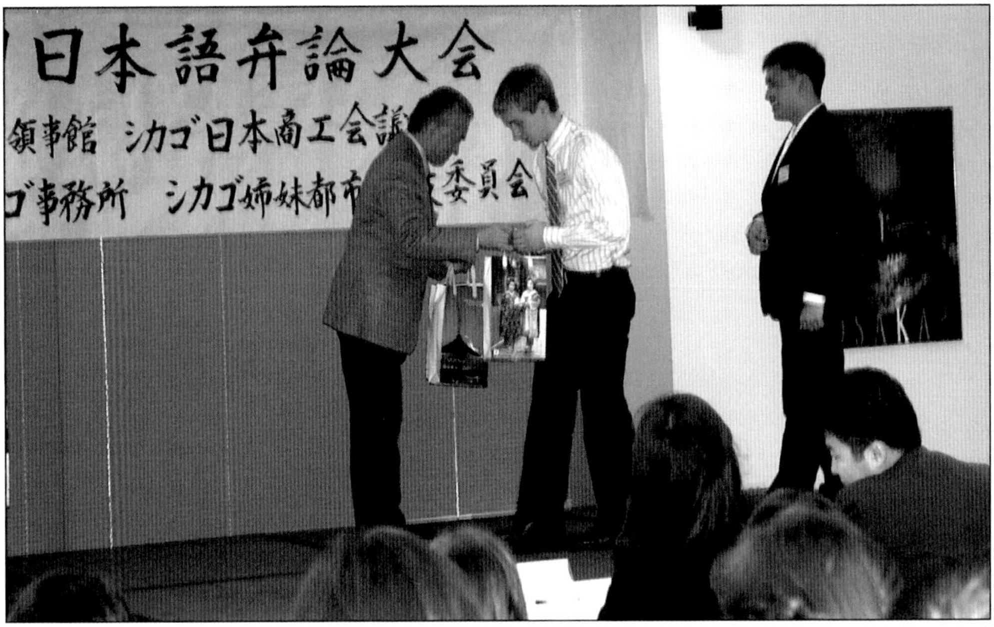

Elk Grove High School junior Tom Tasche accepts the first-place award at the 22nd annual Japanese Speech Contest held at the Japanese Consulate in Chicago on March 29, 2008. The contest was open to all high school students taking Japanese from Illinois, Indiana, Wisconsin, and Minnesota.

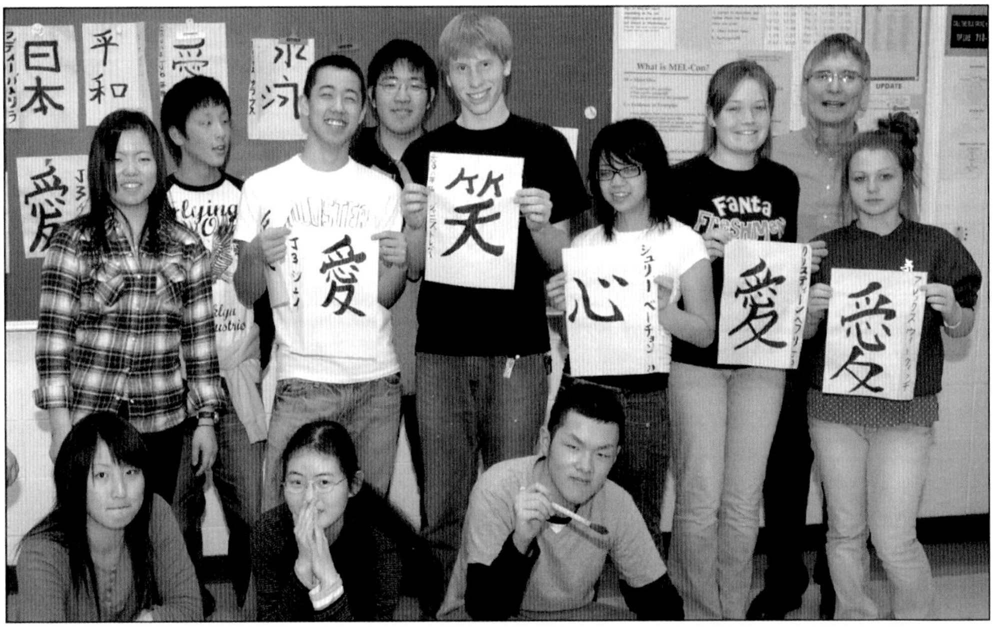

In 2008, the Elk Grove High School Japanese Exchange program celebrates its 20th year. In March, family's hosted students from the Japanese sister schools, Ashikodai and Ashitandai High Schools. In June, Elk Grove Village students traveled to Japan. All families share local customs and traditions. Winners of the calligraphy competition among the advanced students of Japanese pose with exchange visitors who helped them practice their skills in Cliff Darnall's Japanese classes.

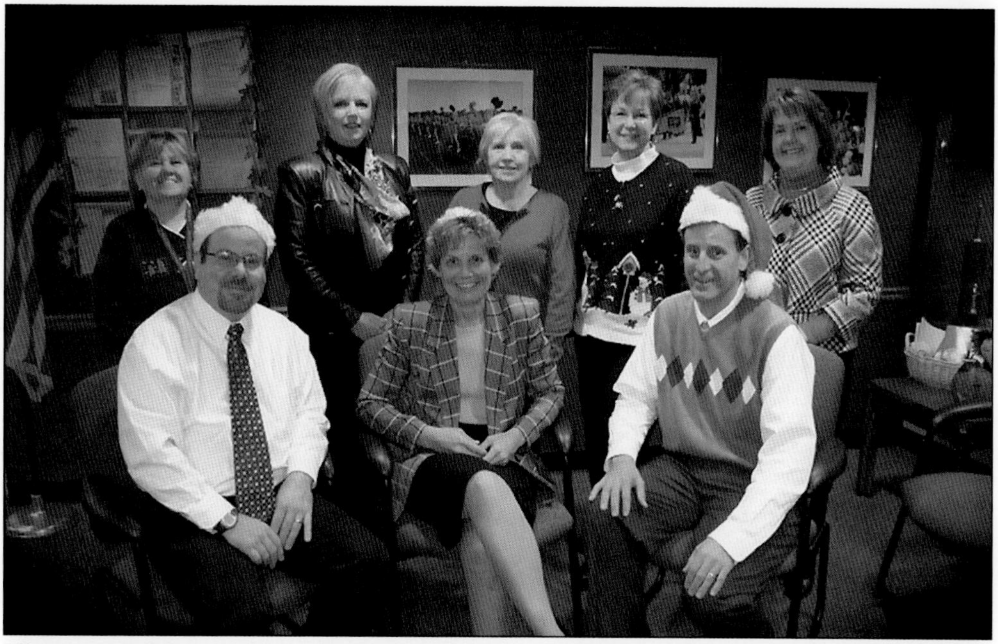

Elk Grove High School main office staff take time for a holiday picture in December 2007. From left to right are (first row) David Travis, associate principal of instruction; Nancy Holman, principal; and Ken Stiff, associate principal of operations; (second row) Nicky Rutka, Denise Sabatino, Mary Holda, Barbara Sittner, and Diane Free, the educational support personnel staff.

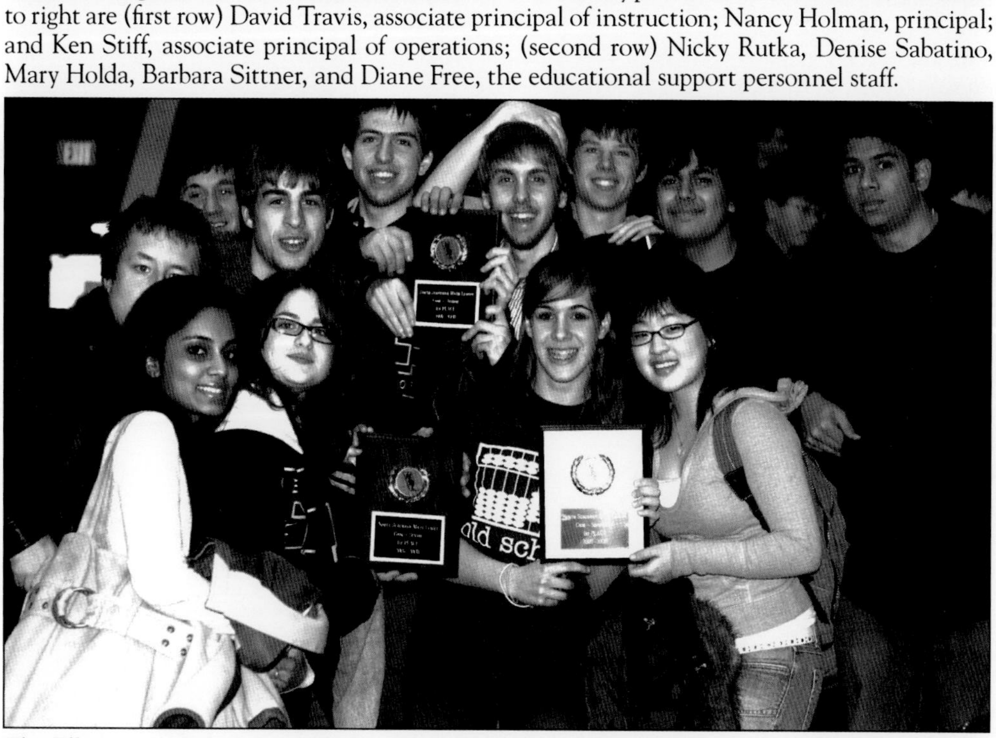

The Elk Grove High School math team proudly shows their awards. In the Cook Division for sophomores, juniors, and senior levels, the team took first place. For the division, the entire team took second place. Throughout the year, students compete in five competitions against area schools. At years end, all mathletes are invited to compete in the Illinois Math League regional competition where students can qualify for the state meet.

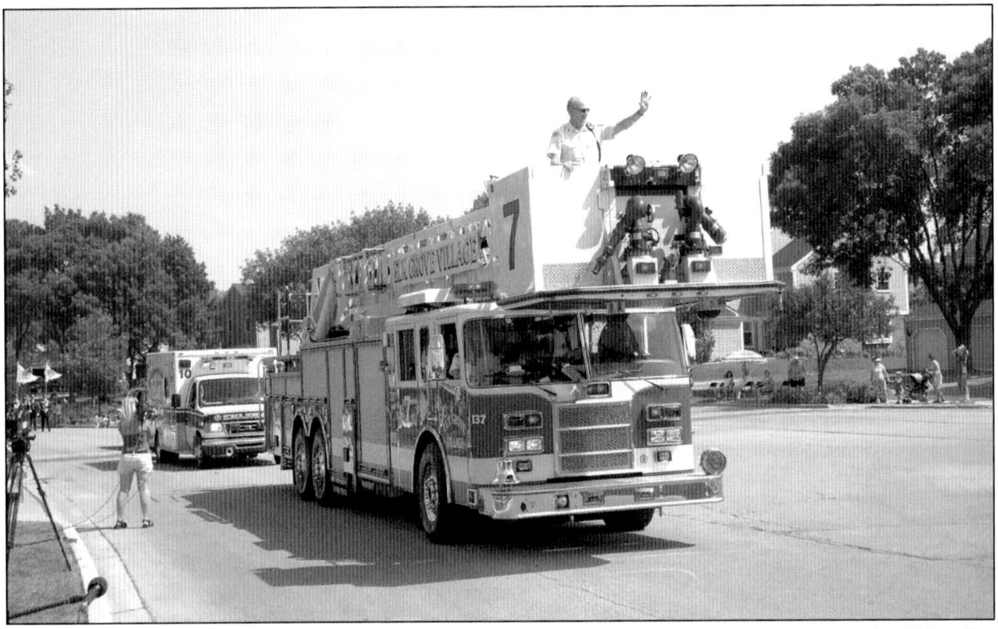

Fire Chief David L. Miller waves to residents during the 2006 anniversary parade. The fire department has come a long way in the last 50 years. One fire engine housed in a barn in 1957 serving approximately 116 people became four fire stations serving over 34,000 people with high-tech equipment. In 1961, there were 40 volunteer firemen sworn in. Today there are 86 sworn personnel, including four female firefighters.

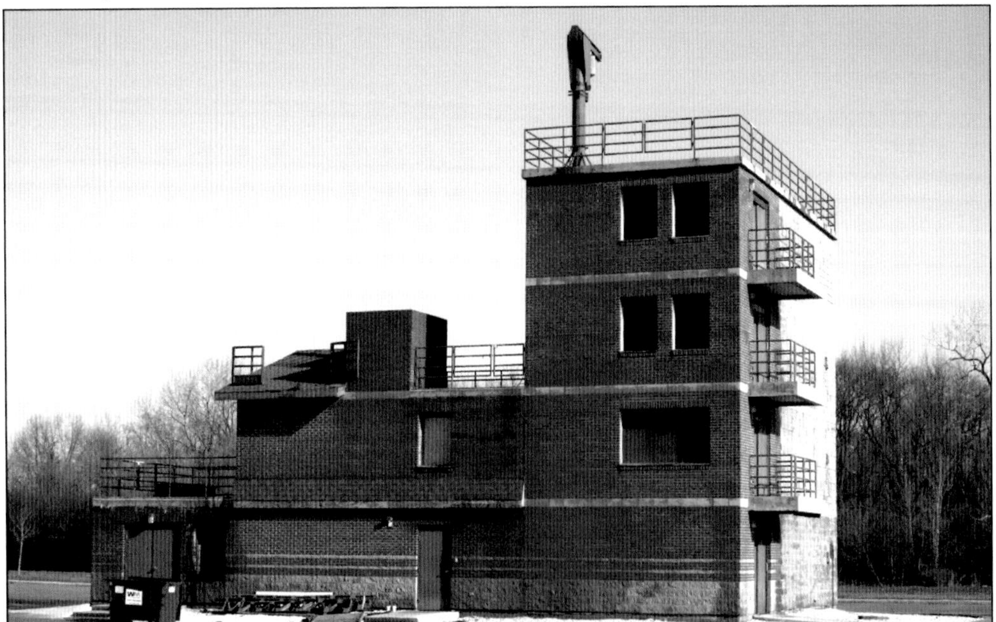

As the only one of its kind in North America, located at 1000 Oakton Street, Station No. 8 has a training building. This hands-on high-tech building is the training site for many firefighters. The four-story building attracts fire departments in other communities, allowing them to train their fire fighters in a hands-on environment as well.

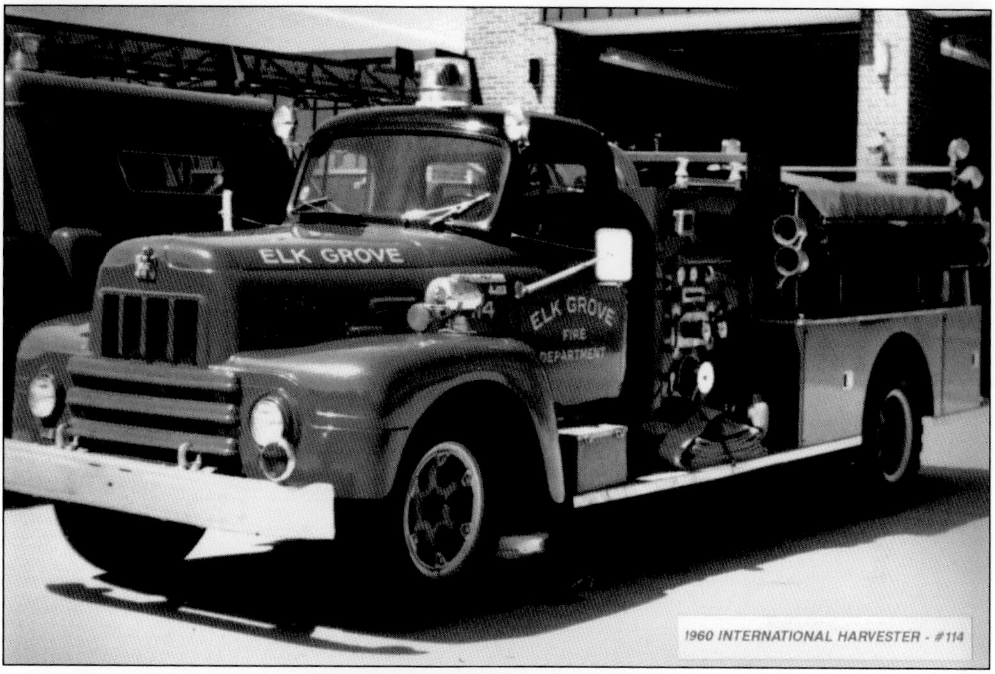

It was not uncommon to see firefighters riding on the back bar of a fire truck. Prior to 1973, the 1960 International Harvester Engine 114 did not have a cab that was equipped to ride passengers. Pictured above is the original 1960 International Harvester Engine 114 without the passenger cab. Below, volunteer firefighter Leonard Zgonina (second from left) became a lieutenant. He retired after 20 years of service. The other volunteer firefighters are unidentified. They are prepared to go out on a call. Today the dangers are doubled by riding on the back of a truck because of the growth of the community and all the well-driven streets.

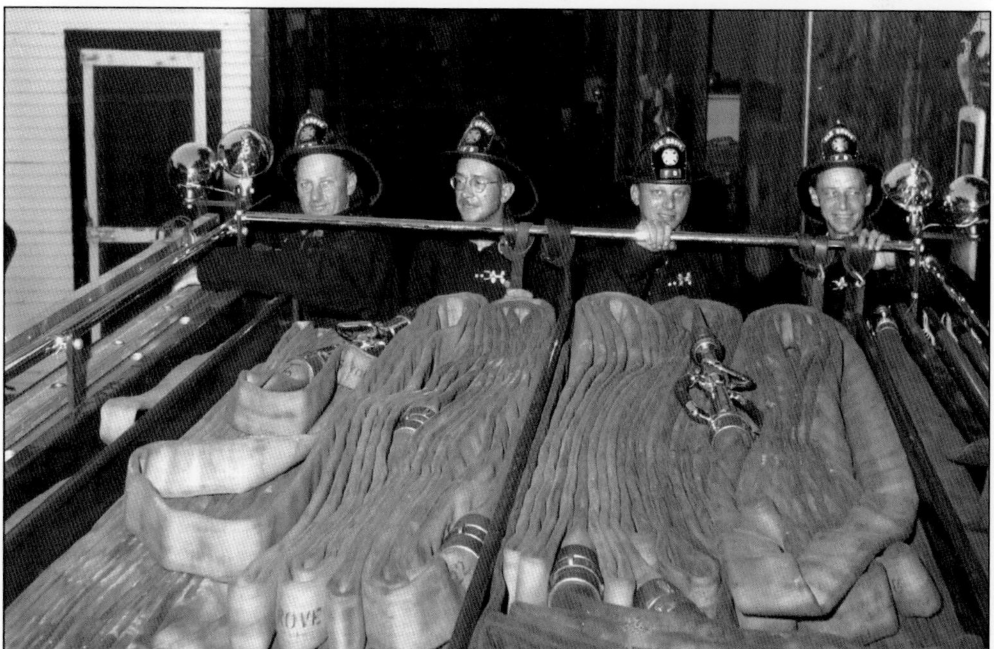

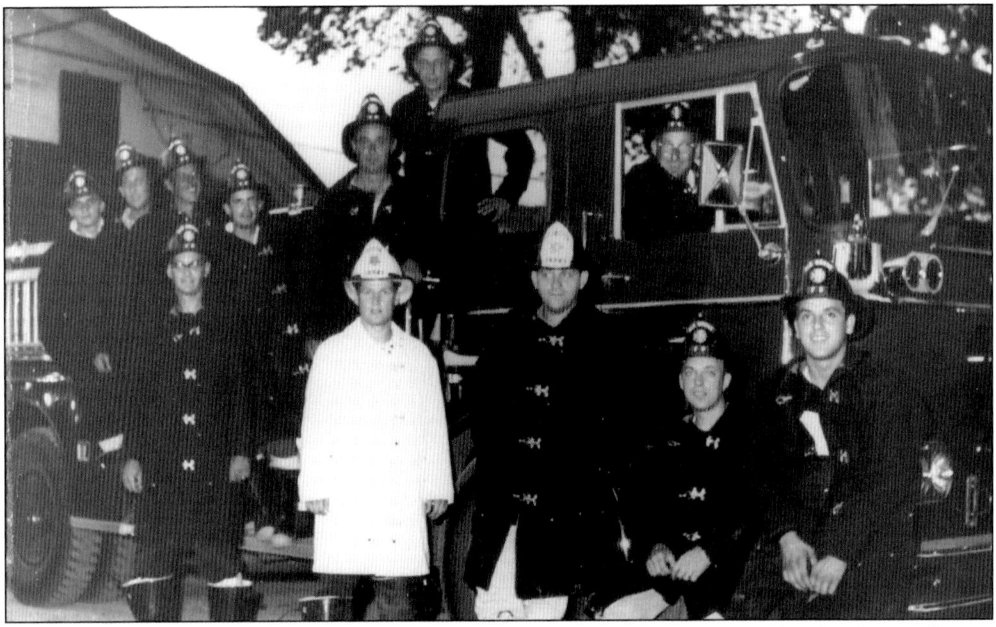

The first fire department began in 1960 in an old barn at 780 Tonne Road. Charles Hodlmair, the first village president, donated the barn. In February 1961, 40 volunteer firemen were sworn in. Space at the new municipal building at 666 Landmeier Road was allocated for the fire department. Fire Chief Al Mergens was happy to move his department out of the barn and into the new building.

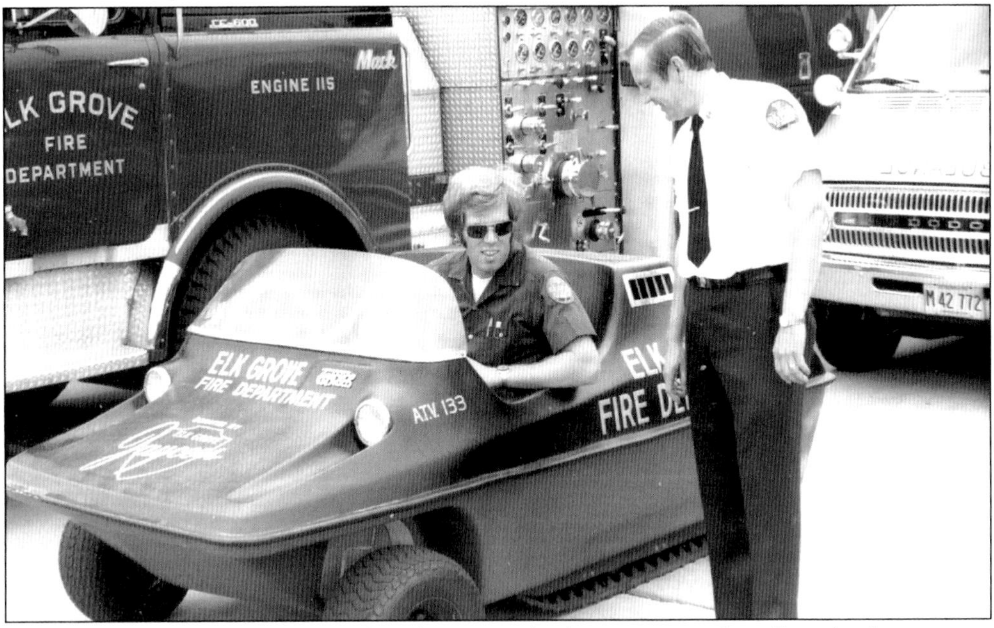

Donated by the Elk Grove Jaycees, this all-terrain vehicle was given to the village fire department. Firefighter Greg Riddle (sitting) and Lt. Donald Langland discuss how the vehicle is prepared to handle different road conditions. The Jaycees have been running community service projects in Elk Grove Village since 1958. The Jaycees teach leadership and personal and professional development to people between the ages of 18 and 41.

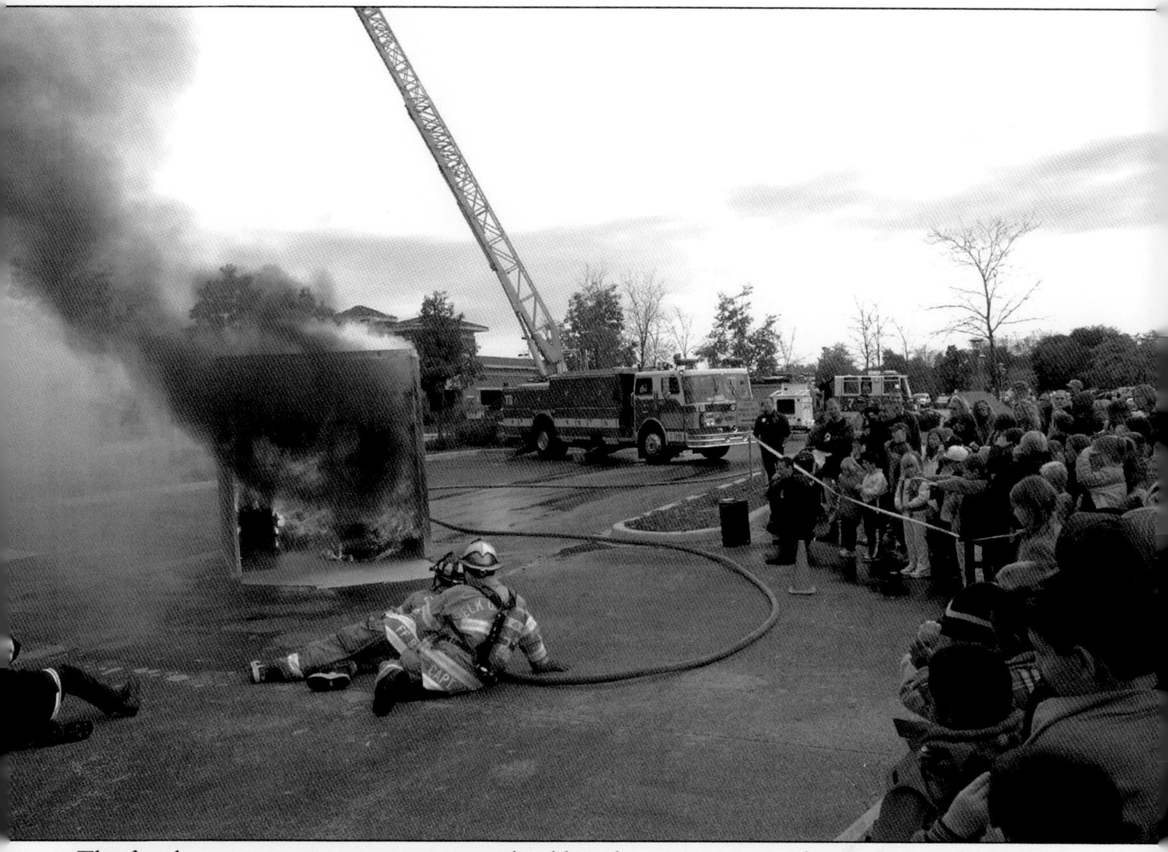

The fire department operates a year-round public education program for residents, schools, and local businesses. The Elk Grove Village Fire Department's annual open house is held during fire prevention week in the second week of October. Visitors may see several safety exhibits, fire apparatus and ambulances, demonstrations from the department's special teams, and they can meet the firefighters and paramedics. The above demonstration shows a live burn house. People see how quickly smoke detectors work and how fast fires spread. A reserve truck, No. 139, can be seen in the background. Battalion Chief William Mark Sellers and Lt. John P. Guglielmo prepare for another demonstration showing how oxygen influences fires. Officer Jeff Andrzejewski and Chief David Miller are in the background. These demonstrations were during the yearlong 50th anniversary celebration in October 2006.

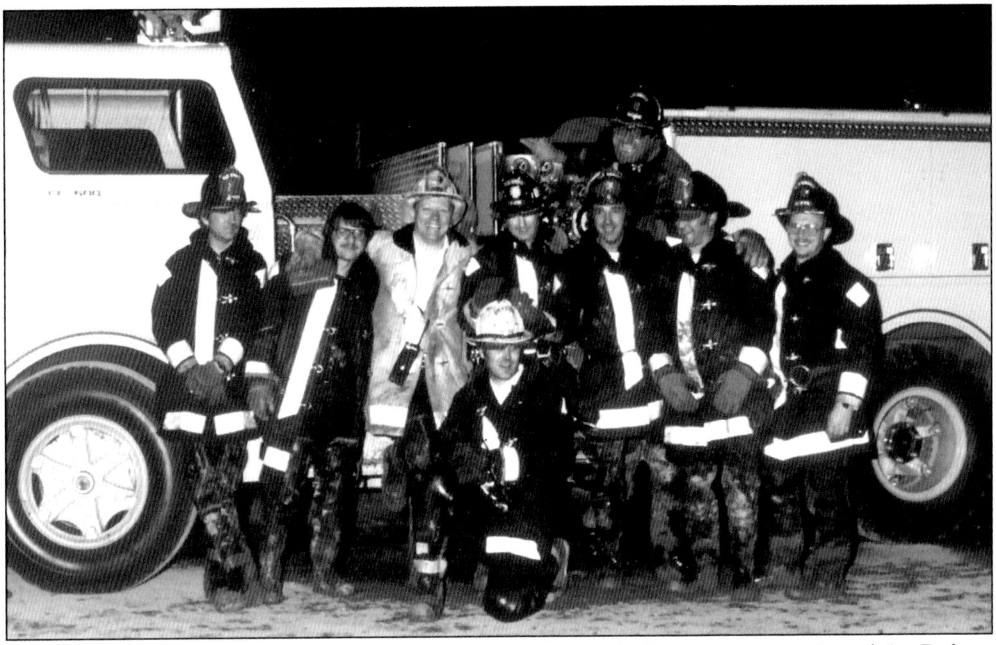

Firefighters (from left to right) David McCulla, Robert Marshall, Capt. Wayne Singel, Lt. Robert Hermann (kneeling), David Miller, Leonard Kopinski, volunteer Louie Tosto (standing on the truck), John Serbec, and Jerry Norris stand in front of Engine 118. The engine was once painted a lime color but then was repainted red.

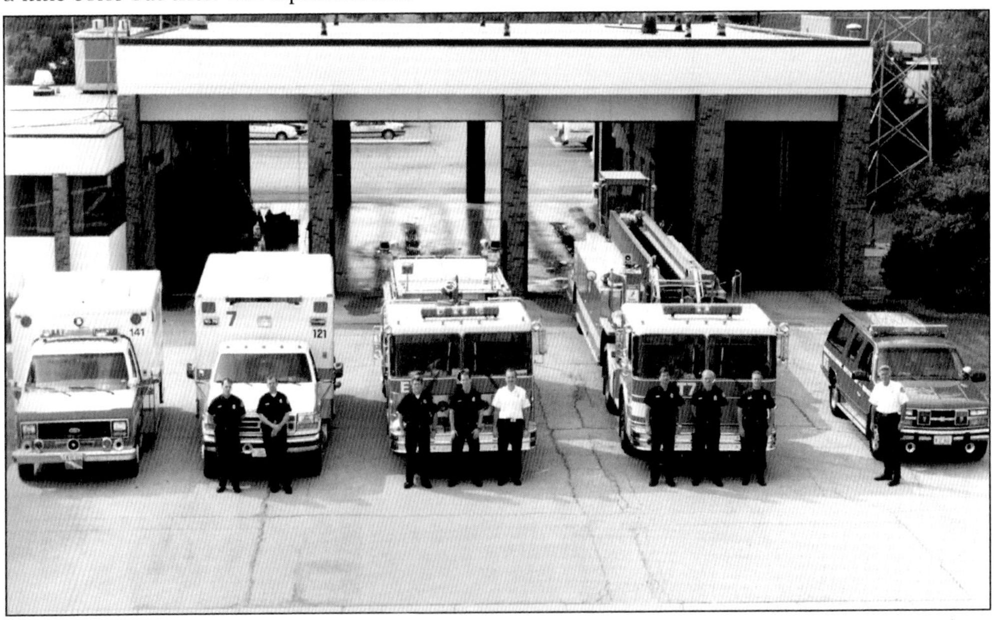

Firefighters (from left to right) Brian McVeigh, Fred Hanselman, William Hopkins, Mathew Reiddy, Albert Vrshek, Michael Harris, Edward Ogorek, Ronald Halvorsen, and Capt. Robert Hermann pose for a picture at Station No. 7, located at 101 Biesterfield Road. There are four stations in the village. Station No. 8 is located at 1000 Oakton Street, Station No. 9 is at 1655 Greenleaf Avenue, and Station No. 10 is at 676 Meacham Road. The administration office is at 901 Brantwood Avenue.

Two

Things to Do, Places to Go

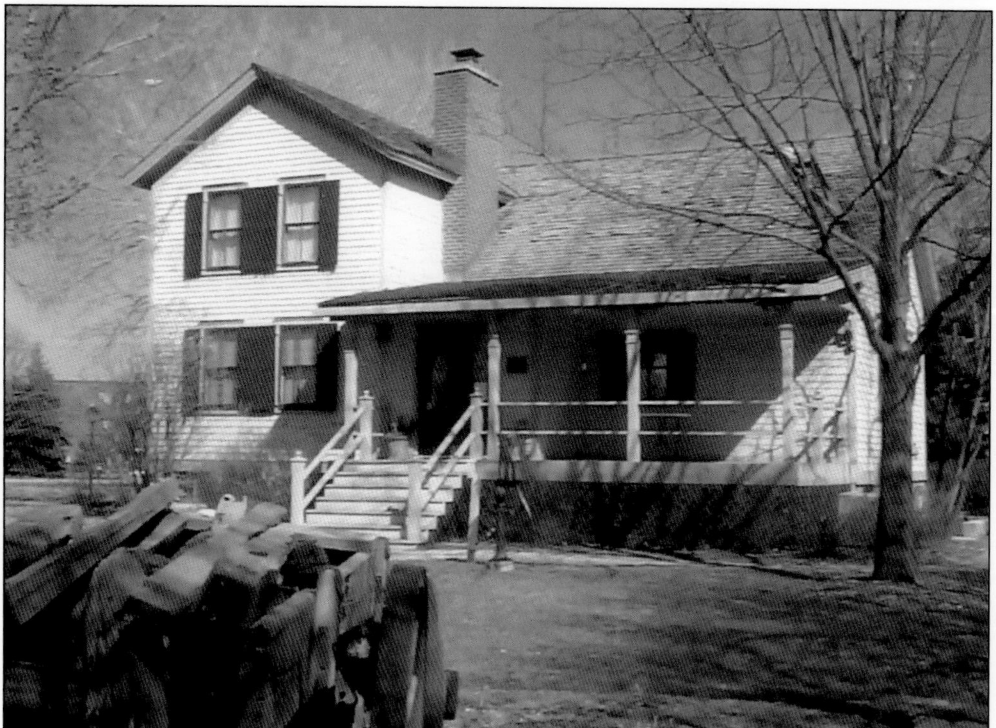

What was once the Henry Schuette farmhouse in the mid-1850s became the Elk Grove Village Farmhouse Museum. The Maiorielle family donated the farmhouse to the Elk Grove Village Historical Society to be used as a museum in March 1976, and it was moved from Clearmont and Arlington Heights Roads to its permanent location at 499 Biesterfield Road. (EGHS.)

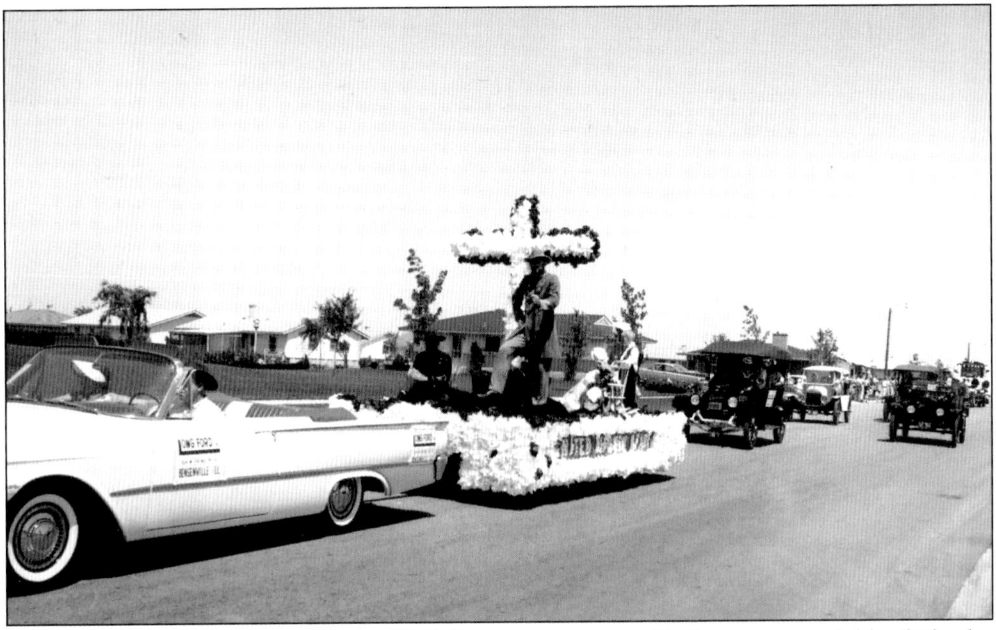

Considered "the Peony Capital of the World," once internationally famous peony fields of Charles Klehm and Sons were located in what is now Northwest Point Corporate Park. Klehm's peony plants used to be so in demand that the crop had to be sold three years in advance. Klehm's always saved one field of peonies to decorate the floats in the village's annual Peony Parade held in the late 1950s. (EGHS.)

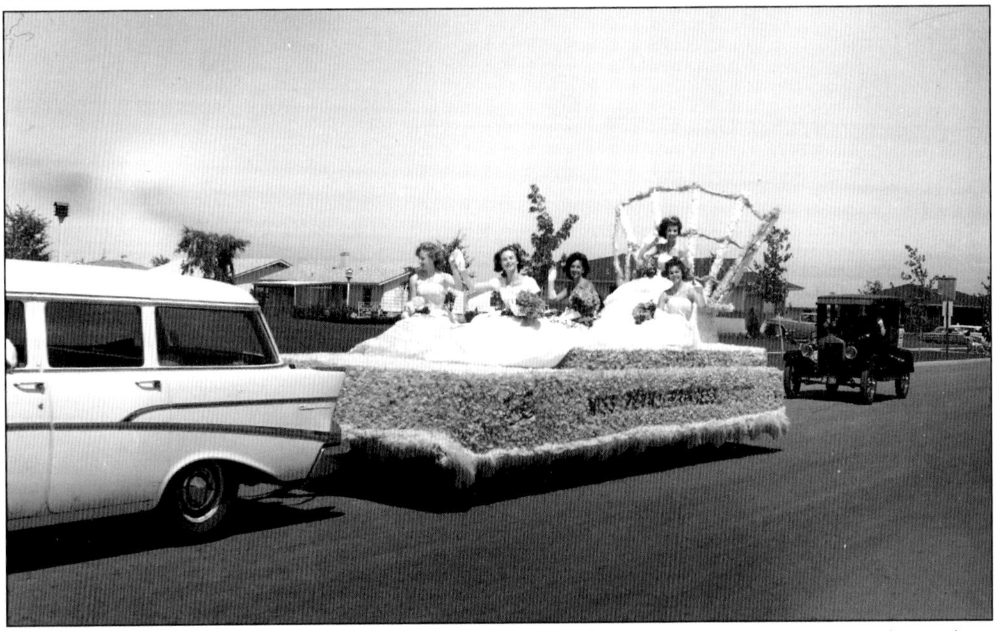

Peony parades were held annually from 1959 to 1974. Prior to its completion, the Park 'n' Shop Plaza at State Street and Higgins Road was the ending location for the parade. Pictured on the float is the 1967 Peony Princess Bonita Gay, with second and third place winners Donnalynn Freund and Diane Neuman. Miss Congeniality Lynda Naones and Sharon Hurley ride beside them. (EGHS.)

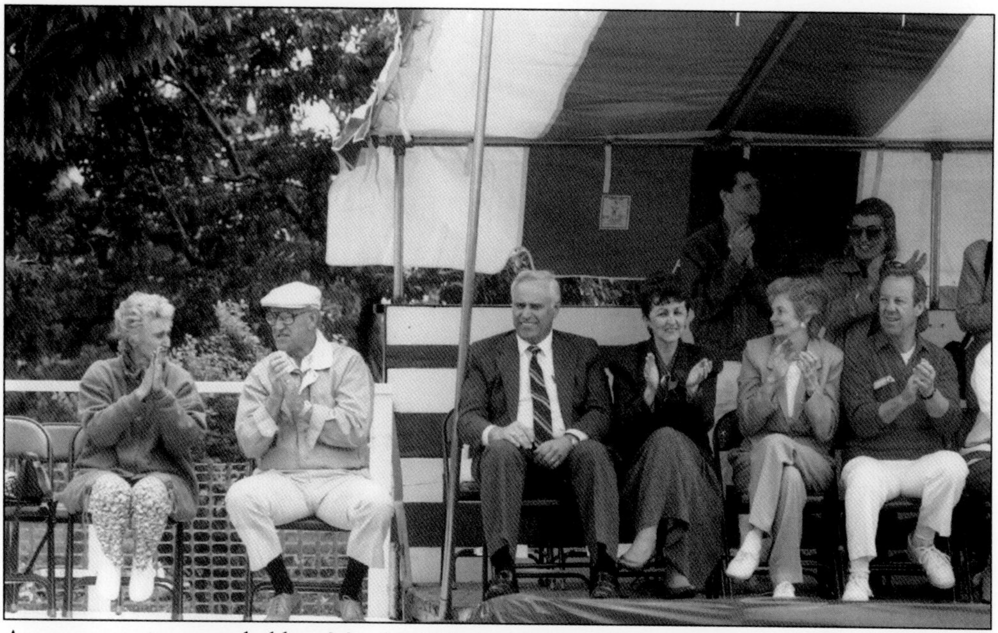

At a community event held on May 20, 1991, Frank Czarnik (wearing a suit and tie) sits next to his wife, Nancy, enjoying the afternoon. They are joined by Jim Heffern (right) and his wife and village president Chuck Zetteck with his wife, Gloria (left). Community officials attend events to support the community in which they serve. (EGHS.)

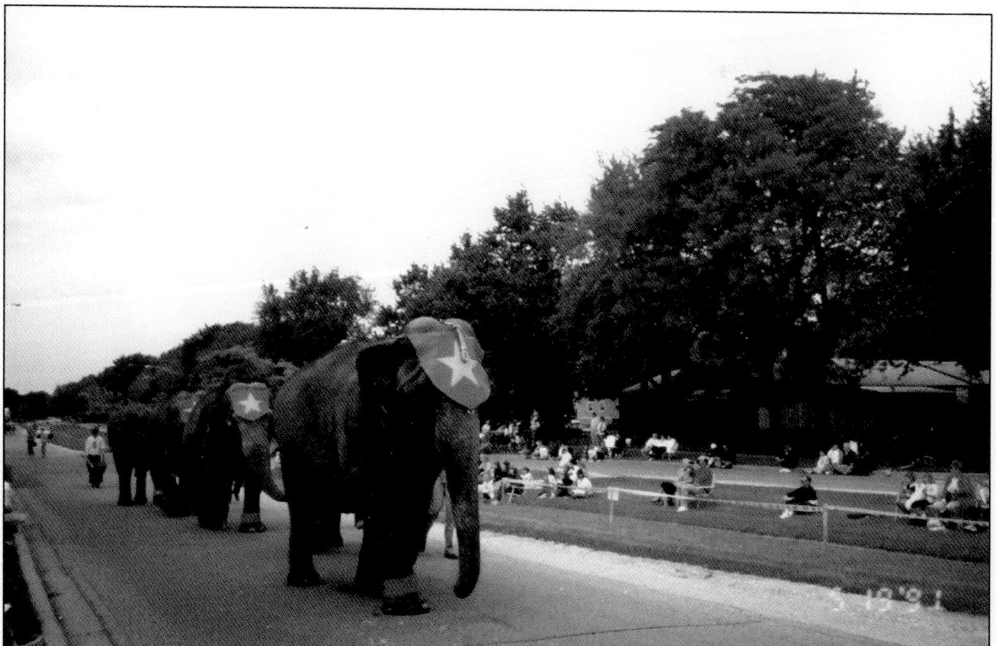

Elk Grove Village officials have held a hometown parade for years, but it was not until they switched it to an evening parade in 2000 that they began to attract record-size crowds. Thousands of residents and visitors crowd the two-mile route starting at Elk Grove Boulevard and Tonne Road, heading west on Elk Grove Boulevard and ending at Lions Drive by the high school.

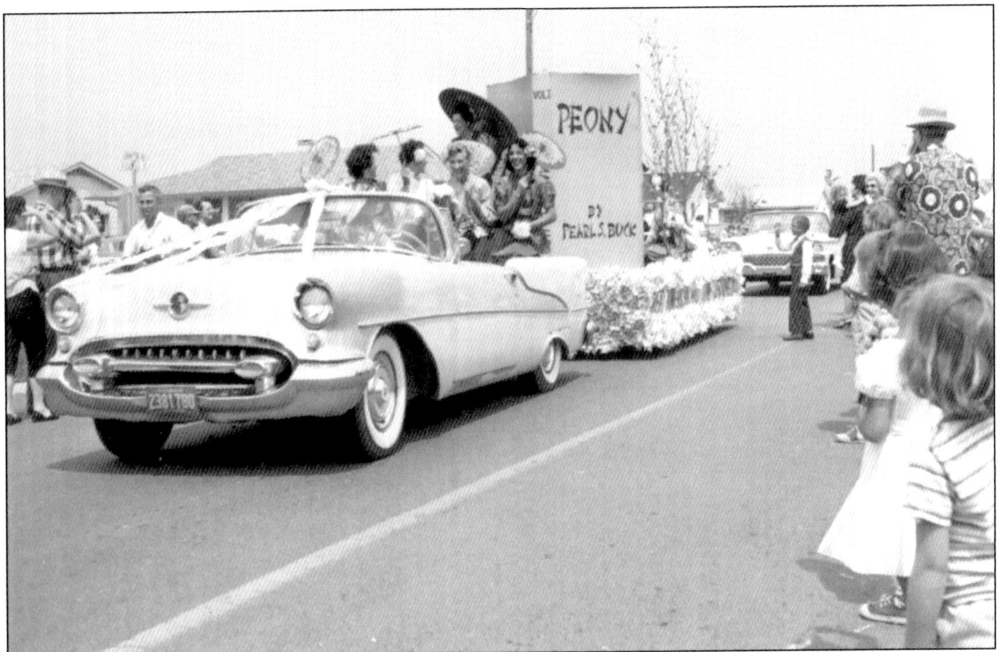

The Peony Parade of 1959 featured a float by the Junior Women's Club. The float was designed by Darlene Greaves and had a theme relating to the club's library affiliation. The float looked like Pearl S. Buck's book, *Peony*, and won first place for the best use of the peony. Several thousand residents watched the parade year after year. (EGHS.)

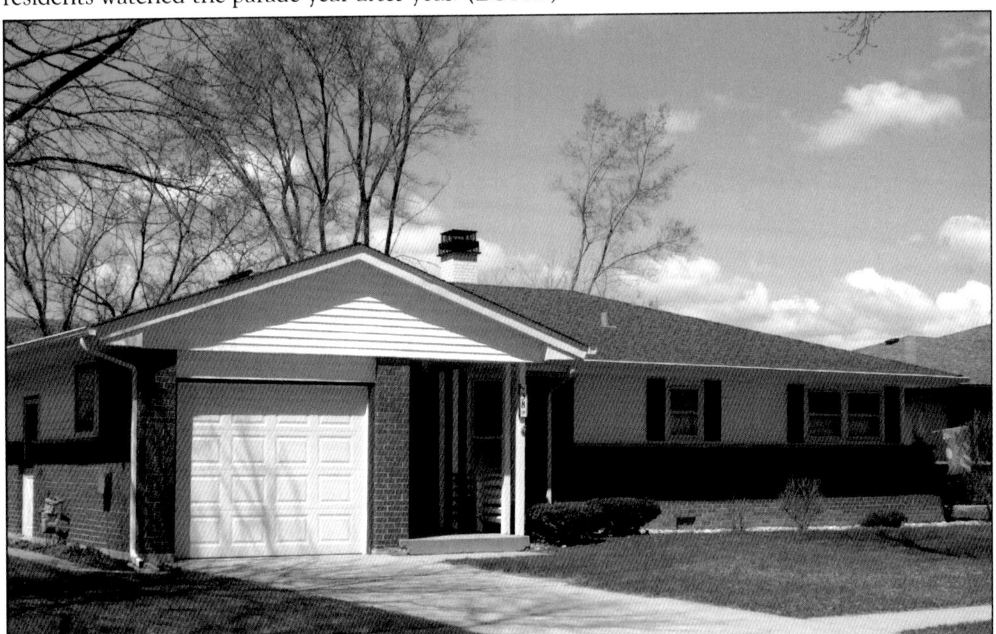

The Elk Grove Village Public Library was founded in 1959 in a house at 38 Forest Lane. Centex Corporation donated the building to the Junior Women's Club for the purpose of a library. The first librarian was resident Evelyn Schmidt in 1961. The mailbox was used as a book return and the bathtub was where books were stored until the volunteers were able to reshelf the books.

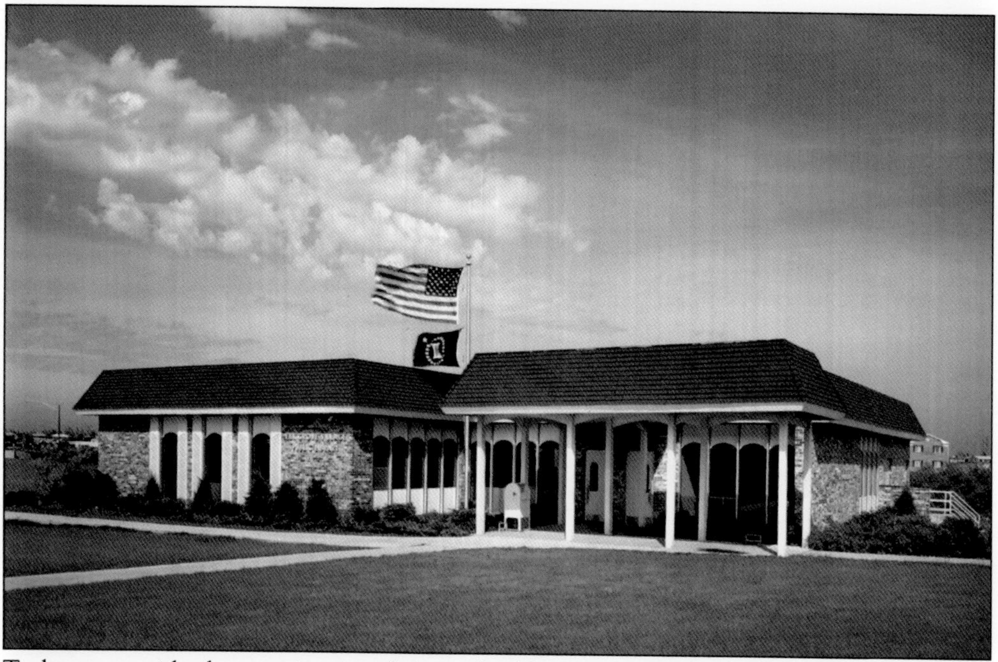

To keep up with the growing population, the library expanded. In July 1966, it moved to 901 Brantwood Avenue. Pictured above is the library on Brantwood Avenue in 1968. In 1990, the library again moved. The fire department administrative offices and the local Channel 6 news now reside in the old library building. (EGHS.)

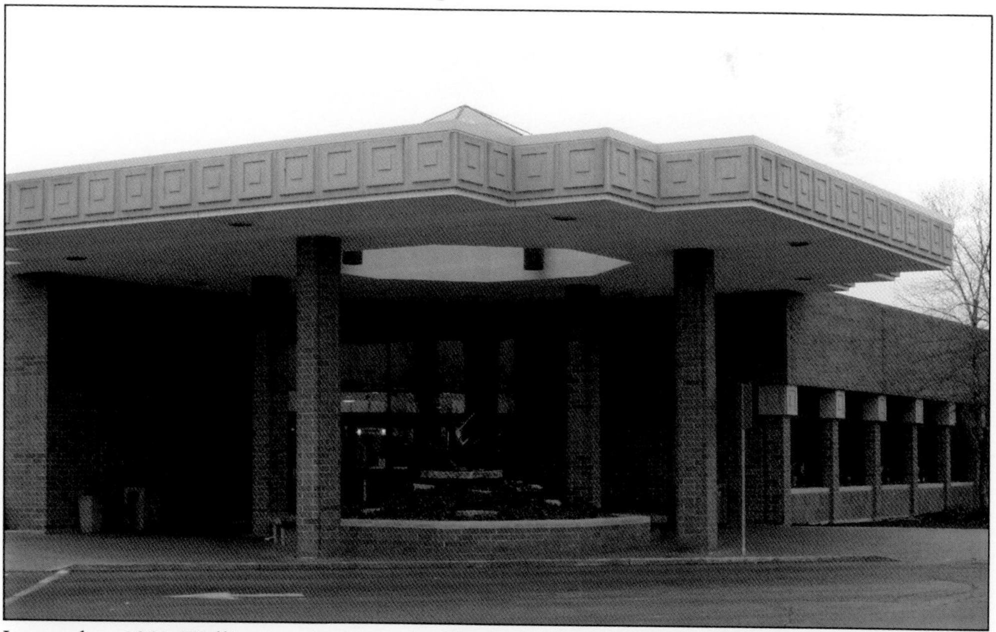

Located at 1001 Wellington Avenue, the Elk Grove Village Public Library opened its current 63,000-square-foot facility in September 1990. Expanding its inventory by adding over 19,000 books and materials annually, the library is considered one of the top five Illinois libraries for per capita use. It has an extensive business collection and has access to 15 million items from other libraries within the system.

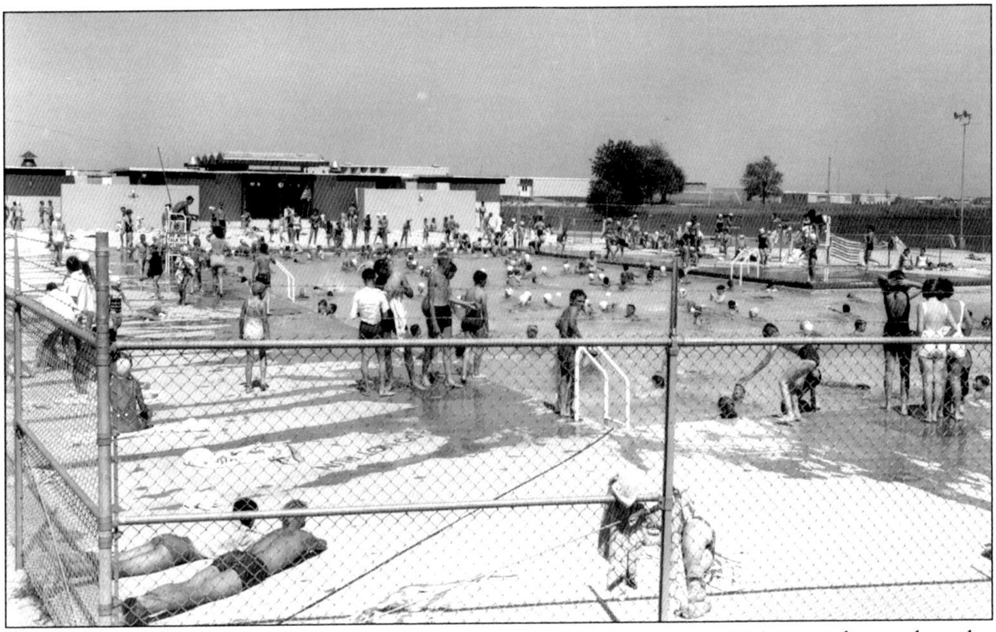

Lion's park and pool, which was built by Lion's Club fund-raising in 1961, was donated to the village park district. Hardworking members of the club took on the tasks of painting, landscaping, administration, and management for the opening and dedication to occur in June. The entire facility was given to the Elk Grove Park District seven years later. In 1986, Lion's pool was converted into Rainbow Falls. (EGHS.)

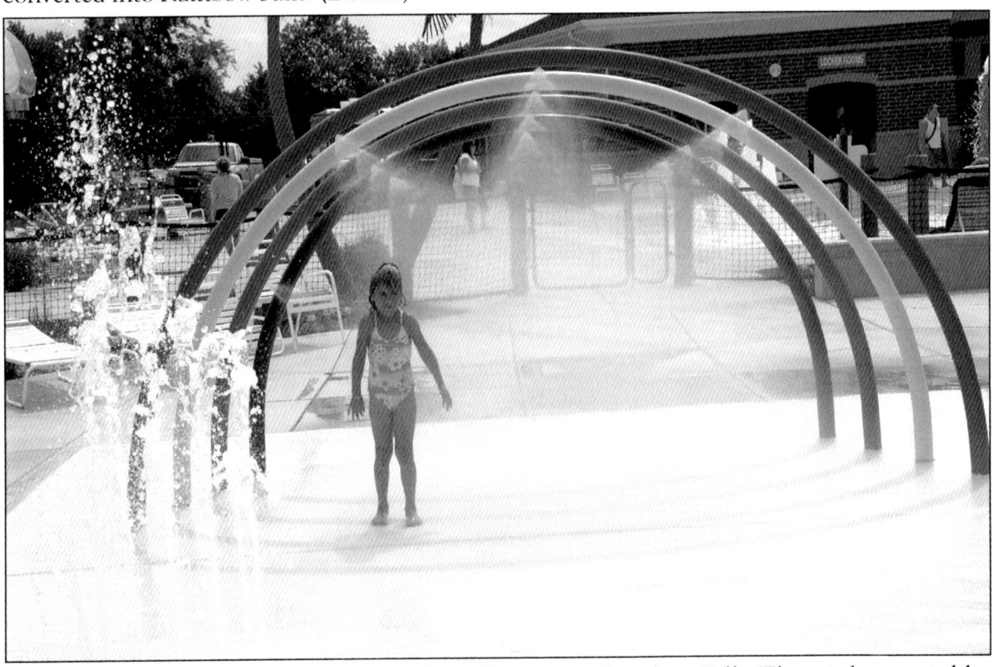

Shauna Snell knows how to cool off on a hot afternoon at Rainbow Falls. The rainbow sprinkler is one of the many water attractions for kids. Rainbow Falls has a little something for everyone from toddlers frolicking in the kiddie pool to adults kicking back for a relaxing ride down the lazy river.

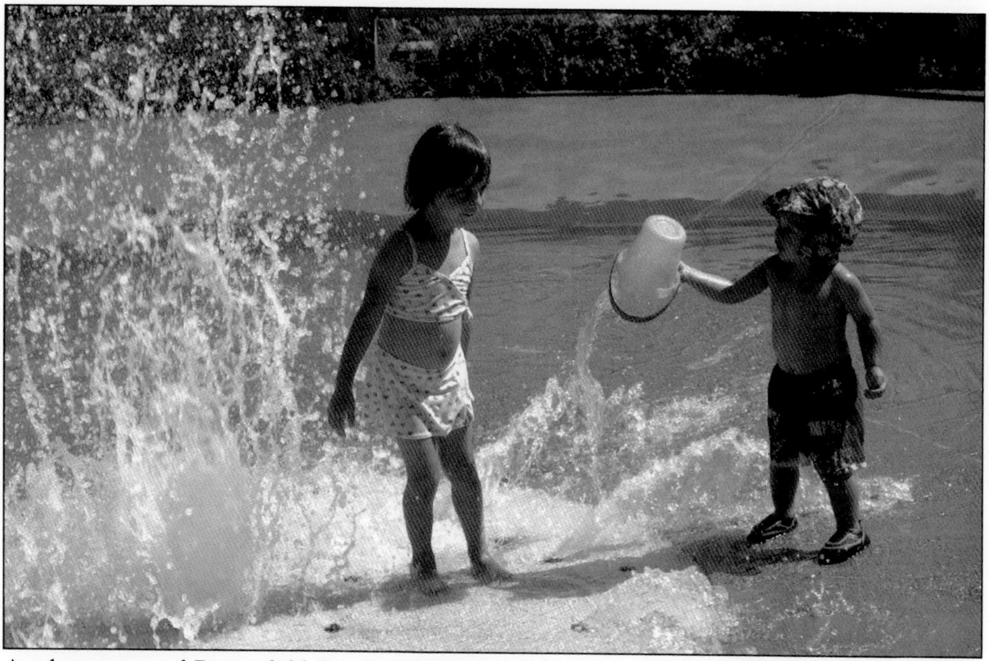

At the corner of Biesterfield Road and Gibson Drive is a popular park for many residents, nonresidents, and youth summer camps. Having two playgrounds, two water playgrounds, a bike and pedestrian trail, and a covered shelter and picnic area, this park is the perfect place on a warm summer day. Summer camps use this park as a place for a morning or afternoon field trip. Snell and Nathan Schiavo cannot resist the cooling water from the fountain in the park, which is on most of the day and into early evening hours. Ryan Hennings is a resident who enjoys one of the two playground areas. At the end of 2007 and into 2008, Fountain Square Park was updated with newer equipment.

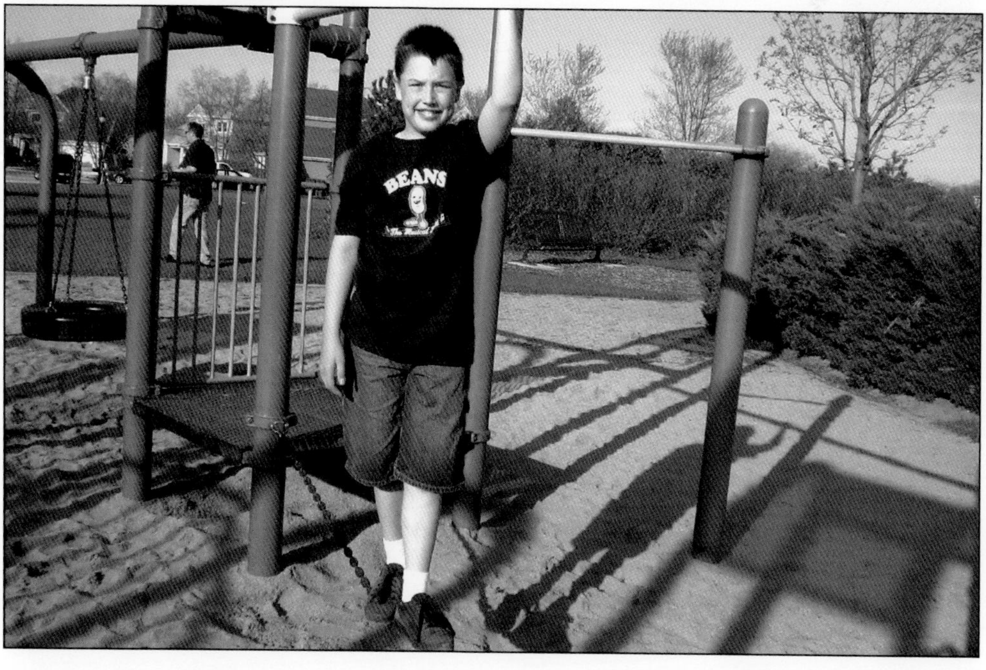

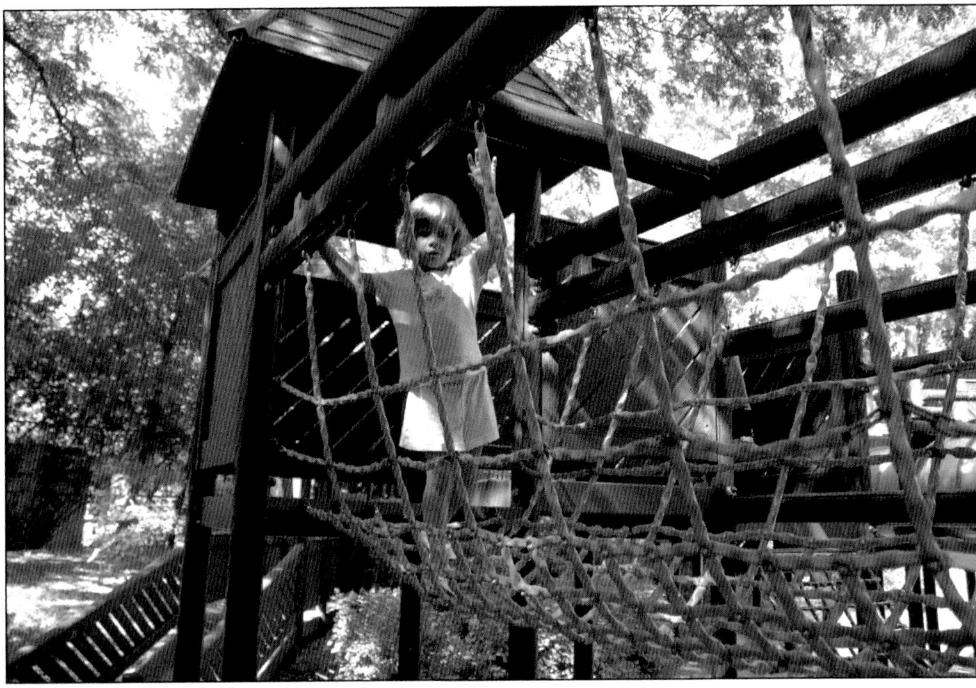

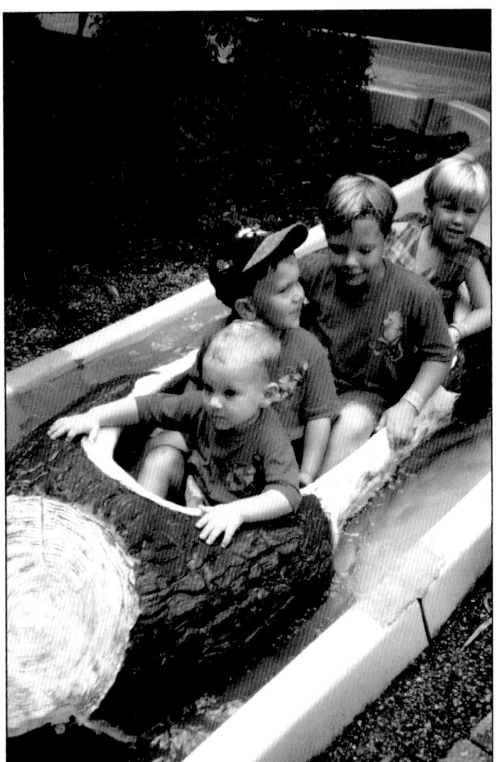

Children between the ages of two and nine will find a hidden treasure known as Pirate's Cove Theme Park. Children can climb through the newly renovated Castle of Camelot, ride down Misty the smoke-breathing dragon, race friends down the Pirate Plunge, scale up the 20-foot-high Smugglers Crag, ride a train through the old Eureka Mine, or picnic on the authentic 18th-century pirate ship. Pirate's Cove first opened in 1983. Over 125,000 people visited it by the end of its second season. Shauna Snell climbs through the obstacle nets in the pirate-climbing arena (above). From left to right, Steven Vicino and Nick Vicino ride with another boy and Diana Zinnel on the log ride in 1995. The log ride has since been replaced by the Safari Train ride.

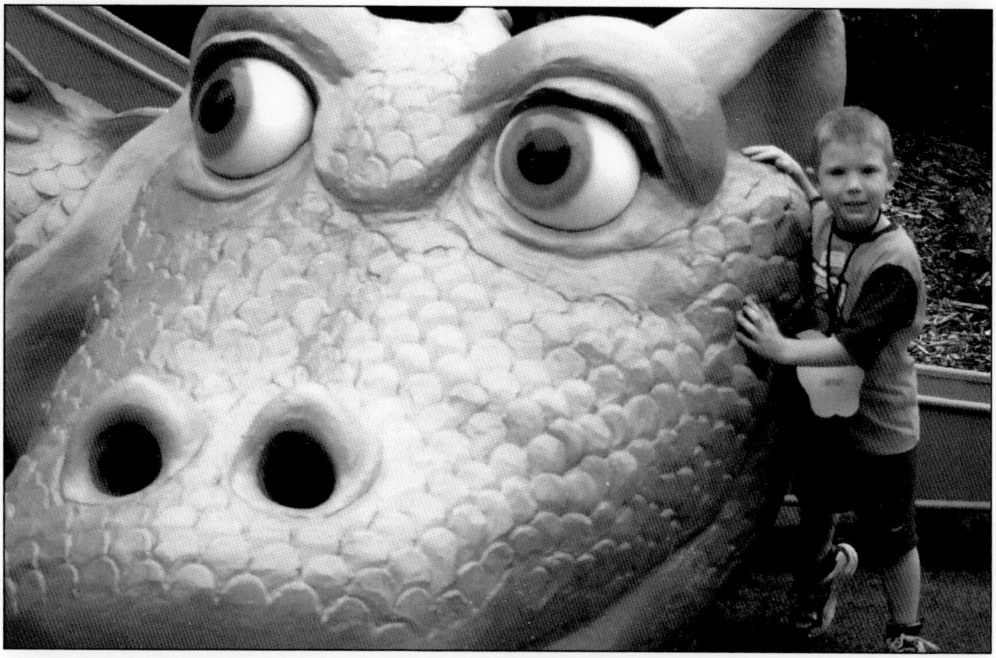

Preschooler Jordan Colby enjoys a fun-filled day at Pirate's Cove. Traditionally, the last day of school for many preschools is spent at Pirate's Cove. The green dragon looks a little intimidating as he guards the castle, but he is friendly, and kids love sliding down his red tongue. The playground equipment, wooden decks, net bridges, tunnels, tubes, and tires are fun no matter the age of the child.

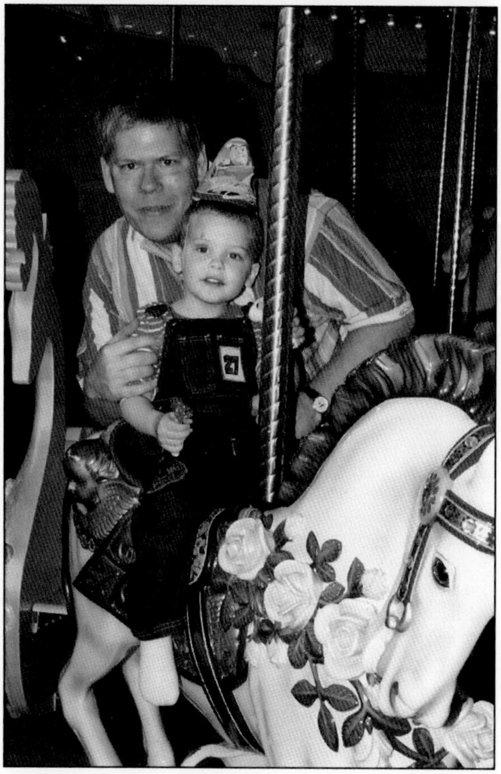

A very popular party location is at the Jack A. Claes Pavilion Carousel. Adults and children both can ride on the indoor carousel. Since the carousel room can be rented for groups or birthday parties for up to 100 guests, it is not unusual for residents to book a carousel party one year in advance. Elk Grove Village resident Bob Behnke and his son Ian celebrate Ian's third birthday.

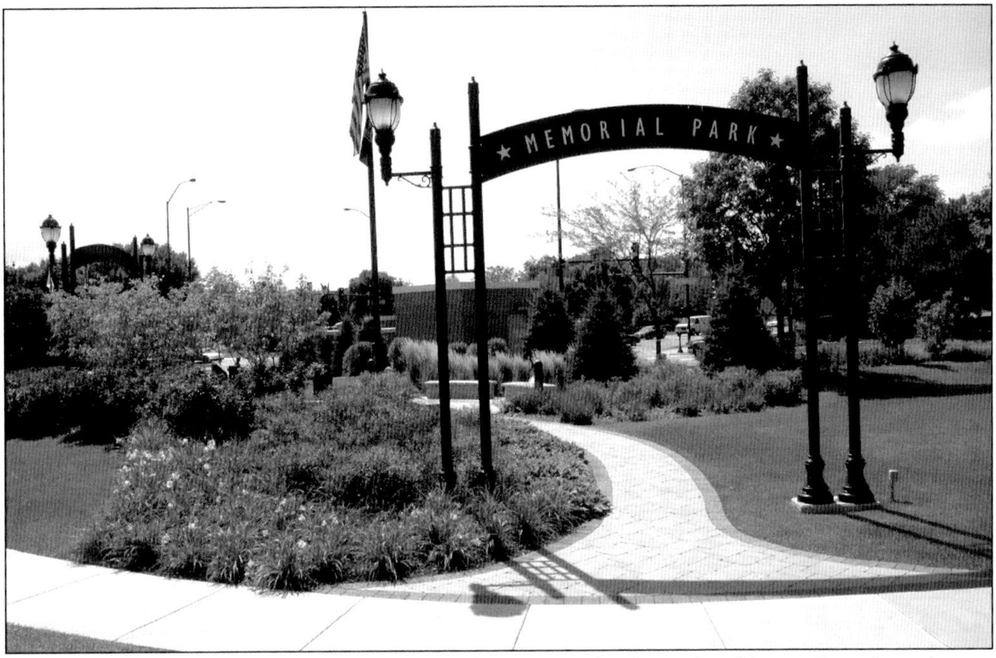

Visitors to the park walk through gateways, known as the "portals of honor," as the relaxing sound of a fountain echoes nearby. It serves as a tribute to the men and women of Elk Grove Village who dedicated their lives protecting liberty and freedom. Each branch of the armed forces is recognized with a granite obelisk. More than two years of planning was needed for Veterans Memorial Park. The park not only honors veterans but also offers a place for reflection for families touched by the service of men and women veterans. The family of George Gullo granted the property for development in his honor. The Veterans of Foreign Wars, Post No. 9284 and the American Legion Post No. 216 helped bring this Veterans Memorial Park to realization.

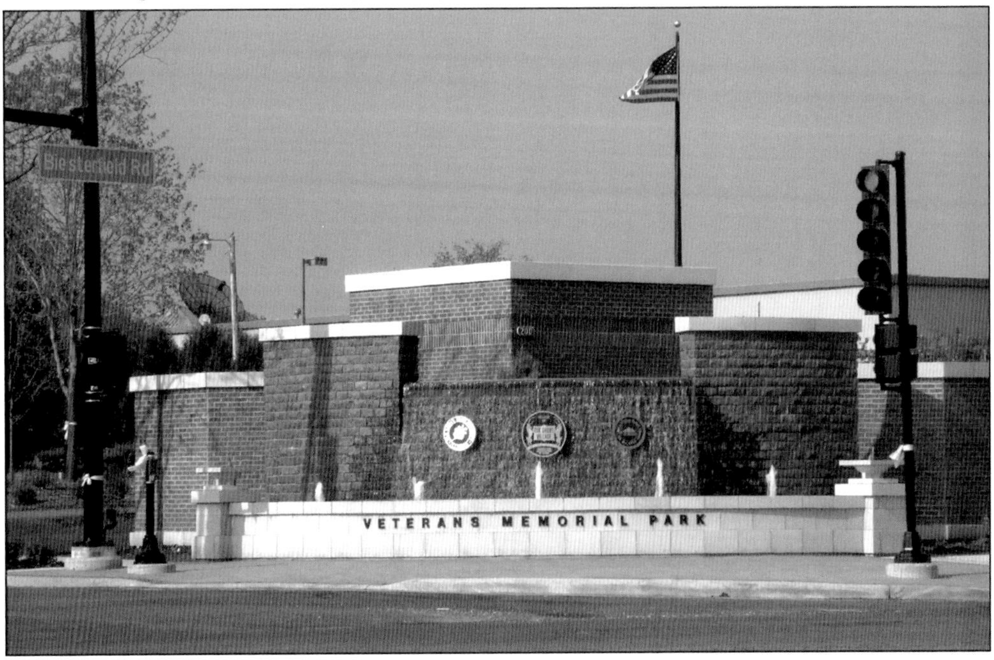

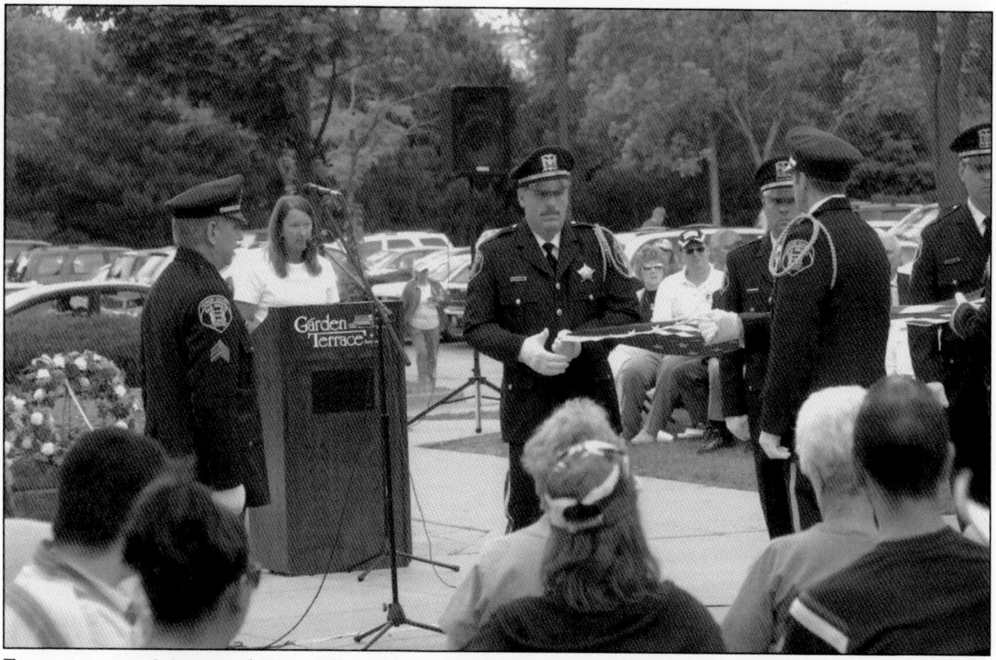

Every year on Memorial Day, Elk Grove Village honors those people who sacrificed their lives for the freedom of the country. In 2007, village trustee Chris Prochno read what each of the 13 flag folds meant as the fire and police honor guard began the flag-folding ceremony. On Memorial Day, the third fold of the flag had special meaning. "The 3rd fold is made in honor and remembrance of the veterans departing our ranks who gave a portion of their lives for the defense of our country to attain peace throughout the world." During the ceremony, a World War II plane flew overhead. The ceremony took place in front of the Jack A. Claes Pavilion by a bronze statue titled *Field of Blue*.

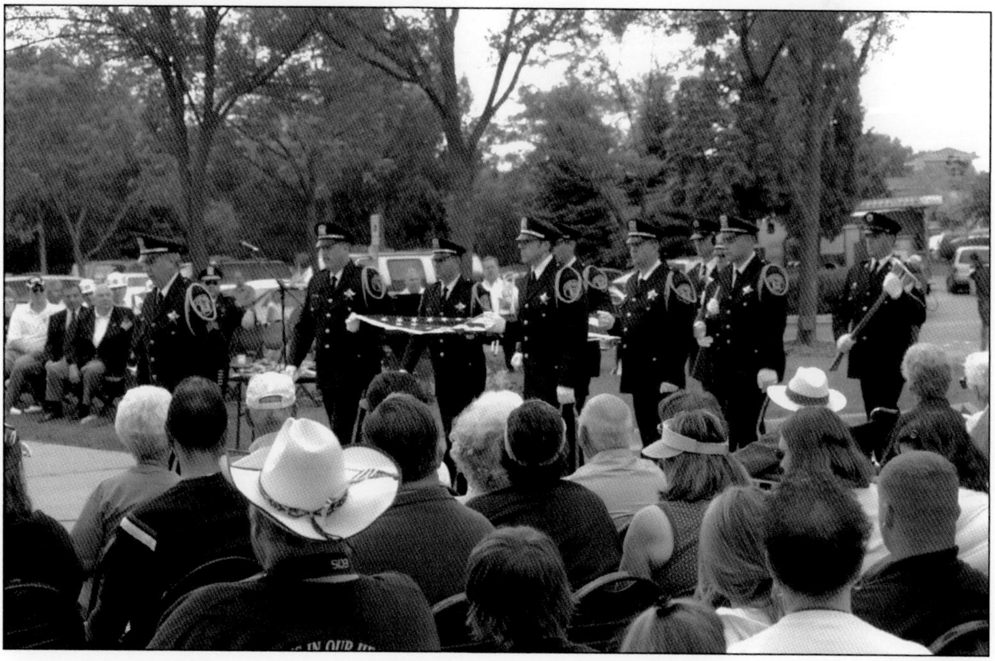

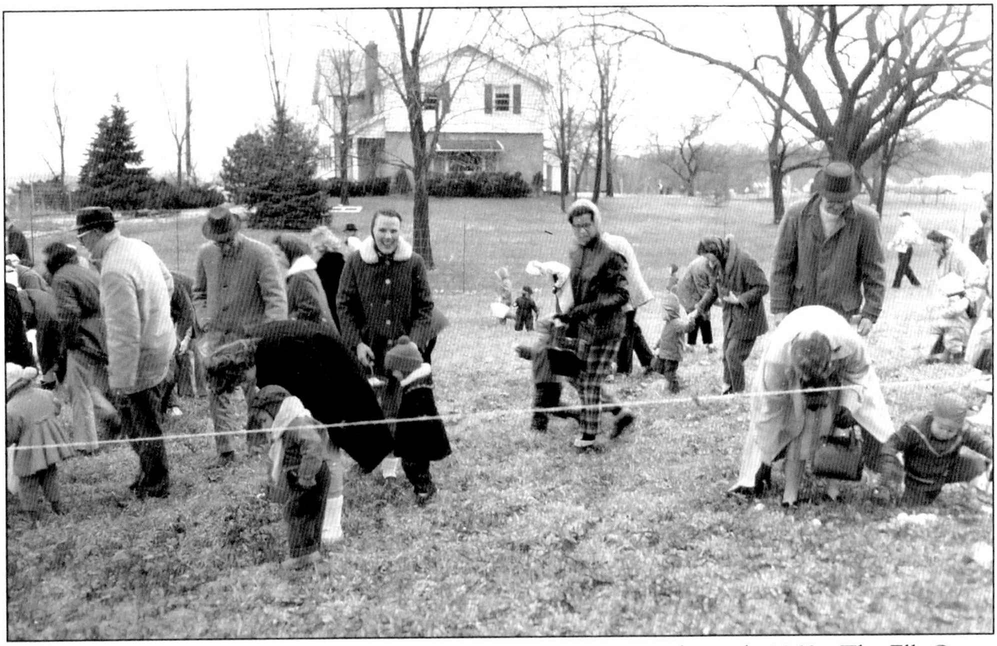

Easter-egg hunts were held in the Ned Brown Forest Preserve in the early 1960s. The Elk Grove Jaycee's sponsored the events. Thousands of eggs blanketed the grass with a sea of beautiful color. Real hard-boiled eggs were used up until the 1970s. Hundreds of families turned out for the event every year with their Easter baskets in hand, waiting to see how many eggs they could gather.

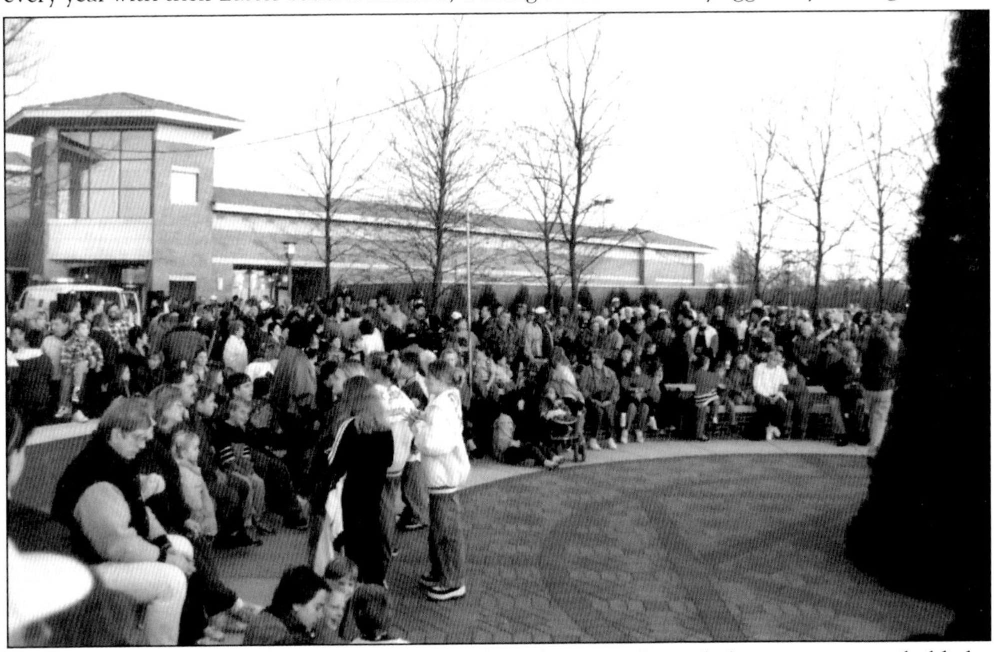

Since 1998, Elk Grove residents look forward to the annual tree-lighting ceremony held the Friday after Thanksgiving. Hundreds of residents and visitors flock to the Elk Grove Village Green to see Santa and Mrs. Claus and to hear the Christmas carols sung by the Elk Grove High School choir. Hot chocolate and cookies distributed by the Lion's Club warms up the chilly evening. A beautiful display of fireworks ends the joyous event.

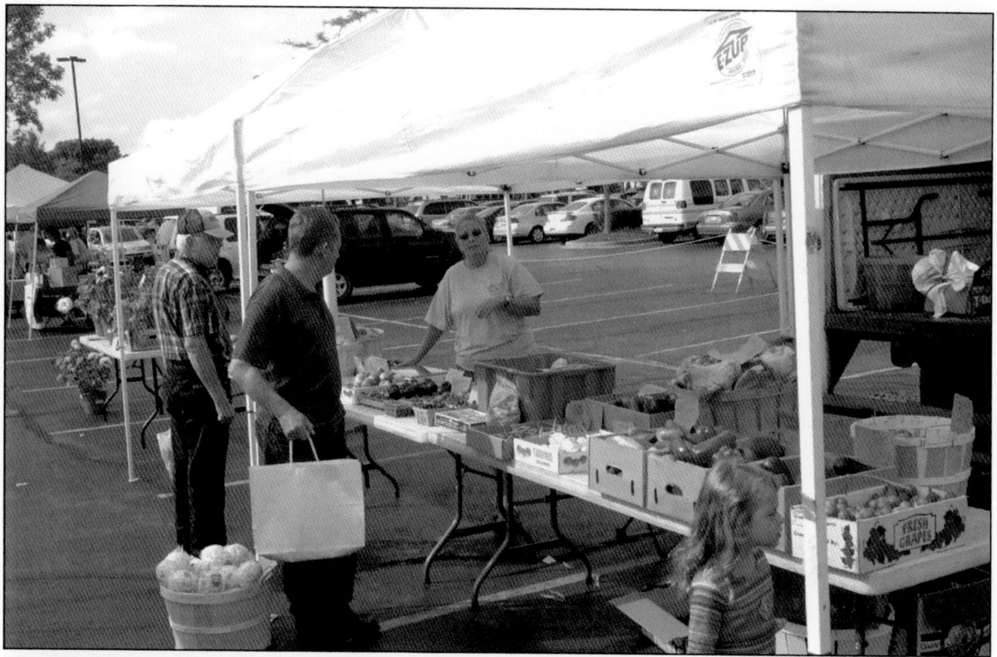

The Elk Grove Village Farmer's Market is located at 1000 Wellington Avenue at the intersection of Wellington Avenue and Biesterfield Road. It is across the street from the village clock tower. Residents can find farm-fresh vegetables, flowers, fruits, honey, salsa, juices, gourmet pet products, and more. It opens on Wednesdays from June until September.

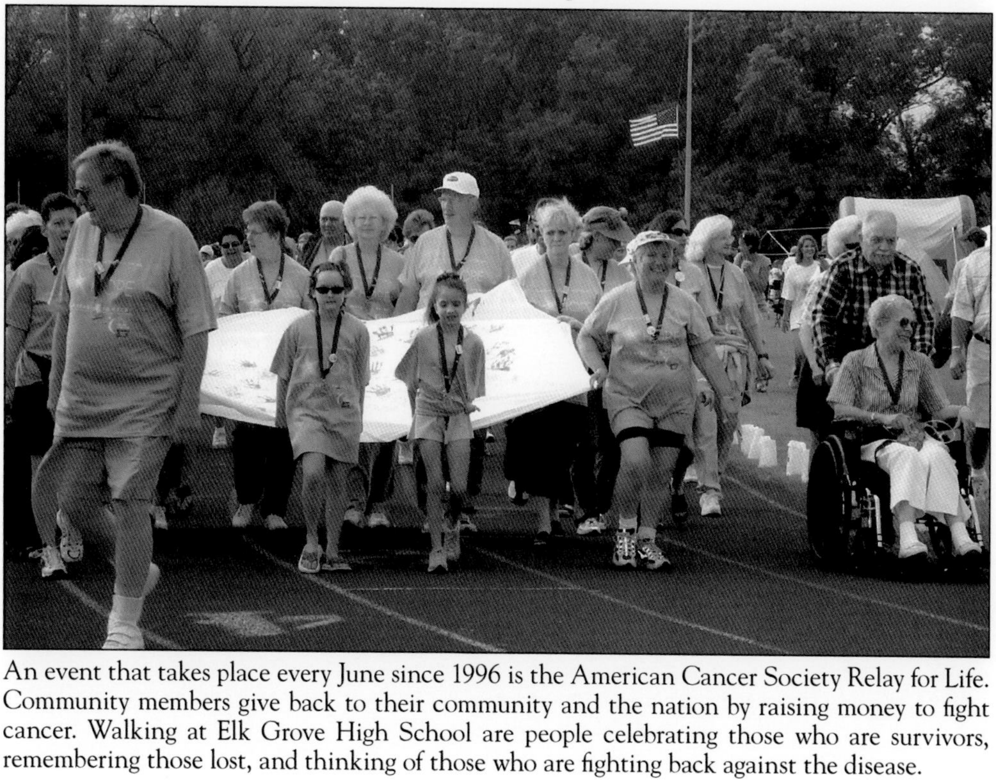

An event that takes place every June since 1996 is the American Cancer Society Relay for Life. Community members give back to their community and the nation by raising money to fight cancer. Walking at Elk Grove High School are people celebrating those who are survivors, remembering those lost, and thinking of those who are fighting back against the disease.

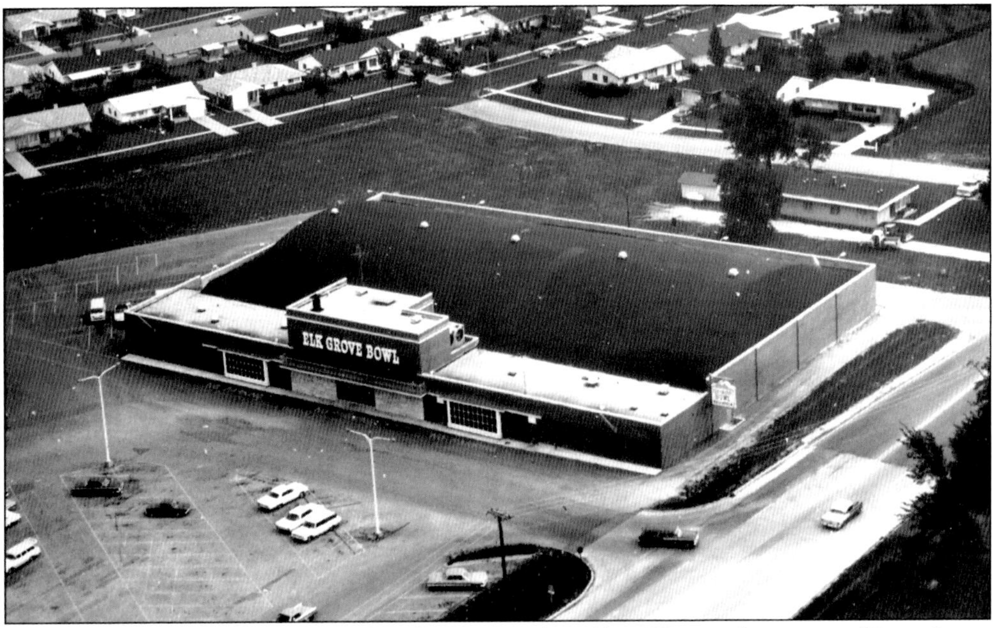

Elk Grove Bowl opened in 1963 in the Elk Grove Park 'n' Shop Plaza at the corner of State Street (now Arlington Heights Road) and Higgins Road. Centex Corporation built the first residential subdivision for Elk Grove Village behind the bowling center in what was considered downtown Elk Grove. Although downtown has since moved, Elk Grove Bowl is in its same location, with a third-generation family member running the entertainment center.

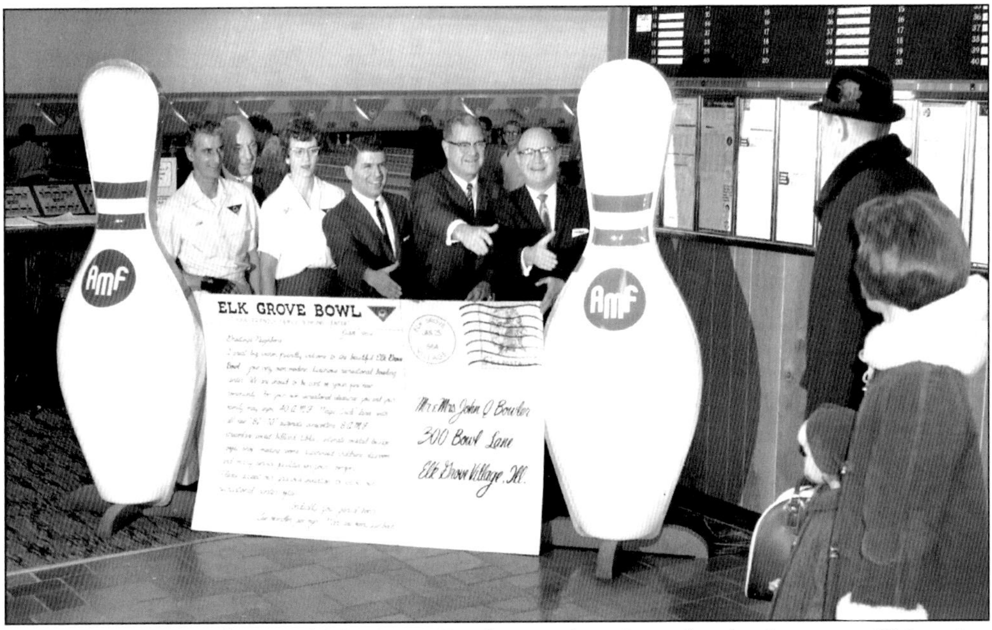

In August 1963, family-owned Elk Grove Bowl opened its doors for the first time. Welcoming customers, from left to right, are professional bowler Jim St. John, two AMF representatives, owner Lewis Handler, owner Marc Auerback, and Henry Auerback. Currently, third-generation family member Debbie Handler owns and operates Elk Grove Bowl. Debbie is the daughter of Lewis and the granddaughter of Marc. Elk Grove Bowl is located at 53 South Arlington Heights Road.

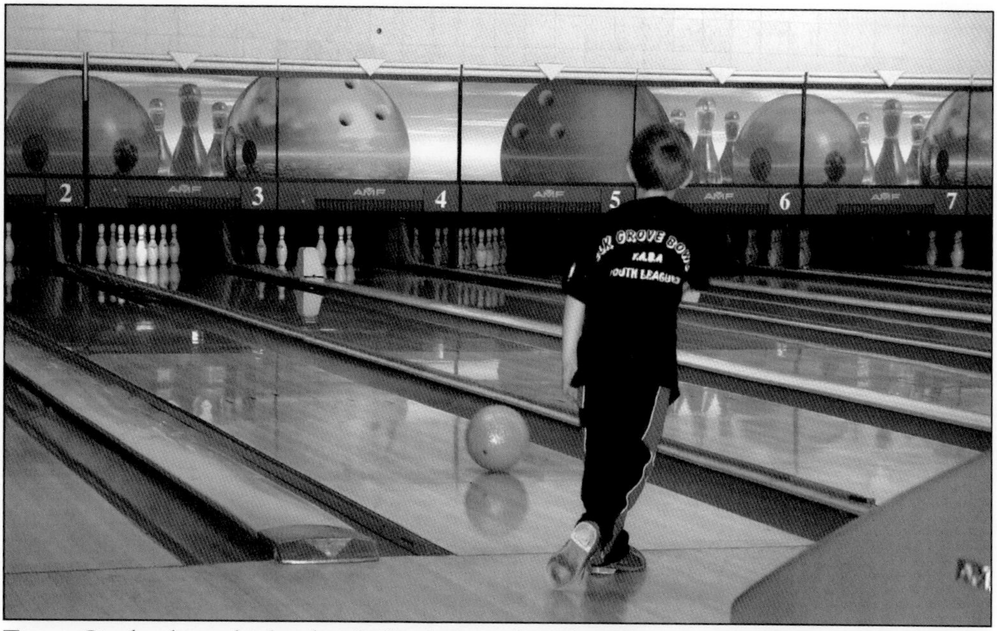

Timmy Sipolt releases his bowling ball in hopes of a strike. Elk Grove Bowl offers many programs and leagues for their young bowlers as well as older bowlers. Youth bowlers can join fun or competitive summer and fall leagues. There are youth tournaments and scholarship programs where youth can earn money bowling for their college fund. Youth bowlers also have trained coaches during the leagues, offering them advice on techniques.

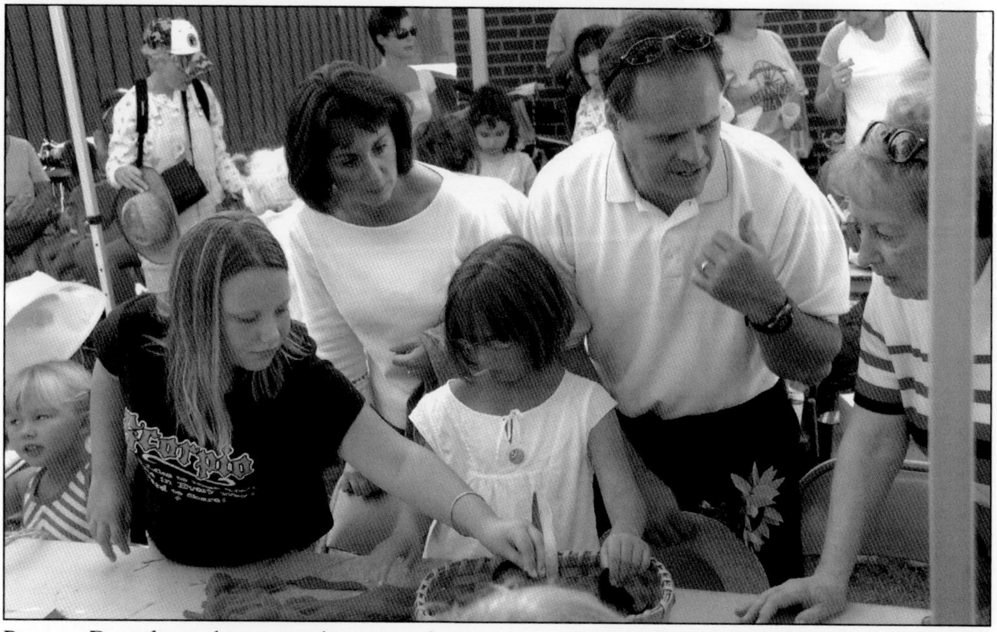

Pioneer Days festival is a popular event that re-creates life in the pioneer era. Starting in 1978, the festival, sponsored by the Elk Grove Historical Society, attracts large crowds of spectators and participants who look for more hands-on pioneer activities to experience. Tours of the museum and farmhouse are also given. Celebrating with blue grass music and square dancing is also available. The Snell family enjoys family time at Pioneer Days.

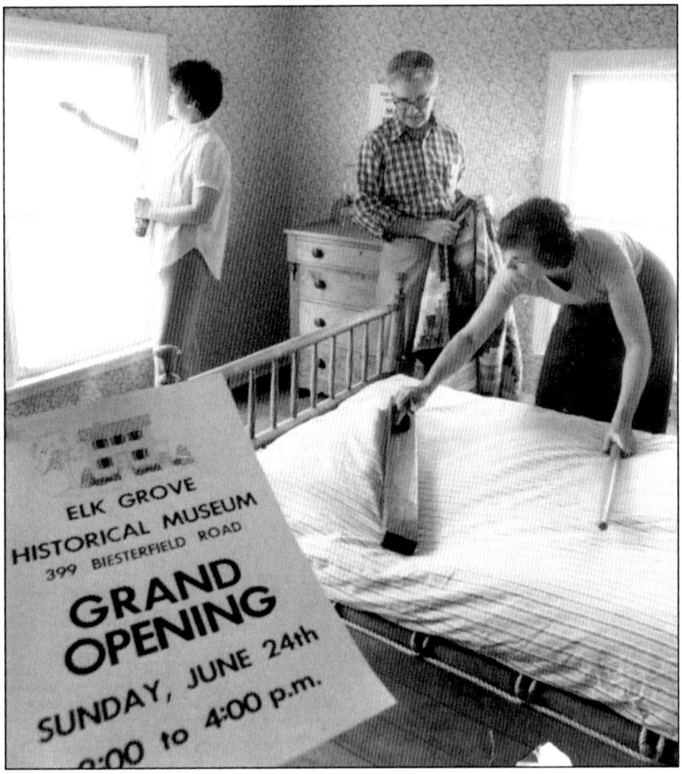

Charter members of the Elk Grove Historical Society Margie Elkins (left), Phil Barry, and Darlene Greaves prepare for the historical museum open house on June 24, 1979. The Schuette-Biermann historic house is the home of the historical society of Elk Grove located at 499 Biesterfield Road. Formed on July 10, 1975, the organization has been an important factor in the preservation of local history. (EGHS.)

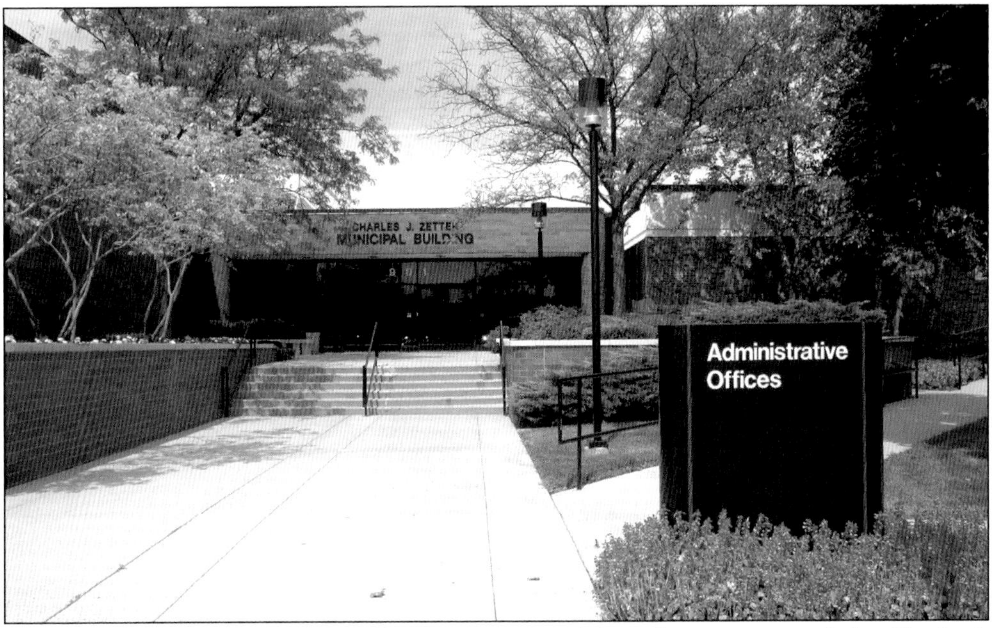

After his retirement in 1993, the Elk Grove Municipal Complex was renamed the Charles J. Zettek Municipal Building. Known for his love of the community, Zettek called Elk Grove Village "the Camelot of the Northwest Suburbs." Although he died at the age of 69, he served the community for 32 years. He was a village trustee for 10 years before serving as the village president from 1971 to 1993.

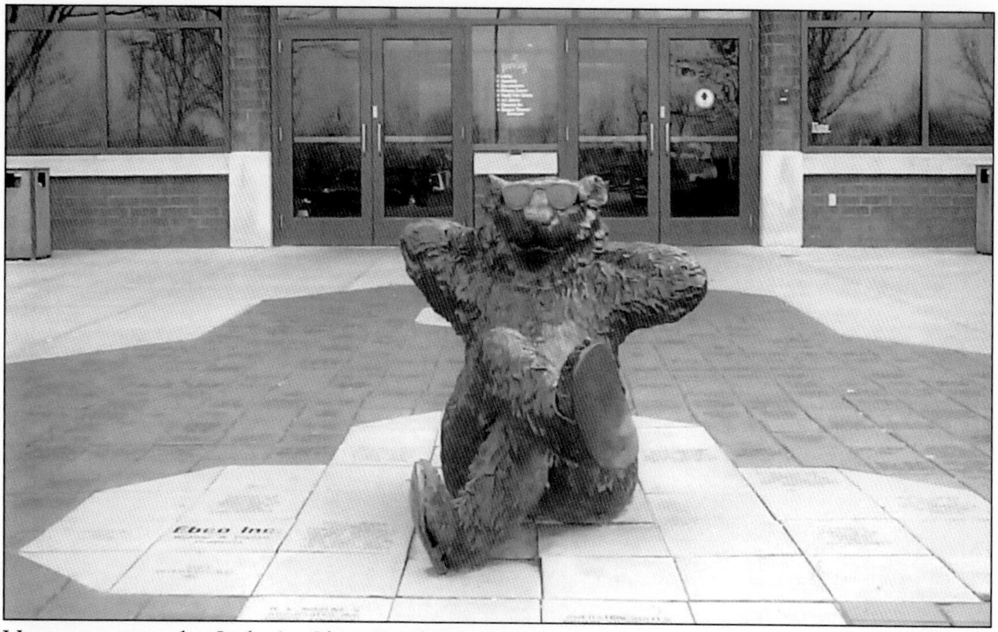

Upon entering the Jack A. Claes Pavilion, guests enjoy memories and personal expressions shared by other community members. Embossed memorial bricks are purchased in celebration of a birthday, announcement of a graduation, a dedication to military individuals, or just to display a company name and trade. In the center of these bricks sits a welcoming bear statue named *Shades* that entices children of all ages to jump on his lap.

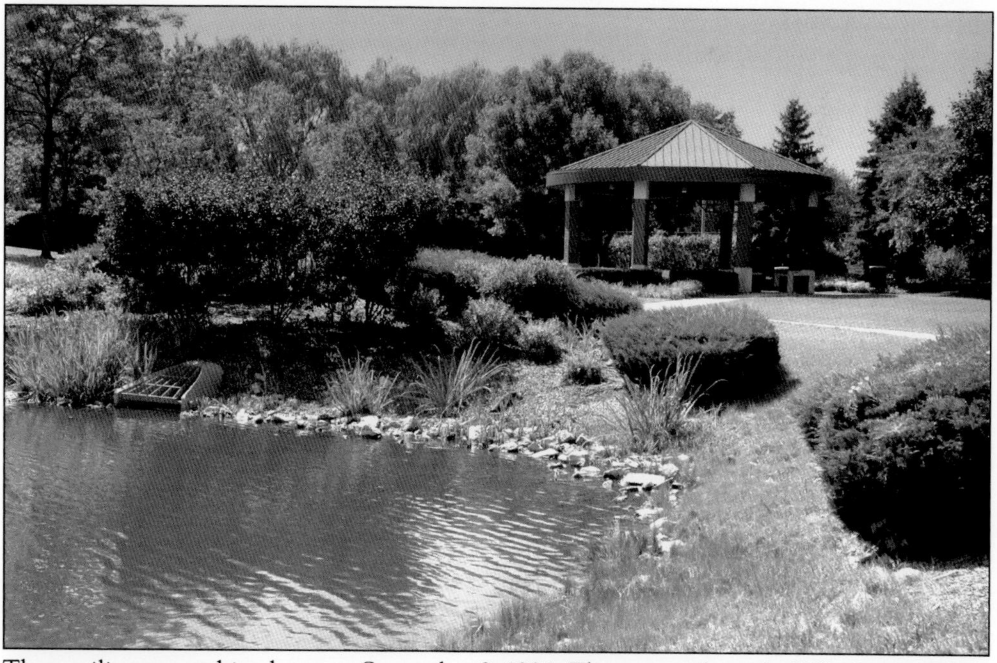

The pavilion opened its doors on September 9, 1994. The crowned jewel of Elk Grove Village has become the center of community activity. Over a quarter million people a year pass through its doors to enjoy the many events and activities held daily. The gazebo on the grounds is often used for weddings.

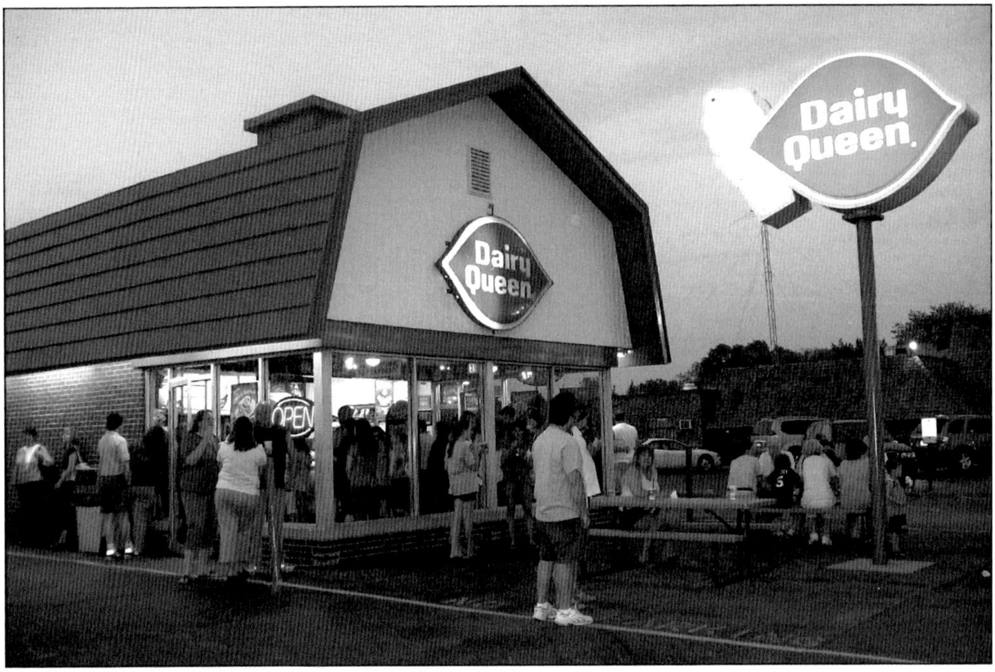

Built in 1965 at 20 East Devon Avenue, Dairy Queen has served as a central location for families, friends, and sports teams to gather together for fun and celebration. Rob and Jennifer Jordan, residents since 1989, opened their family-owned business to the community in the spring of 1990. Since then, they have given back to the community by sponsoring many sport teams and employing hundreds of teenagers looking for work from Elk Grove and Conant High Schools. Many of these teenagers work from their freshman year in high school to their senior year in college. From left to right, Alex Montague, Linda Beaudoin, Tim Furlong, Paige Bostedt, and Ryan Jordan are a few of those teenage employees.

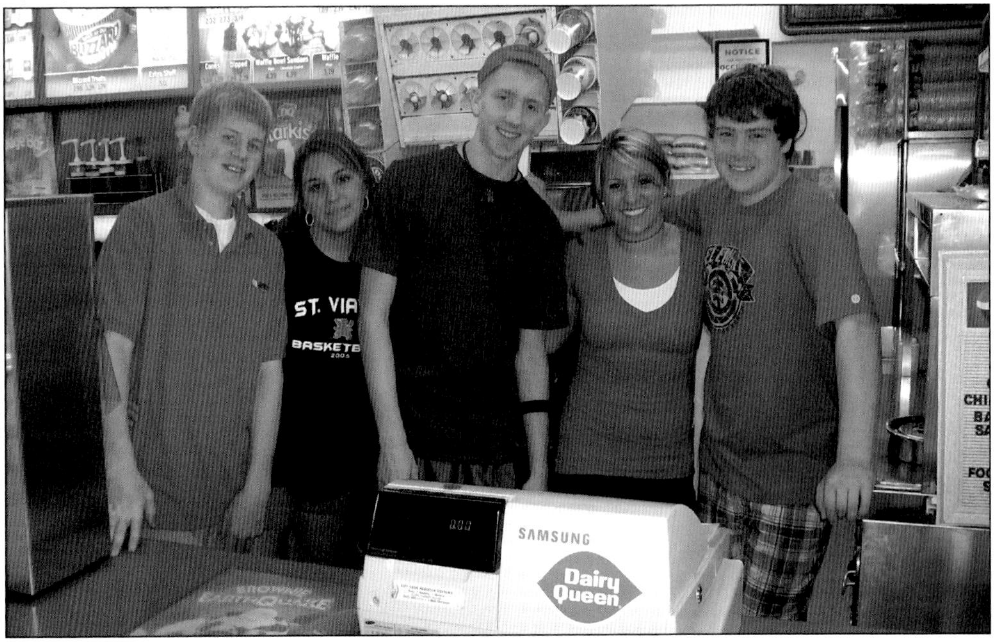

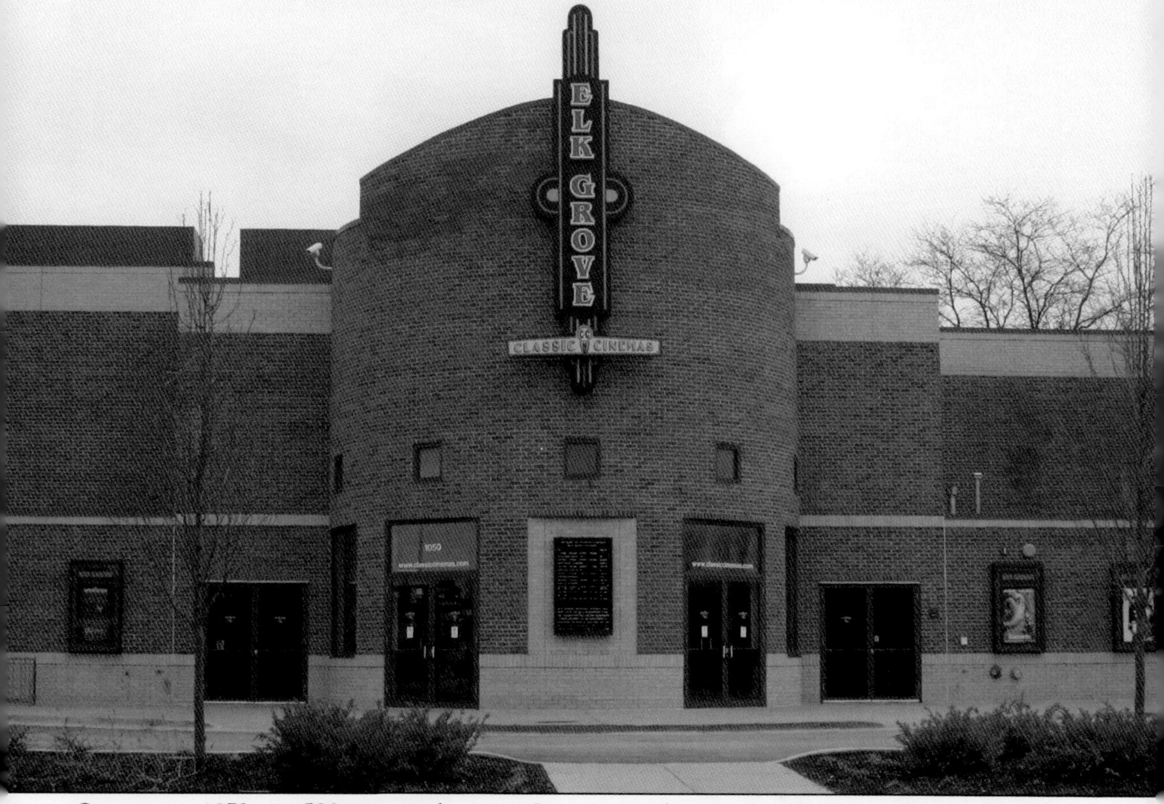

Opening in 1972 as a 500-seat single screen Jerry Lewis theater, the Elk Grove Theatre closed a few years later. After being vacant for many years, Classic Cinemas started a total-reconstruction project in October 1986. The theater reopened April 17, 1987. In 1997, Classic Cinemas bought the theater and started construction again to add four more auditoriums. Reopening in April 1998, the theater has the latest amenities. The Elk Grove Theatre is the first in the country to install the Kodak Digital Cinema System, producing almost twice the screen quality of other systems. In 2007, the theater expanded again to include two big-screen auditoriums, stadium seating, digital sound, and two new handicapped-accessible party rooms.

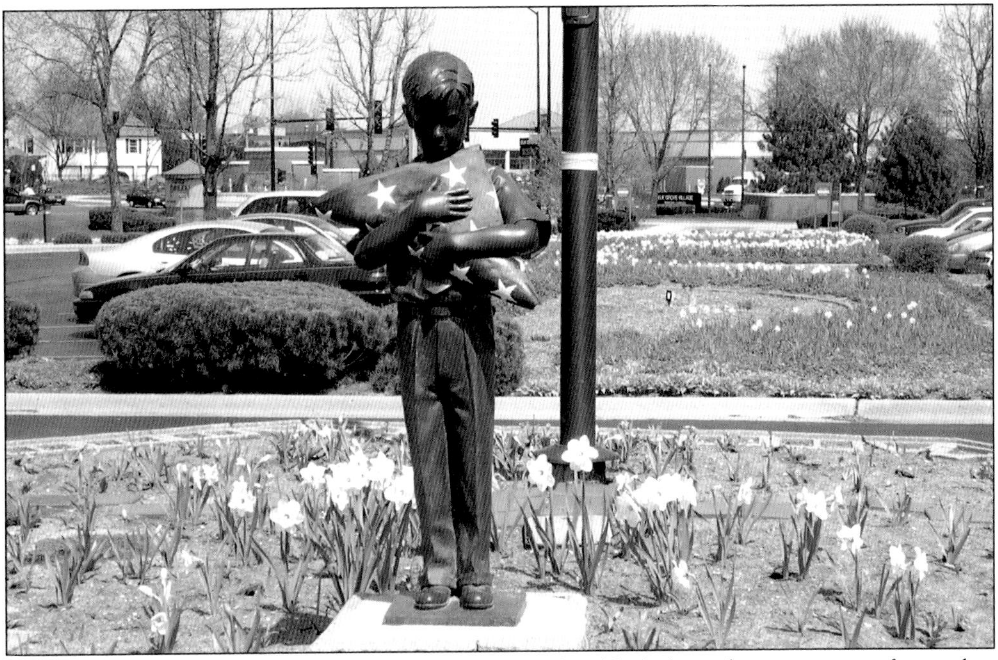

The Veterans of Foreign Wars Post No. 9284 donated *Field of Blue*, a bronze statue of a somber boy holding a folded American flag. The statue stands in front of the park district pavilion for many to see. *In the Shade* and *Sip and Splash* are also outside. Statues inside the pavilion are *Chealsea*, a ballerina, and *Boy on the Turtle*. These were bought for beautification purposes.

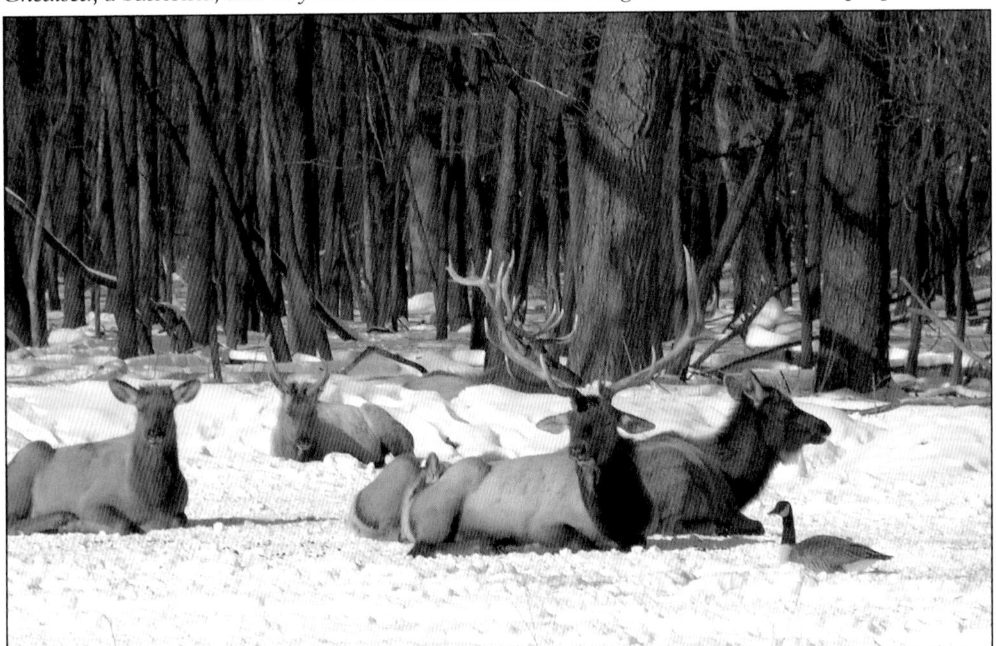

For all the elk enthusiasts, at the corner of Arlington Heights and Higgins Roads, people may visit the herd of elk that reside in the forest preserve. It is a great place for both children and adults to watch the elk in their natural home. When the elk get close to the fence, people are only an inch or two away from looking at these majestic animals.

Three

Just Playing the Game

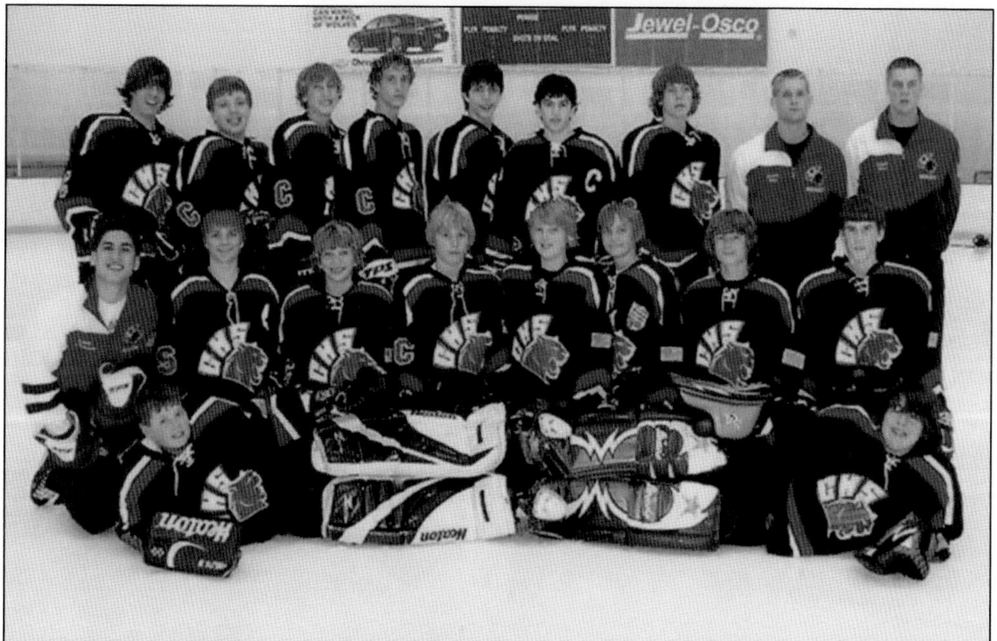

Back Row: Kevin Pollack, Chris Galuszka, Mark Anders, Jay Scheer, Adam Reninger, Anthony Altosino, Ryan Colby, Matt Turinsky and Brian Marek.
Kneeling: Vince Conenna, Kyle, Cornier, Connor Reed, Conor Donahue, Jimmy Donovan, Shane Hahn, Alex Rymarz and Tom Strahl
Goalies: Jeremy Palucska and Emmet O'Malley

CHS High School is a combined high school team consisting of Conant, Hoffman Estates, and Schaumburg High Schools. In 2005, Conant combined teams with Hoffman Estates and Schaumburg, bringing together three very strong hockey competitors, definitely a force to be reckoned with. The 2008 Chicago Metropolitan High School Northwest Junior Varsity Founders Cup champions were coached by former Conant student Vince Conenna, Matt Turinsky, and Brian Marek.

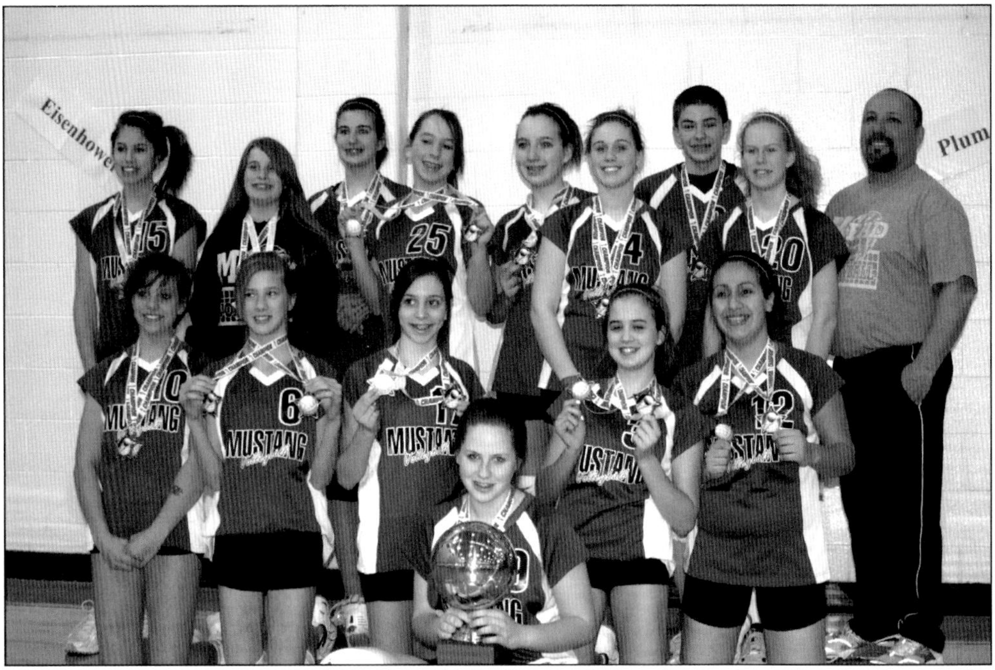

Although the local junior highs offer volleyball to girls, in the 2007–2008 school year, the Margaret Mead Mustangs had a boy successfully try out for the seventh-grade team. Margaret Mead Junior High supported the student and Title IX of the education amendments of 1972, proving once again that Elk Grove is an exceptional community. The seventh-grade team had a great year. Not only were they district 54 conference champions, but they were also tournament conference champions. Above from left to right, showing off their medals and trophy are (first row) Gabi Vaia, Laura Sue Jensen, Alyssa Altosino, Kylie Behnke (sitting), Suzi Loznjakovic, and Sarah Thompson; (second row) Ali Wright, Carly Guierri, Callie Kopp, Jessica Batio, Kelli Romero, Breanna Esmael, Brendan Pasbrig, Kelly Hartsfield, and coach Paul Beranek.

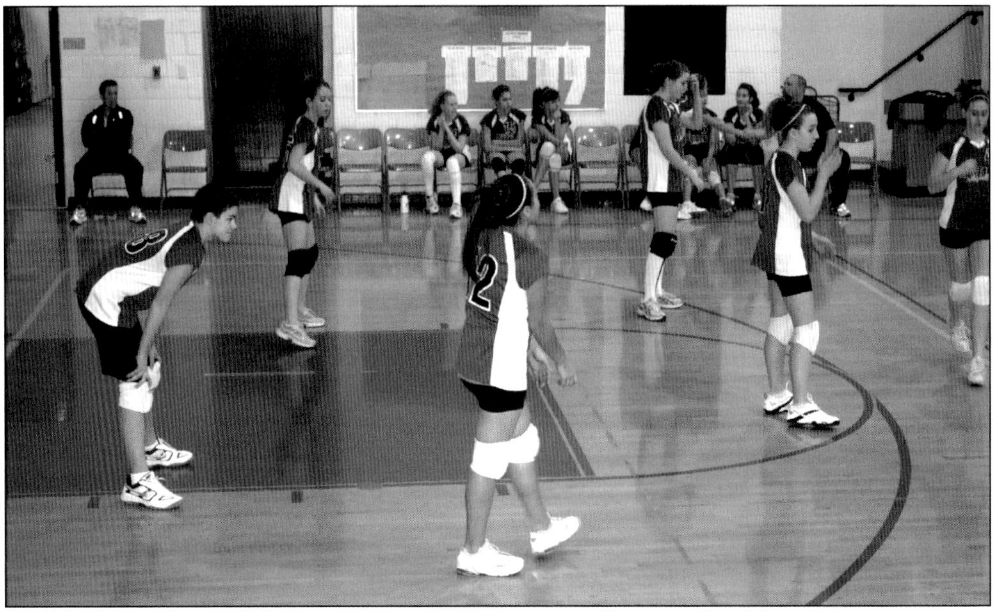

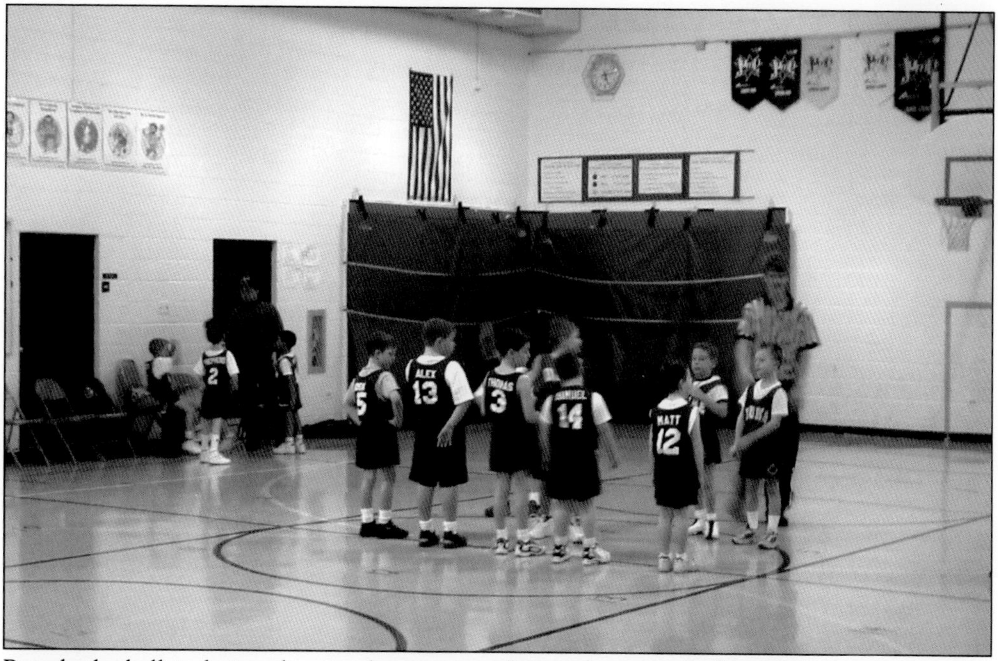

Boys basketball is designed to teach sportsmanship and teamwork through learning the basic skills of dribbling, shooting, passing, and defensive work. Classes are offered for toddlers through high school level. The third- and fourth-grade teams are strictly instructional and developmental. A draft process selects students in grades five through eight.

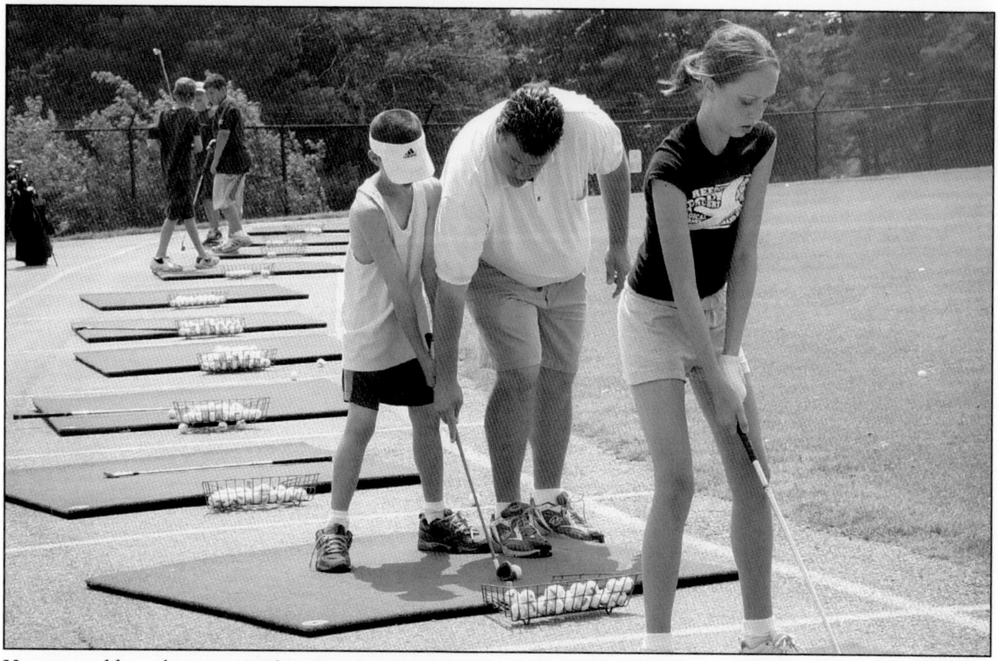

Young golf enthusiast Mike Sipolt takes lessons through the park district. Built in 1984 by William Newcomb, Fox Run Golf Links is a championship 18-hole course set on 124 acres of land. The course is located at 333 Plum Grove Road and is guaranteed to challenge any level of player because of the many lakes, sand traps, and trees.

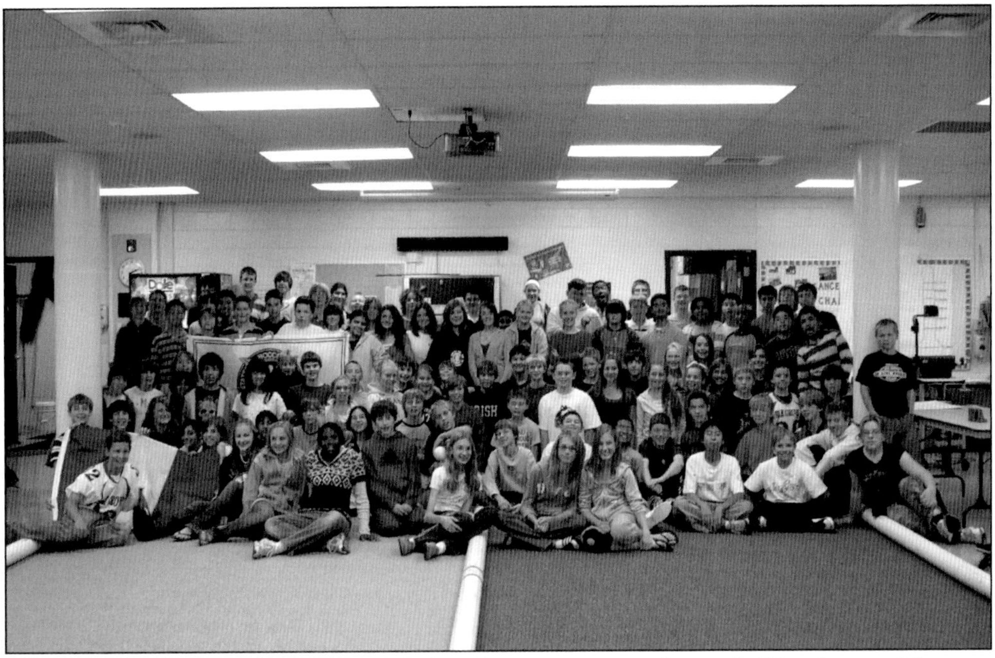

Margaret Mead bocce ball participants gather for a team picture. Bocce ball has been at Margaret Mead since 2004. It started out small with just one court, but because of all the enthusiasm and love for the sport, it has grown to two courts. All of the T-shirts, bocce balls, and carpet have been donated from the United States Bocce Federation. The pipe was donated from De Franco Plumbing in Palatine. Do to the generosity of all the sponsors, the school has not paid for anything. The courts are set up in the cafeteria and taken apart at the end of each practice. One of the traditions of the Bocce Club is the infamous naming of the team. Mike Coy is the bocce ball coach. Below, from left to right getting ready to shoot are Jordan Murphy, Jake Nelson, Nick Palasz, and Michael Bernacki.

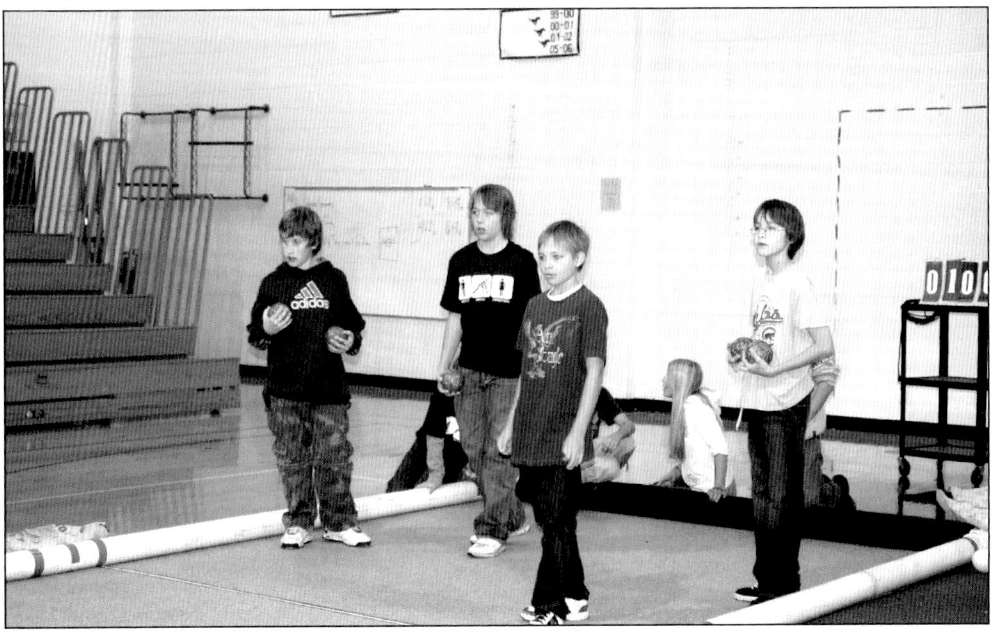

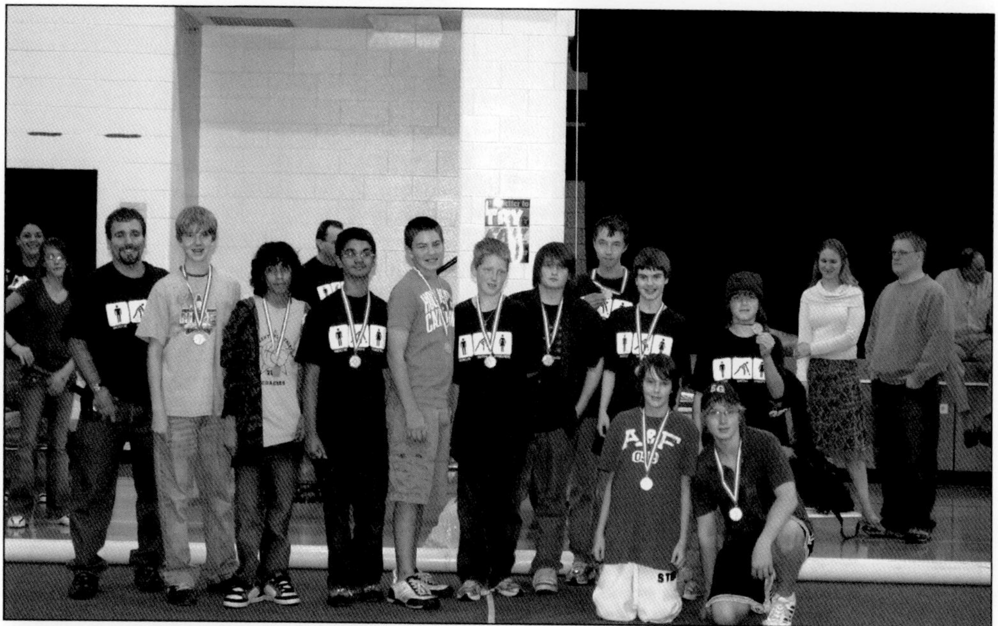

Winners of the fall Margaret Mead bocce ball season proudly display their highly achieved first, second, and third place metals. Each team consists of four players that make up about 30 teams of seventh and eighth graders. The students put the courts together, referee the games, and run the tournaments. There is fall and spring bocce everyday after school with the exception of Wednesday.

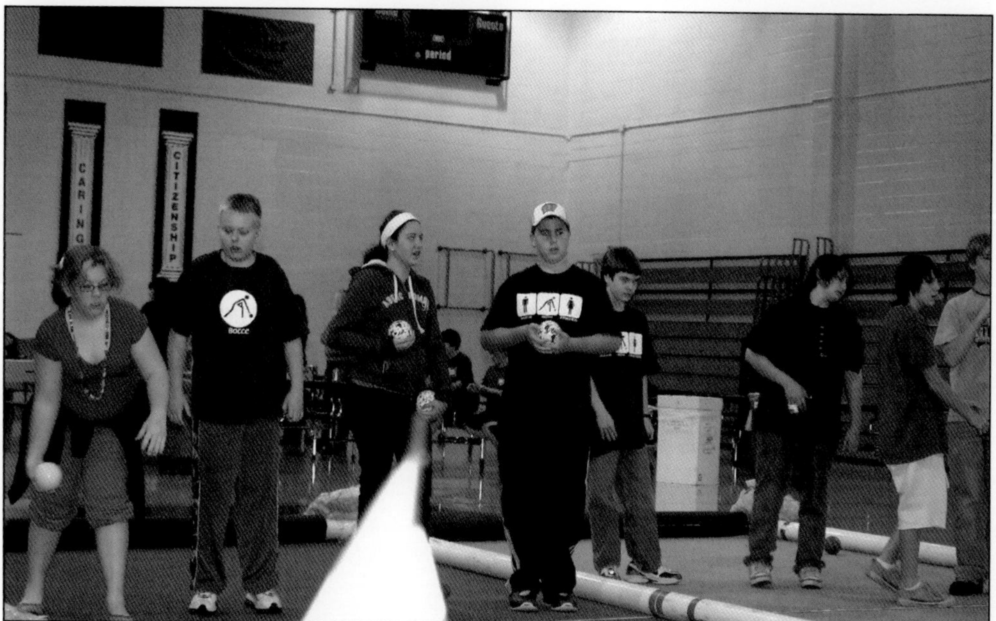

Competing in the semifinal match are Alexis Turnet (left) and Ryan Glathopher (second from left) on the Bocce Bowler team. Dominque ? and Alex Pope (center), on the Don Chew team, are brand new to bocce ball this year. The seventh graders finished in fourth place. The boys directly to the right are Daniel Loftus, Daniel Legut, and Brandon Donaldson. The green and white shirt Pope is wearing is the club T-shirt.

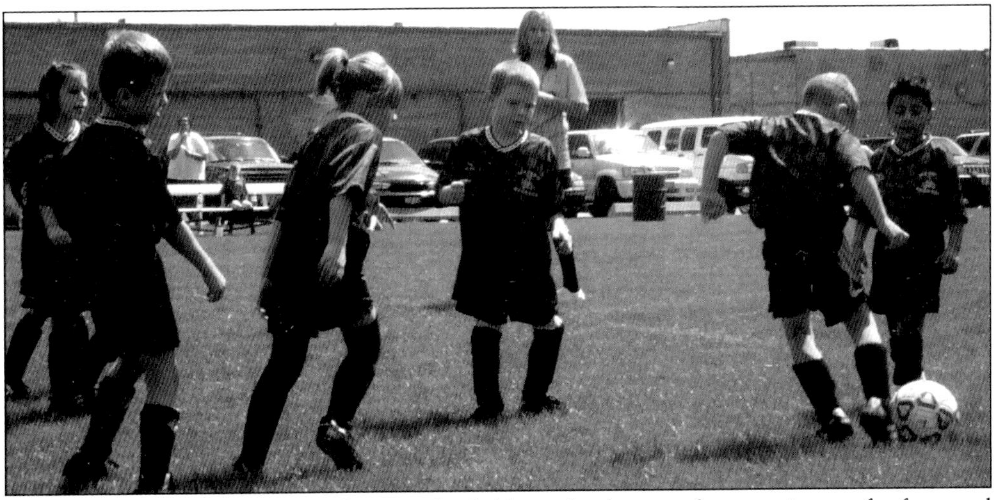

The soccer program is designed to teach children the basics of soccer in a safe, fun, and exciting environment. In the spring, the teams are coed, and they are single gender in the fall if enrollment allows. They also host competitive indoor soccer leagues during the winter months. The programs start as young as kindergarten. Travel soccer is a spring and fall combined season starting with tryouts in May.

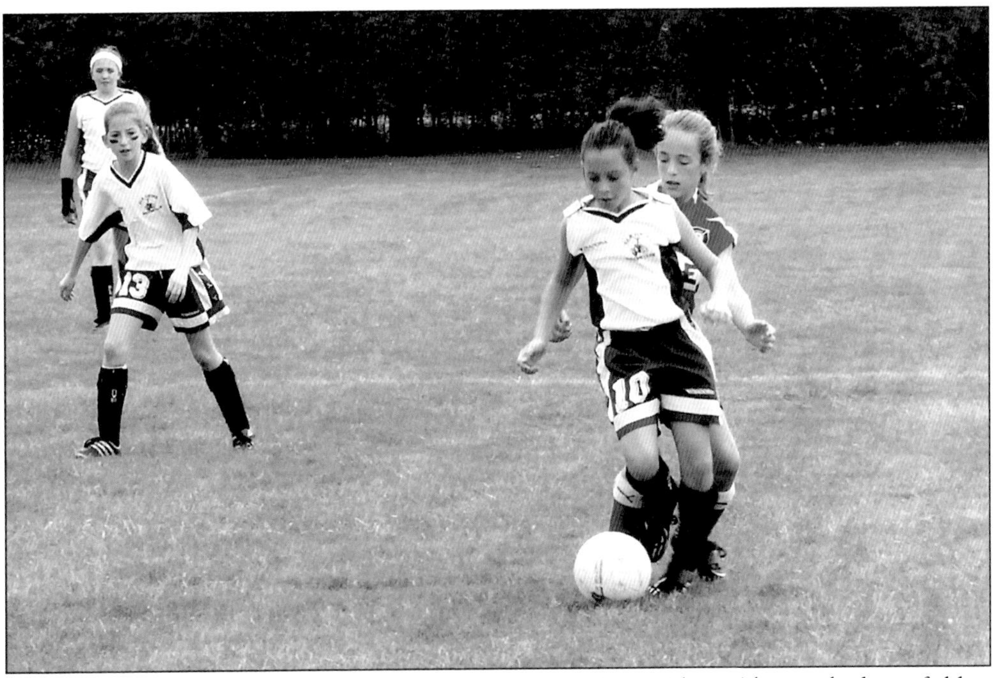

After stealing the ball from the Glen Ellyn Chicago Fire player, Alyssa Altosino looks up field to advance the ball. Teammates Sam Armando and Natalie Kutrumanes are ready to help out. In park district travel soccer, teams range from U10 (under 10 years old) up to U18 (under 18 years old). The Elk Grove Thunder belongs to the Illinois Women's Soccer League. In the 2005 spring season, the Thunder travel team played games every Sunday.

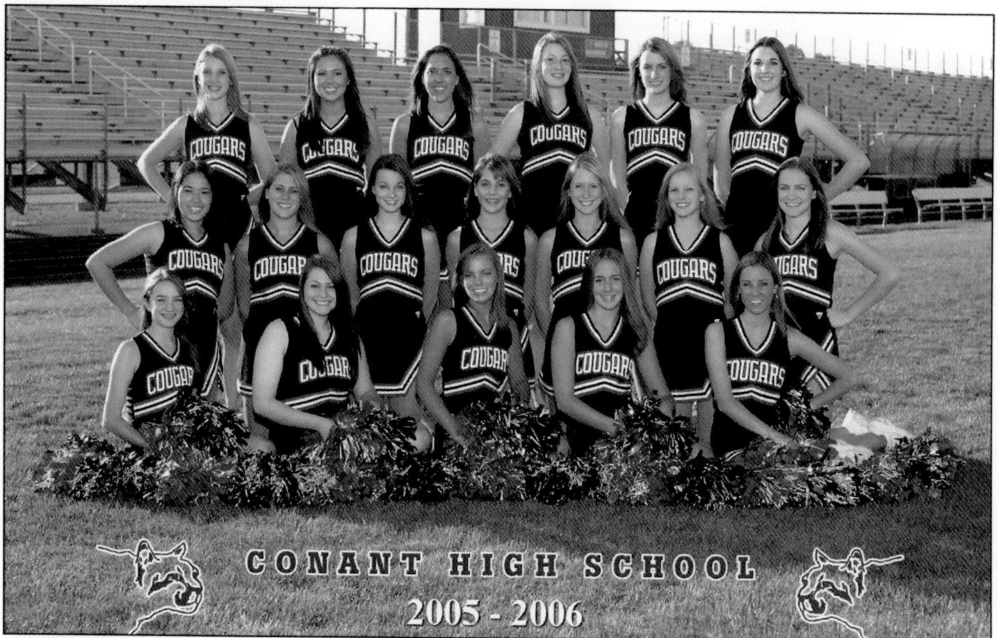

Poms, otherwise known as Charrelles, is a popular club at Conant High School. The team consists of 18 girls who like to put dance into their routines. Practice is year round. They perform at all football and basketball games. The club also competes against other schools. For fun, the Charrelles bake cookies for the football players during homecoming and surprise them during their first-period classes. The 2005–2006 squadron includes (first row) Caitlin Harrison, Sharon Brandys, Stephanie Drnek, Nicole McNulty, and Brianna Williams; (second row) Nicole Wilson, Kim Blecha, Jaclyn Ford, Lindsay Zavala, Becca Simantz, Diana Zinnel, and Elisabeth Zimmerman; (third row) Holly Baker, Maris Miller, Amber Mrkvicka, Alexis Burdick, Jessica Kascewicz, and Michelle Sitrick. Pictured below is Emilee Suchomski from the 2006–2007 squadron. (Above, Visual Image Photography.)

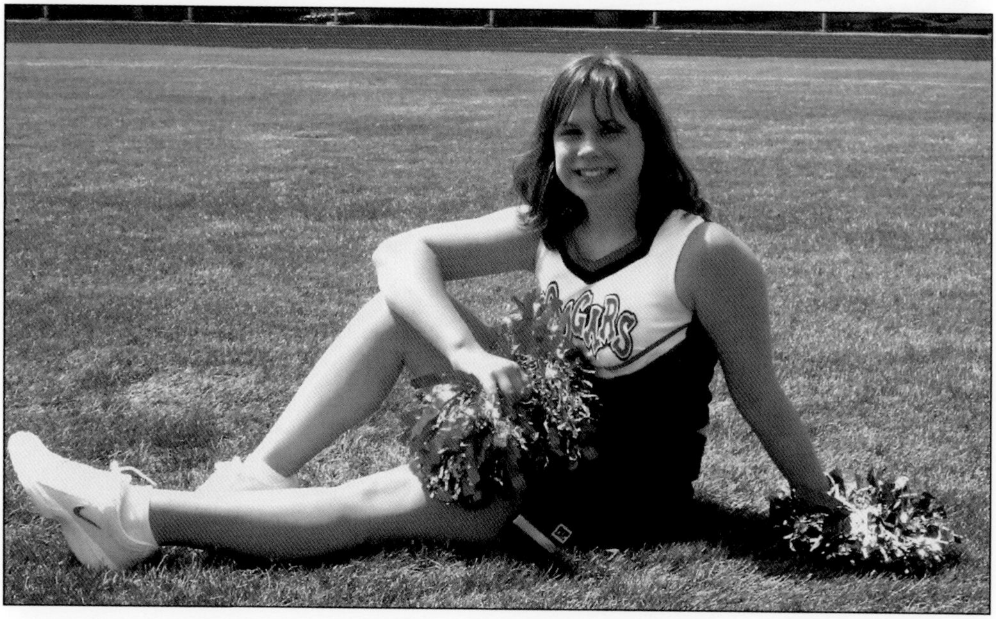

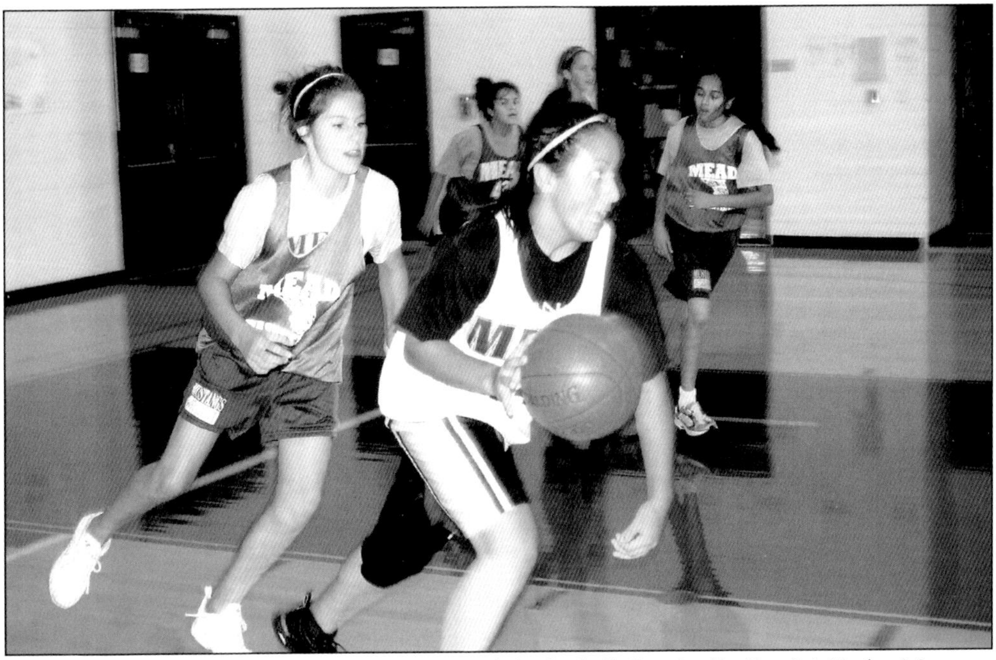

Another popular sport at the junior high level is girls' basketball. Coached by Erin McKinley, Margaret Mead Junior High seventh graders Allie Wright (left) and Sabika Haq chase Sarah Thompson as she tries to make a fast break. In the background are Alicia Senase (left) and Bridget Wijas racing to catch them. The girls practice against each other to prepare for the upcoming games.

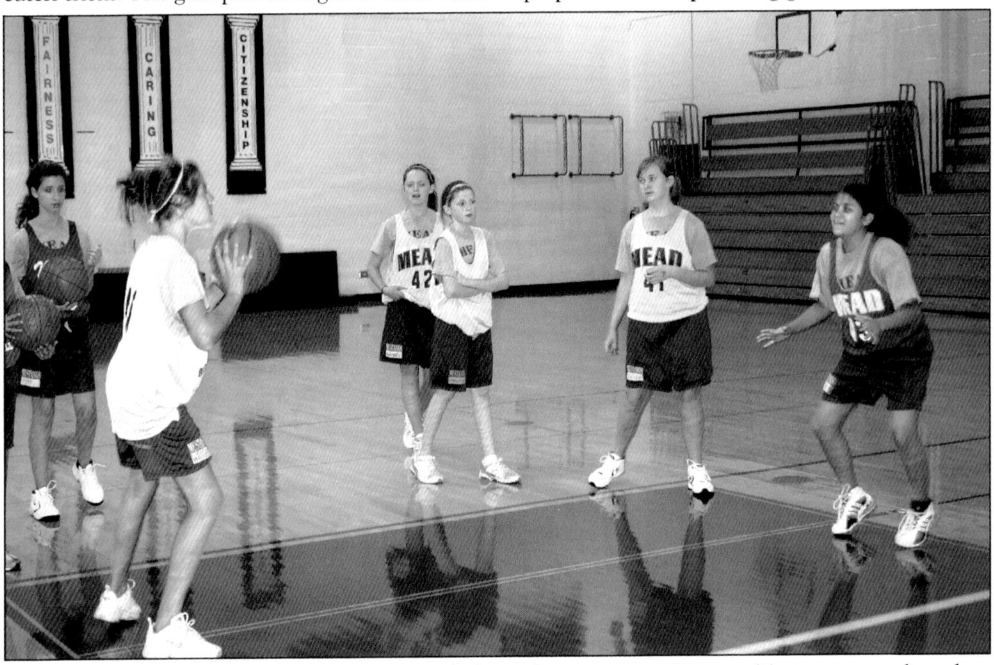

This picture was taken during practice, and the girls are wearing reversible jerseys so that they can scrimmage against each other. Wright (left) and Senase are starting a basketball passing drill. Behind them are Kelly Barry (left) and Ellen O'Malley waiting their turns. After they begin passing, Emily Bunescu (left) and Wijas will take their turns.

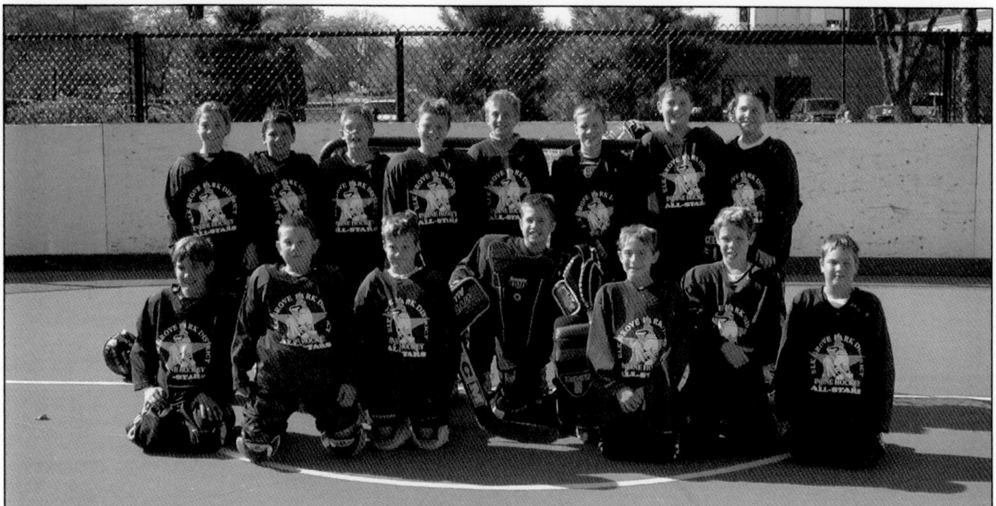

Standing: Maggy Fries, Ryan Chiero, Ryan Colby, Anthony Lauria, Mark Anders, Ryan Basic, Kyle McDevitt and Reed McDermit
Sitting: Brandon Zastrow, unidentified, unidentified, Kyle Kingsmill, Tyler Popp, Chase O'Connel and Sean Major

The Elk Grove Park District 2002 in-line all-star hockey team is pictured at the Audubon In-line Hockey Rink. At the end of the season, the kids on each team vote for the top three players. The top two players are then picked to play in the annual all-star hockey game. It is an honor to be chosen by teammates to play in such a prestigious game.

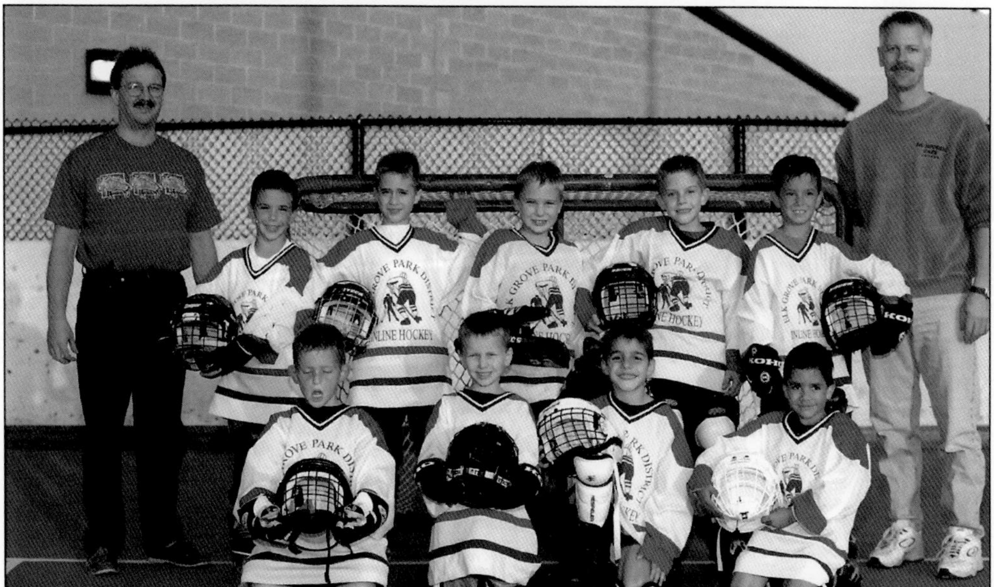

The 2000 Elk Grove Park District Canadian in-line hockey team was coached by Scot Colby and an unidentified assistant coach. From left to right are (first row) Kyle McDevitt, unidentified, Shawn Buckel, and Peter Kinsella; (second row) unidentified, unidentified, Kyle Kingsmill, unidentified, Ryan Colby, A. J. Rukavina, and Scot Colby. Girls and boys play on the same team. The coaches work with the kids to learn all levels of play by rotating the players in different positions, making them more versatile players.

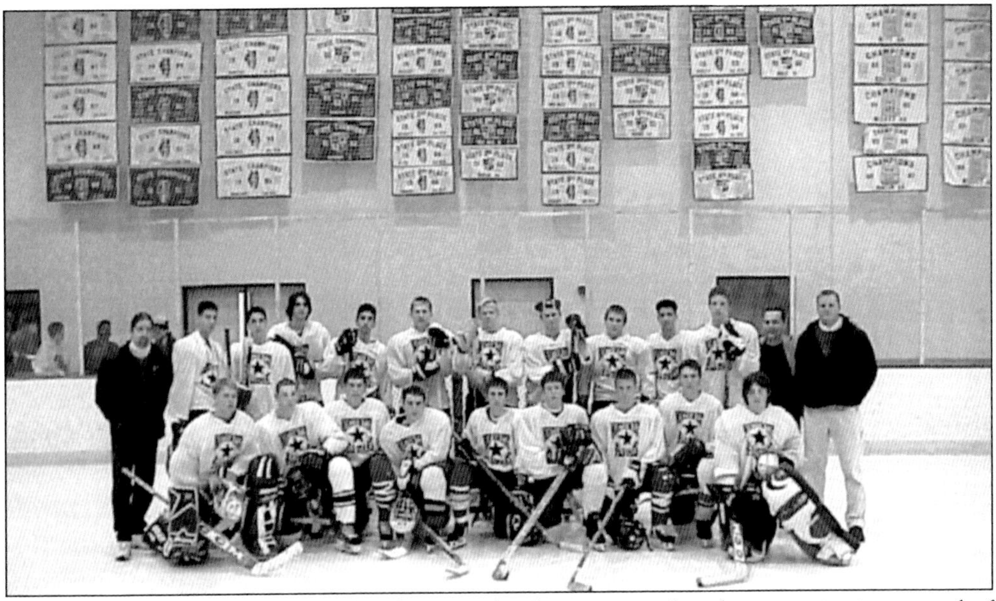

The 2004–2005 Conant High School Cougar hockey team took a division-winning record of 22-4-2. Allowing less than three goals per game, the Cougars defense was stronger than ever. Vince Conenna was an outstanding contributor on the offense with 22 goals and 12 assists. Exceptional goaltending by Evan Markewitz kept loses to a minimum, along with another turning point to the season sparked by Matt Szenda and Joey Carcerano.

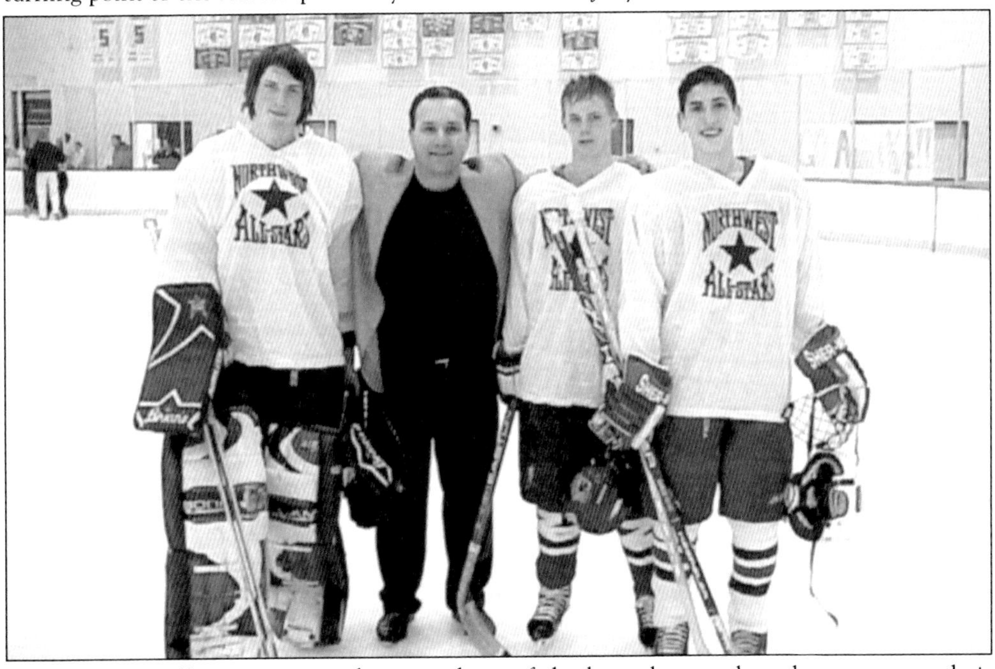

These Conant all-star team members are three of the best players selected to represent their school. Pictured from left to right are goalie Evan Markewycz, coach John Conenna, right-winger Matt Szenda, and center Vince Conenna. The coach's love for hockey became evident at the age of seven. His passion and commitment for hockey runs deep in his veins. Long after the game has ended, one can still hear the echoes of his voice commanding the team to victory.

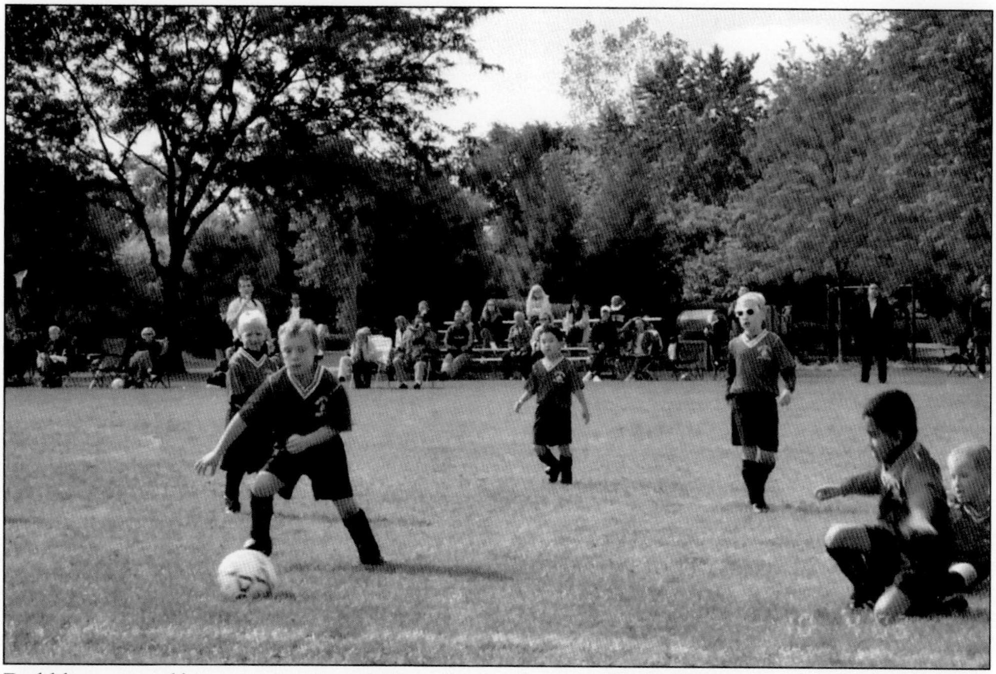

Dribbling toward his opponent's goal, Tony Sapyta from the Fireballs tries to move the ball forward to keep it from the other team and from going out of bounds with defenders in hot pursuit. These first and second graders played at Appleseed Park in the 2004 park district fall league.

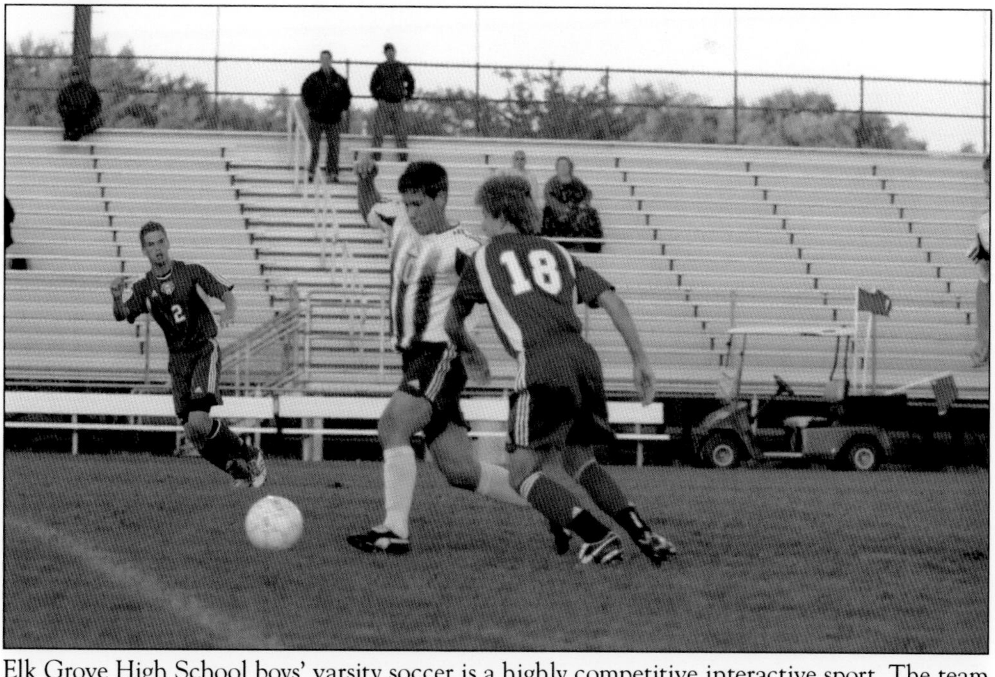

Elk Grove High School boys' varsity soccer is a highly competitive interactive sport. The team consists of 11 players and is widely considered to be one of the most popular sports in the world, gaining more momentum each year. The prestigious soccer cup is highly coveted at the end of the high school season in mid-October.

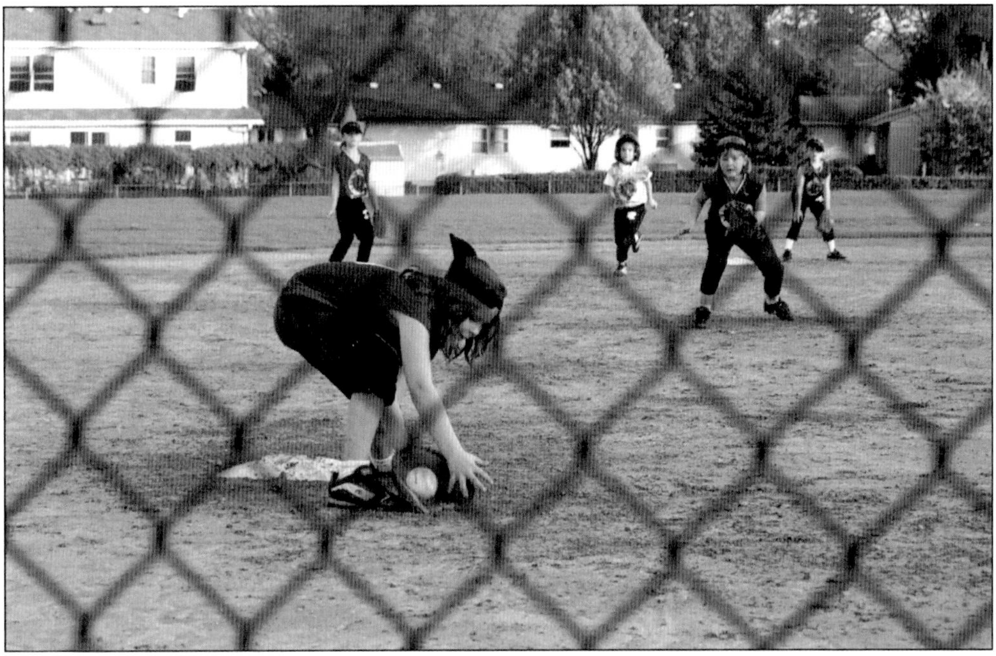

The Elk Grove Park District organizes the Elk Grove Village Girl's Softball League. Girls can sign up for softball as early as first grade all the way through high school. First grade girls are on instructional teams. Shown above are two instructional division teams playing against each other. In the foreground is Kylie Behnke picking up a ground ball to get the runner out at third base.

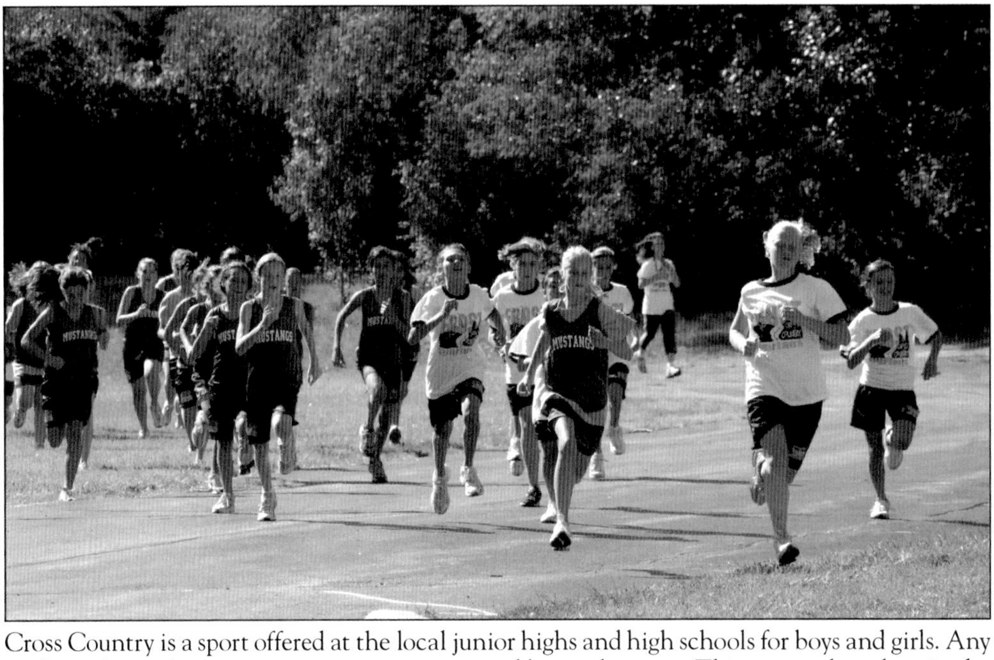

Cross Country is a sport offered at the local junior highs and high schools for boys and girls. Any student who wishes to participate may sign up and be on the team. This sport takes place in the fall. Students practice daily, running more than two miles a day to prepare for meets. Pictured above is Margaret Mead Junior High and Roert Frost Junior High seventh grade girls just starting their meet.

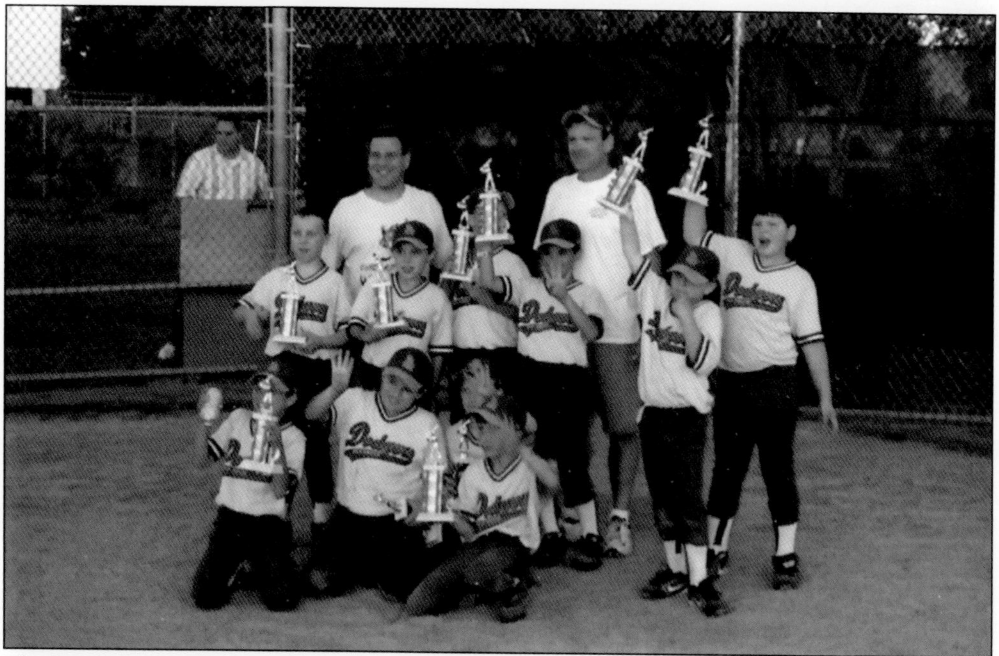

The baseball organization provides a program for all levels of players from house to travel leagues for boys and girls ages 5 through 14. Young players focus on the basic fundamental instruction of the game with a challenging game schedule. Leagues are divided into divisions, including peewee, pinto, mustang, bronco, and pony. The older division competitive leagues include all-star games, playoffs, and a championship game. The seasons typically run April through July. Pictured above is a boys' team called the Padres showing off their hard earned first-place trophies. Below is a peewee team made up of boys and girls showing off their awards for their accomplishments. In younger age divisions, all players receive participation trophies to emphasize that everyone is a winner who tries hard and learns the game.

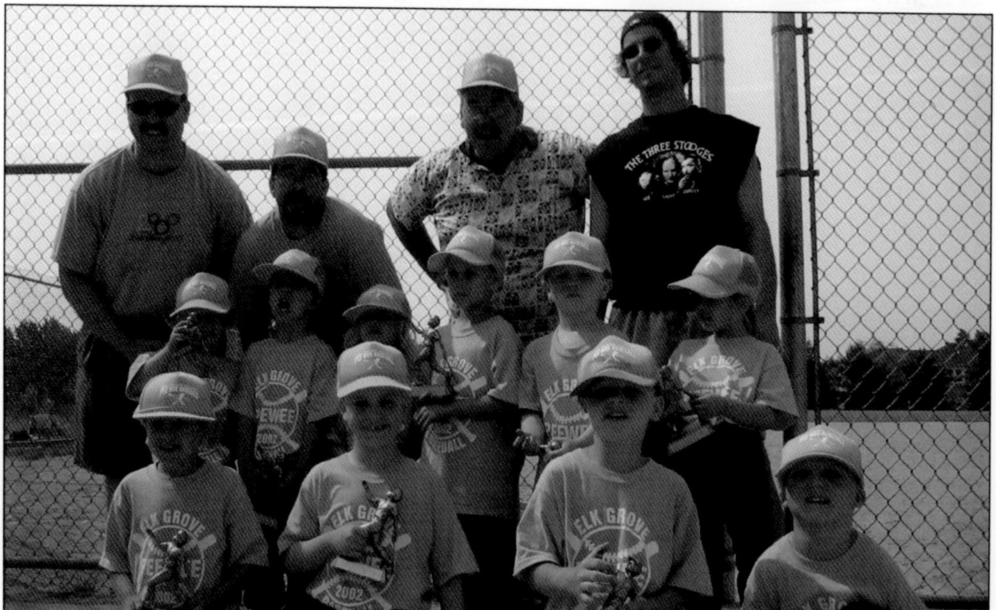

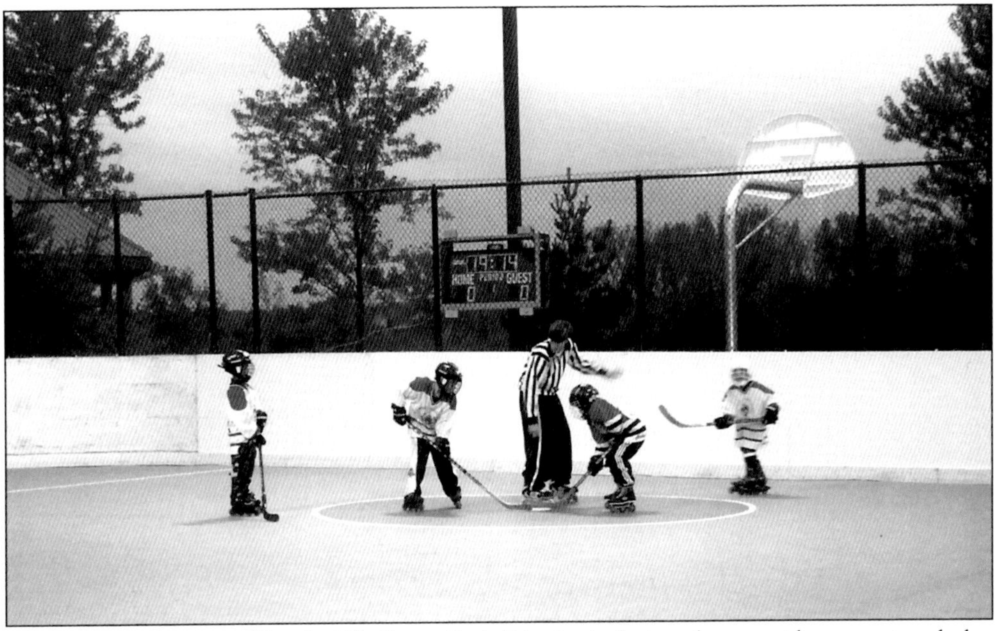

In-line hockey organized by the Elk Grove Park District is designed to provide recreational play in a team setting for boys and girls of all skill levels from kindergarten through high school. Center Jordan Colby gets ready to face off with his opponent at the Mead in-line hockey rink.

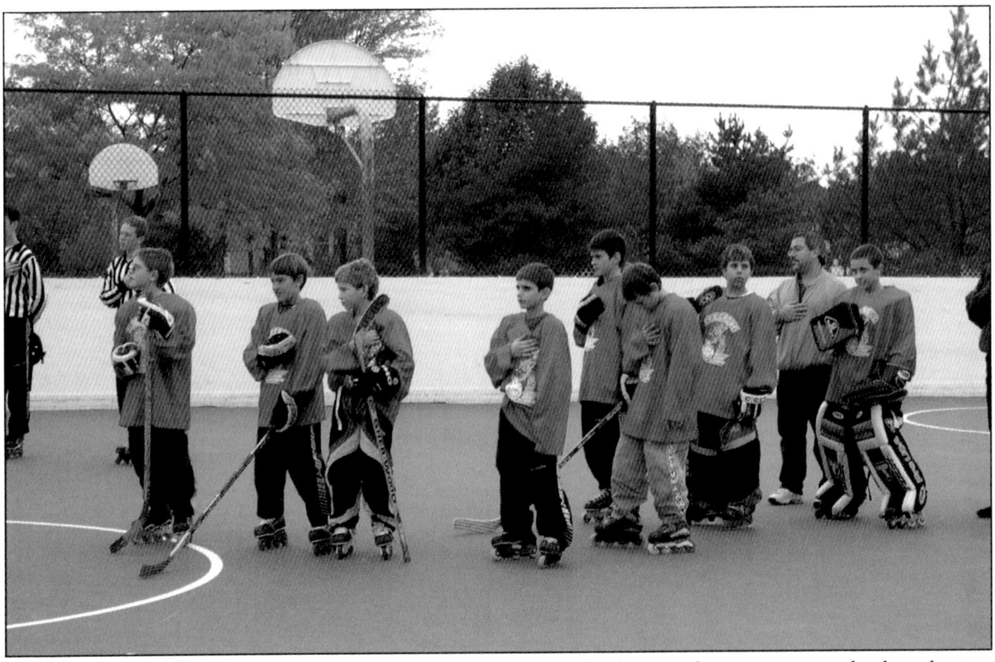

The 2003 all-star in-line hockey team proudly lines up to honor the country with the playing of "The Star Spangled Banner." From left to right are Ryan Colby, Brandon Zastrow, Connor Reed, Steve Kruesch, Ben Rathman, Nick Bania, Michael Martire, and Jake Esma. There are two in-line hockey seasons, spring and fall.

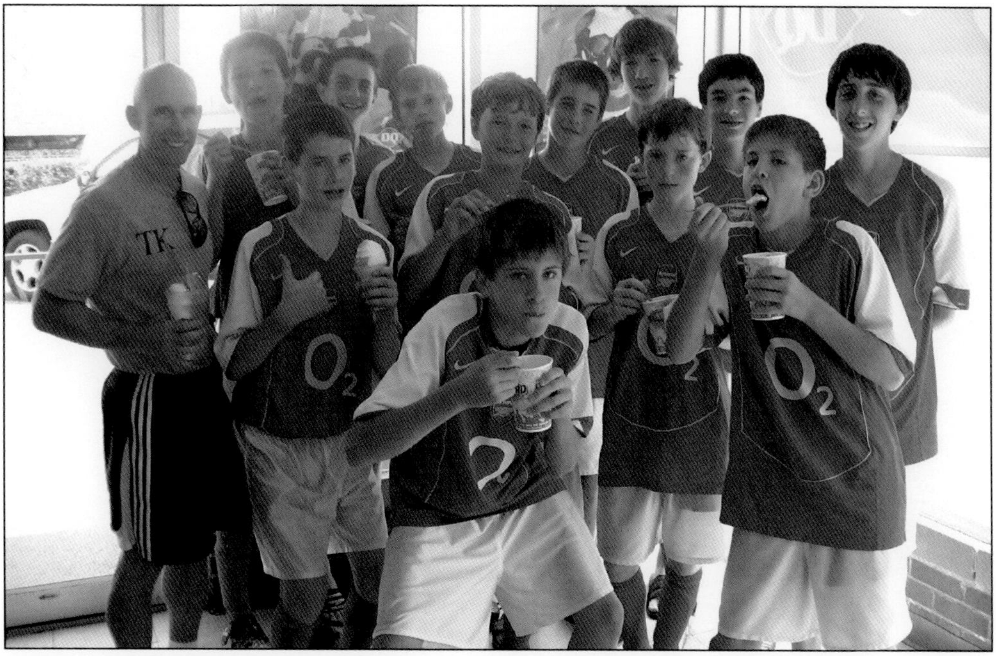

As a resident for 43 years, Tony Kees knows the importance of youth programs. Arsenal Soccer Club founder and director since 1993, Kees has fond memories from his childhood going to the local Dairy Queen after Little League games when he was eight years old. After an impressive end-of-the-season win on a 95-degree day, Dairy Queen hit the spot for the 2007 Elk Grove U14 boys' soccer team. Above, players include Ben Stram, Nick Jordan, Mike and Matt Ginter, Jack Simpson, Danny Cortese, Kyle Krzeski, Jared Lappa, Mike Zentner, Mike Miller, Bobby Potratz, and Thad Struggles. Pictured below is Ryan Fillingim (left) from the Arsenal Soccer Club for the older boys. The club is affiliated with the park district, so it is open to residents and nonresidents.

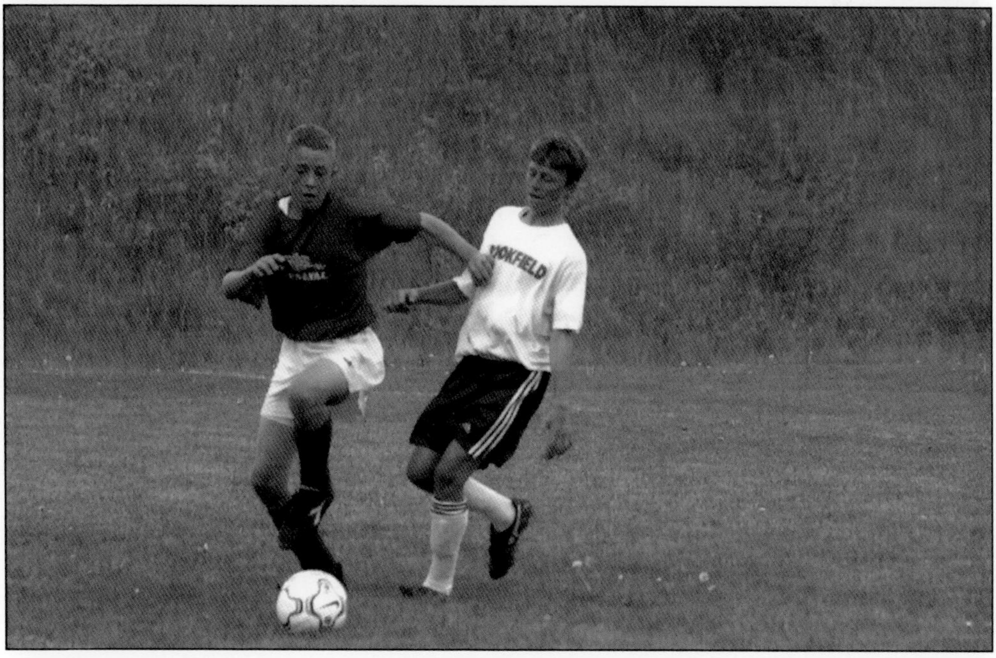

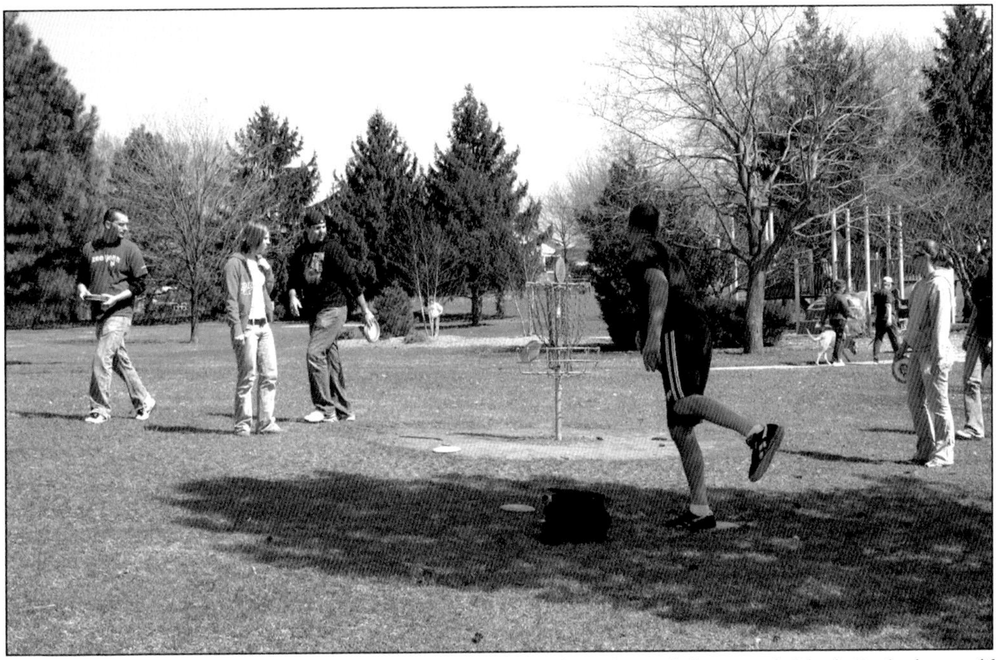

Disc golf is played like traditional golf but with a Frisbee-shaped disc, and Clark Park disc golf course in Elk Grove Village is a place the young and old can enjoy. This well-designed nine-hole course is full of obstacles to make it challenging. If nine holes are not enough, for a more serious player, go to the beginning and play the course twice.

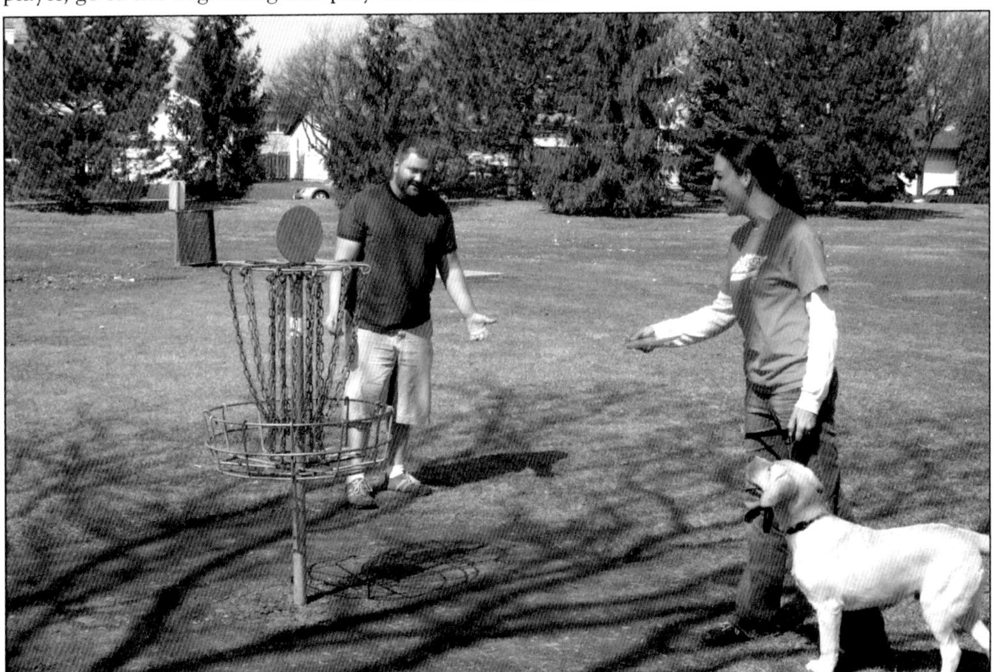

For a relaxing afternoon spent in the sun, Rolling Meadows residents Andrew and Mary Staehlin prefer taking their dog Isaac to Clark Park for a round of disc golf. The couple has been playing disc golf for four years. Isaac keeps an eye on the disc as Mary aims to toss it in the hole.

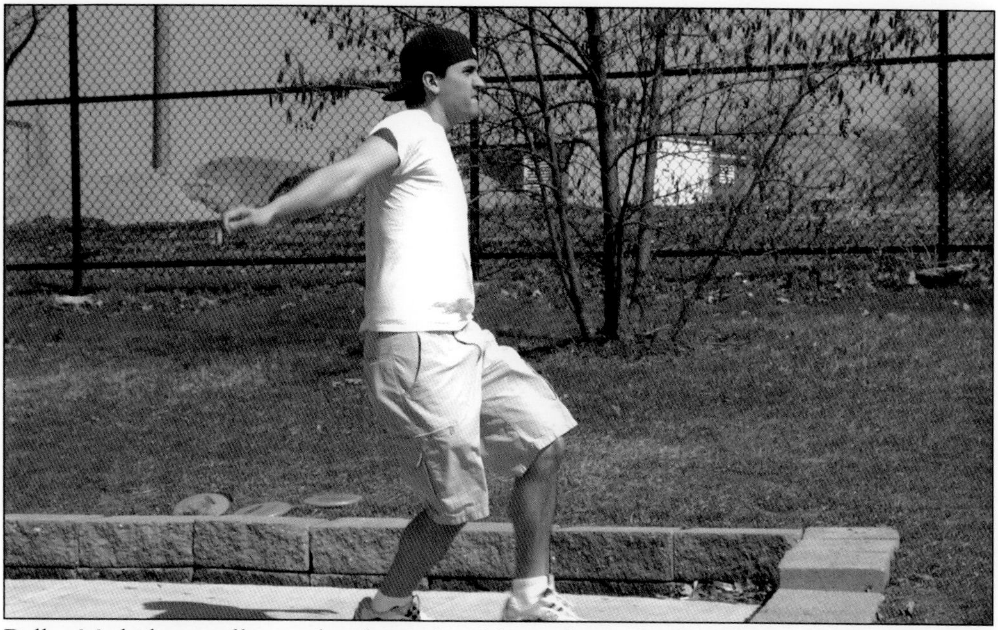

Dallas Madrid tees off using his driver. Just like traditional golf, there are different types of discs. Discs like putters and drivers have many different weights and thicknesses for multiple situations. Some discs are weighted to glide longer in the air for farther distances. More serious players not only have more equipment, but also enter in disc golf tournaments to earn thousands of dollars of prize money.

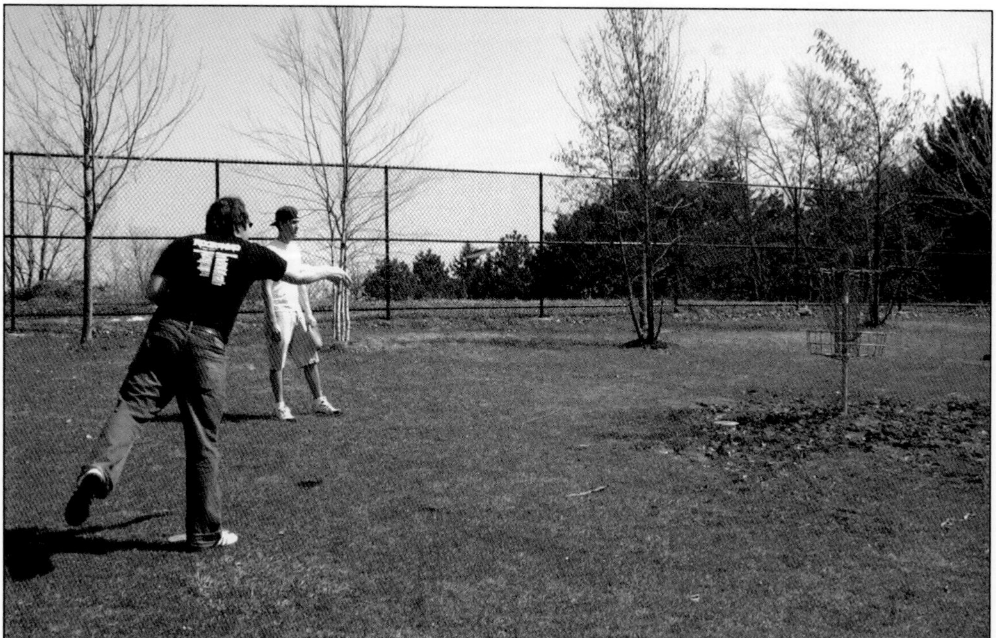

For over three years, friends Mike Gagen and Madrid have been playing disc golf at Clark Park. The Roselle residents enjoy playing in Elk Grove Village because of the difficulty of the course. Trees, playground equipment, tennis courts, baseball fields, and many people all serve as obstacles. Gagen throws his disc hoping to make one under par as Madrid watches.

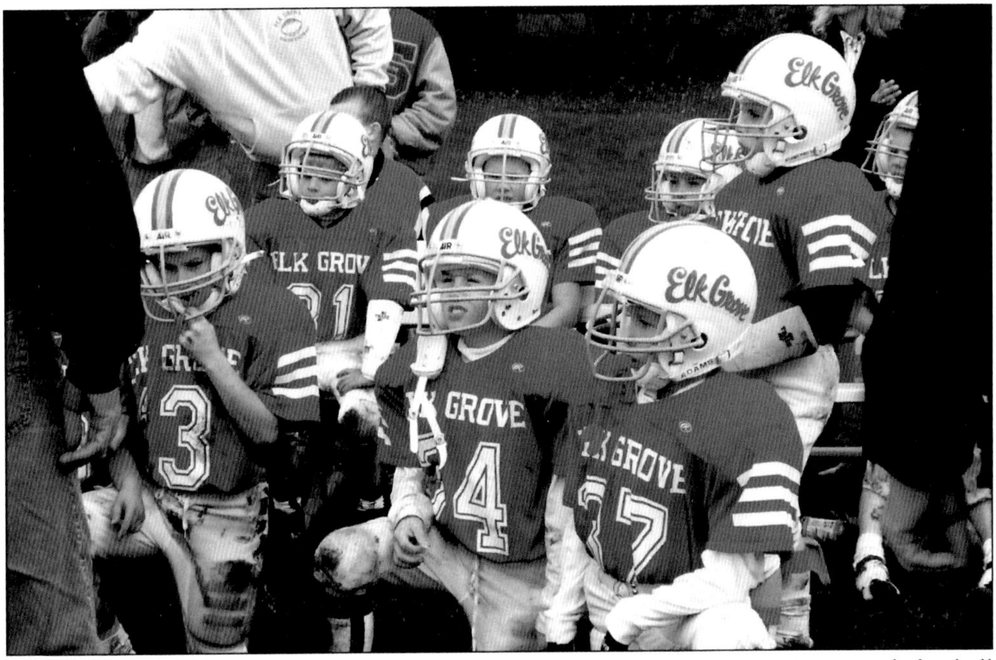

Playing at the community athletic fields and in other neighboring communities, youth football is a favorite among boys of all ages. Mike Sipolt (center) along with his team, the Panthers, listens to their coach after a winning game in 1998. The season starts in August, with practices held approximately three times per week, and games are played through October.

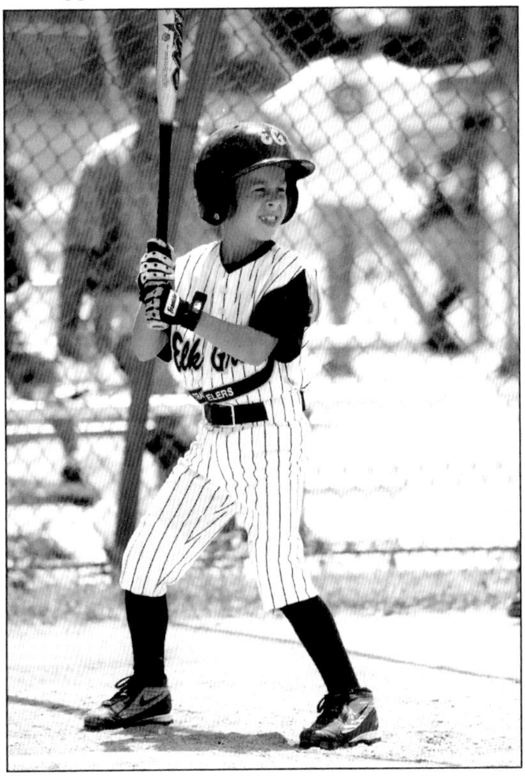

Elk Grove Village baseball is very fortunate to have an old warehouse that allows teams to start practicing in the winter, equipped with fields and batting cages. Instruction and guidance by professional players helps strengthen teams. Resident Ben Suchomski is up at bat during the 2004 travel baseball season.

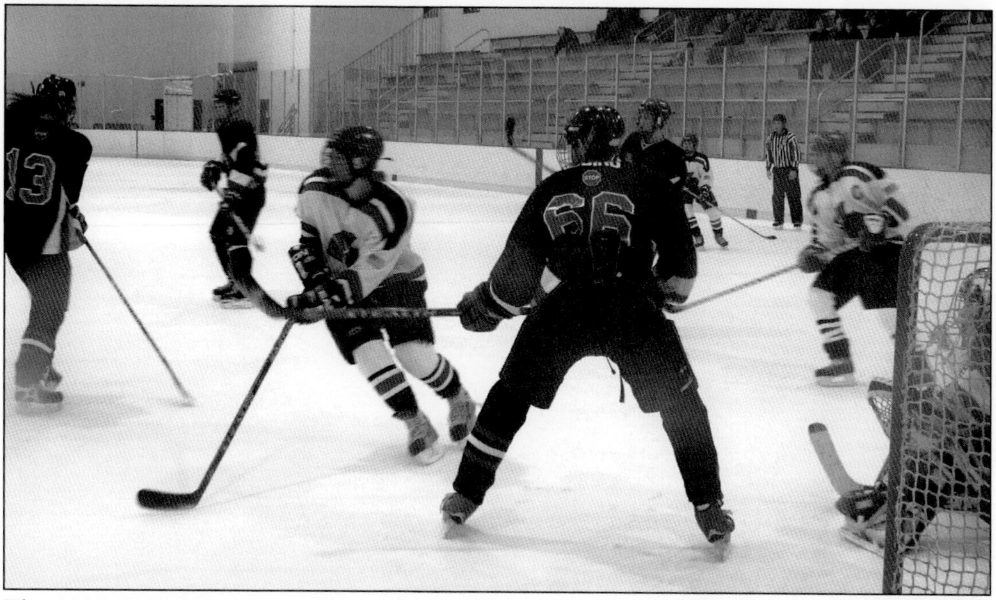

The 2008 CHS (Conant, Hoffman Estates, and Schaumburg High Schools combined team) junior varsity hockey team offensive players Ryan Colby and Anthony Altosino try to regain control of the puck in the offensive zone. The team ended the season by taking fifth place. The structure of the playoff tournament is a typical round robin; the top four teams went on to play in the Scholastic Cup, and the bottom four played in the Founder's Cup. The team started out struggling but respectfully ended the season by winning the 2008 Founders Cup.

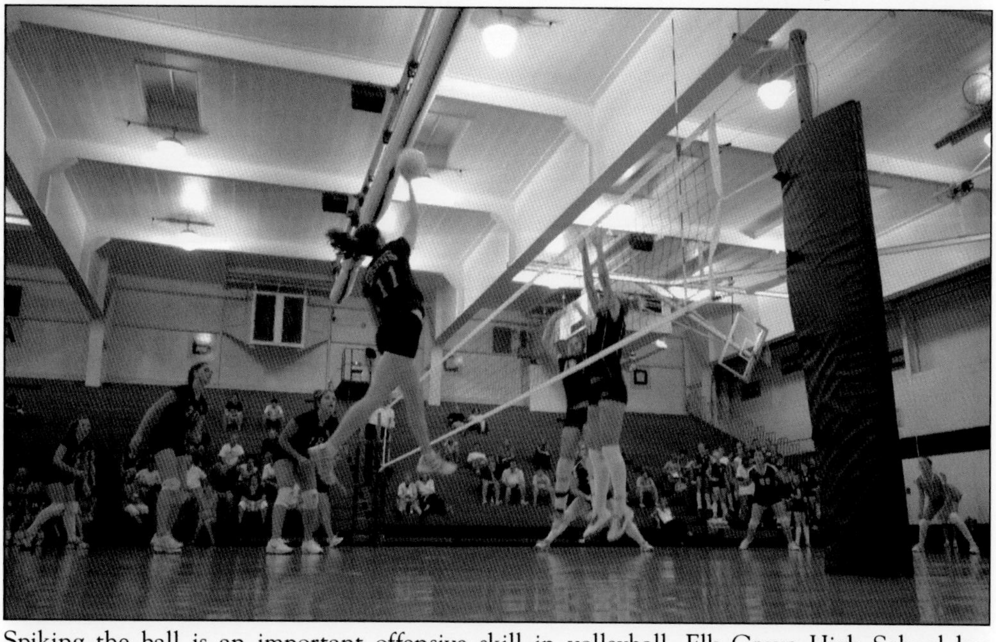

Spiking the ball is an important offensive skill in volleyball. Elk Grove High School has girls' varsity and junior varsity teams, which compete against other local high school teams. The season runs from August to November. Other skills to work on include jumping, setting, bumping, and blocking. Students can participate in camps as well as park district programs to sharpen their abilities before trying out for school teams.

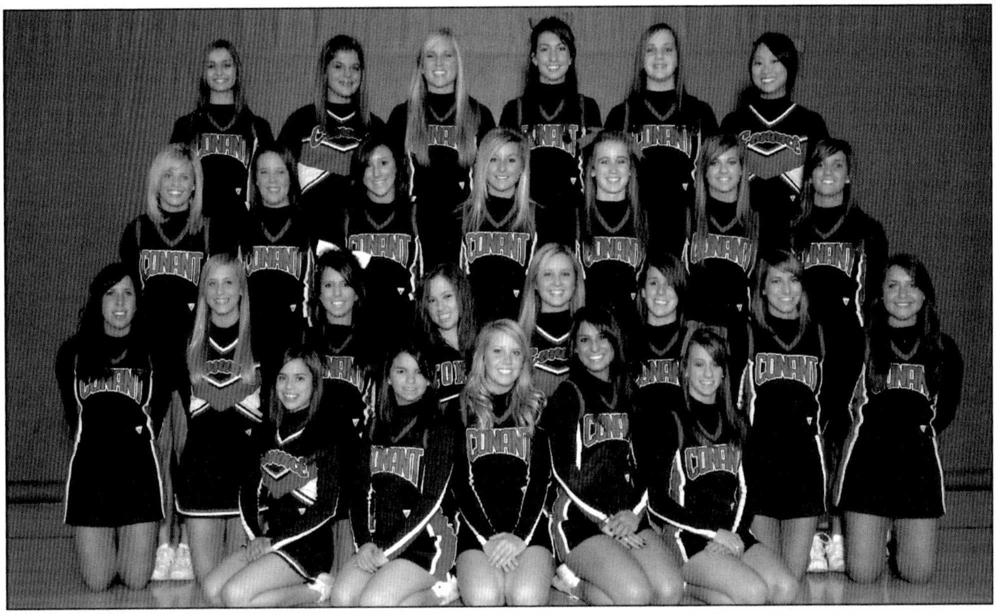

Cheering their teams to victory are the James B. Conant cheerleaders. From left to right are (first row) Danna Lopez, Antoinette Raimondo, Staci Horstmann, Julianna Conenna, and Terie Colletti; (second row) Alyssa Ironside, Melissa Cox, Allie Caiafa, Ana Senyk, Kristen Dolbeare, Jessica DiVito, Lisa Parente, and Gina Cannistra; (third row) Katie Rice, Amy Halden, Allie Paladino, Krista Firnbach, Jackie Smith, Jessica Anselmo, and Nikki McCarthy; (fourth row) Jackie Crivlare, Christina Anderson, Kelsey Abbott, Rachel Jankowski, Michelle Wisser, and Gina Kerstens. (Visual Image Photography.)

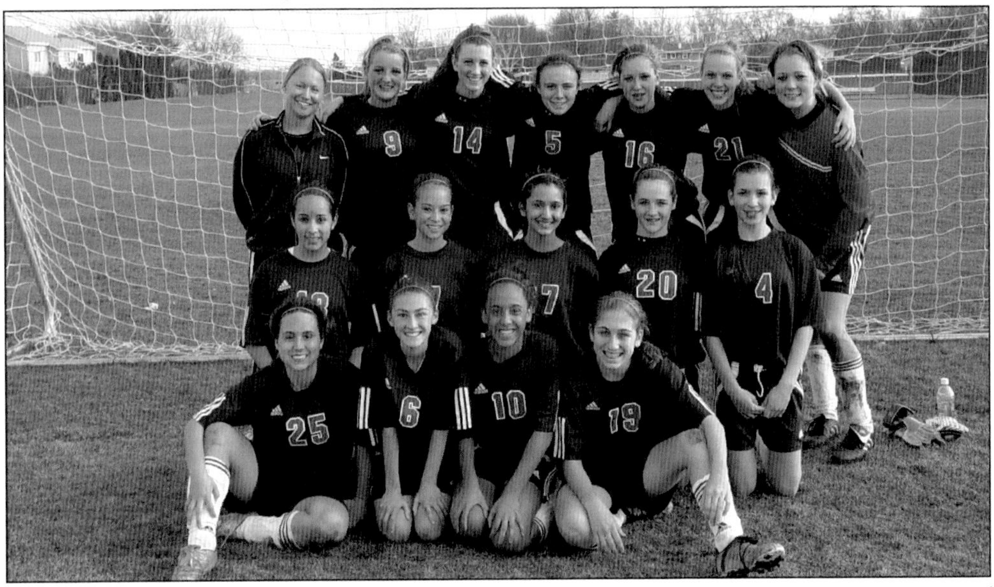

Pictured is the James B. Conant High School's freshman girls' soccer team for 2008. Many of these athletes began their soccer careers playing together as kindergartners in the Elk Grove Soccer Club. They continued playing soccer together in Elk Grove Soccer Club's travel program. Elk Grove players pictured include Lindsay Fillingim, Alyssa Rawleigh, Nina Piscopo, Kelly Lomas, Stacy Boskelly, Hailey Andress, Kate Kauffold, and Caitlin Chiero.

Four

Two Cities Share One World

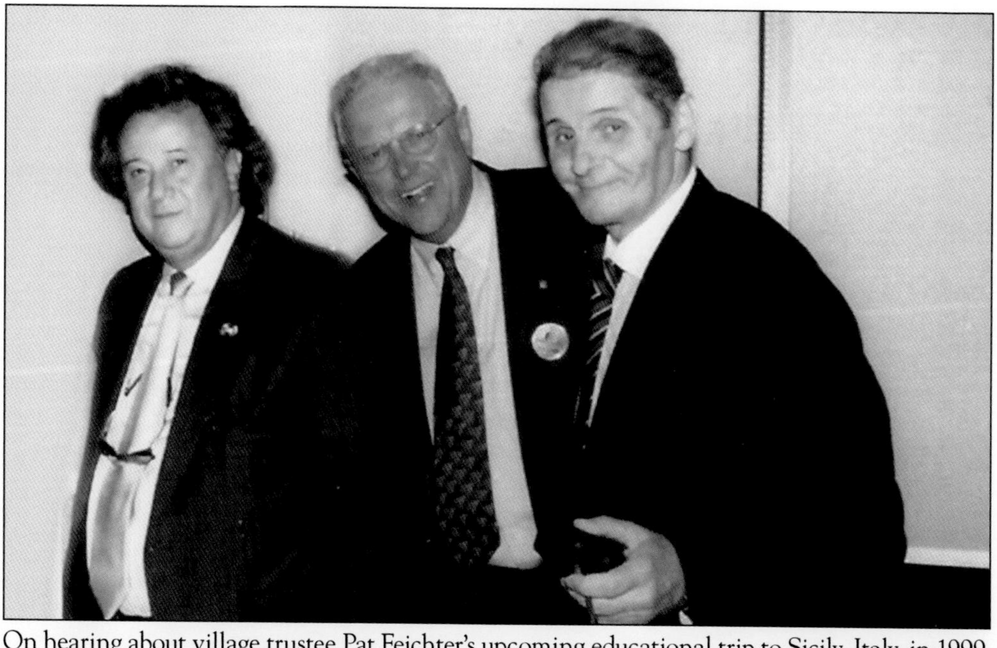

On hearing about village trustee Pat Feichter's upcoming educational trip to Sicily, Italy, in 1999, Giovanni Gullo offered to meet Feichter there to show him what the city had to offer. While in Sicily, Gullo, Feichter, and Giuseppe Lombardo (pictured), the founders of Elk Grove Village Italian Sister Cities, realized a sister city union could be made possible. The three men understood the need to educate people of the village of Elk Grove and surrounding suburbs with a richer understanding of other cultures. Toward that goal, the founders of Elk Grove Village Italian Sister Cities were excited to present their findings at the next village board meeting. Through perseverance and many months of hard work, Sister Cities incorporated on July 20, 2000.

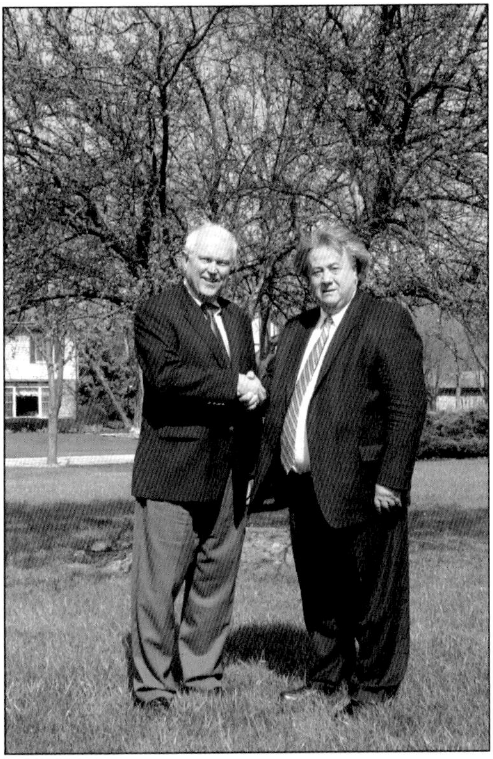

Pat Feichter and Giovanni Gullo, longtime residents of Elk Grove Village, wholeheartedly believed in the sister city concept. After months of many meetings and long days, their vision of a sister city was cultivated. Even to this day, cofounders Gullo, Feichter, and Giuseppe Lombardo are committed to the sister city values and beliefs.

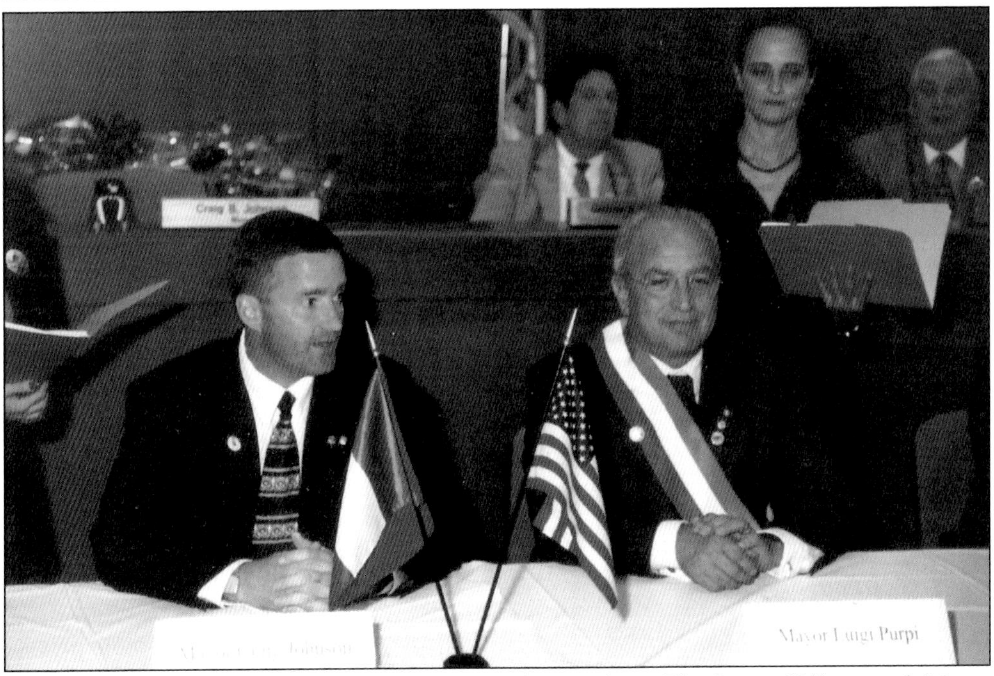

On October 10, 2000, officials Mayor Craig Johnson from Elk Grove Village and Mayor Luigi Purpi from Termini Imerese, Sicily, Italy, signed the official documents solidifying the relationship between the two communities. This occurred in the boardroom at the Charles J. Zetteck Municipal Building.

Twenty schoolchildren from Elk Grove Village volunteered to draw pictures on fabric portraying what living in Elk Grove Village means to them. The quilt, "What Elk Grove Village Means to Me," was presented to the Termini Imerese delegates at an Elk Grove Village board meeting in October 2004. This quilt resides in an elementary school in Termini Imerese.

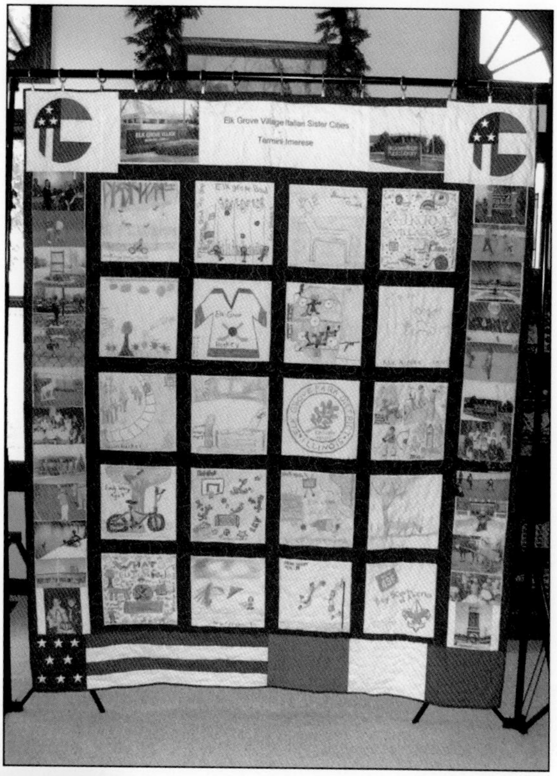

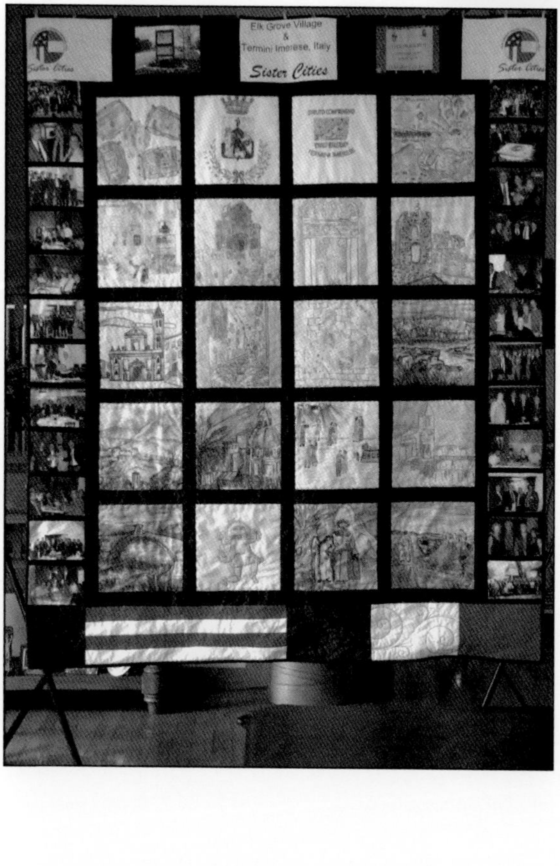

Twenty school children from Termini Imerese drew pictures on fabric portraying what living in Termini Imerese means to them. At a welcoming ceremony in October 2007, the quilt, "What Termini Imerese Means to Me," was presented to Mayor Craig Johnson. The quilt will reside at the Charles J. Zettek Municipal Building after the construction is finished.

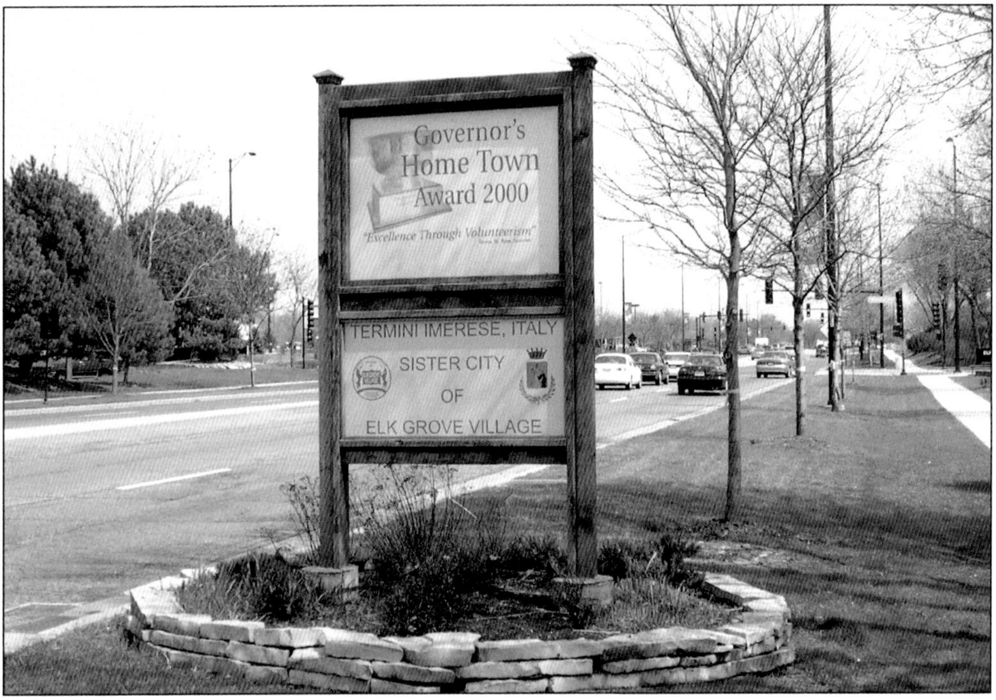

Above is the Elk Grove Village Italian Sister Cities sign proudly displayed in front of the Jack A. Claes Pavilion on Biesterfield Road. Below is the sister city sign in Termini Imerese, displayed on a major highway welcoming everyone to the city. Their sign translates to, "Termini Imerese, city of the thermal hot baths, twin with Elk Grove Village."

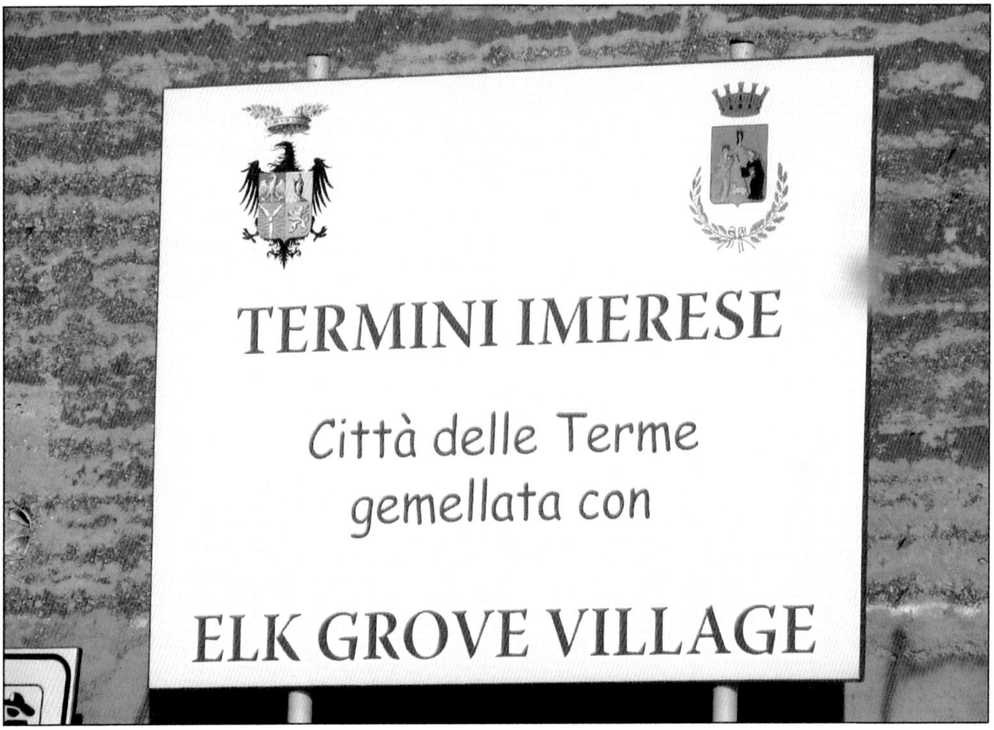

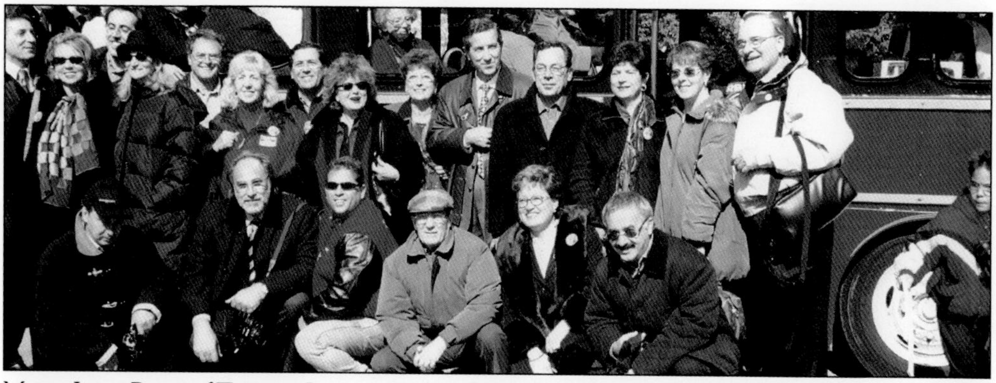

Mayor Luigi Purpi of Termini Imerese and 26 delegates arrived in Chicago on October 7, 2000, for a week of bringing two communities together as sister cities. This visit allowed the development of an ongoing relationship so the two communities can be enriched by this exchange and future exchanges, both economically and professionally.

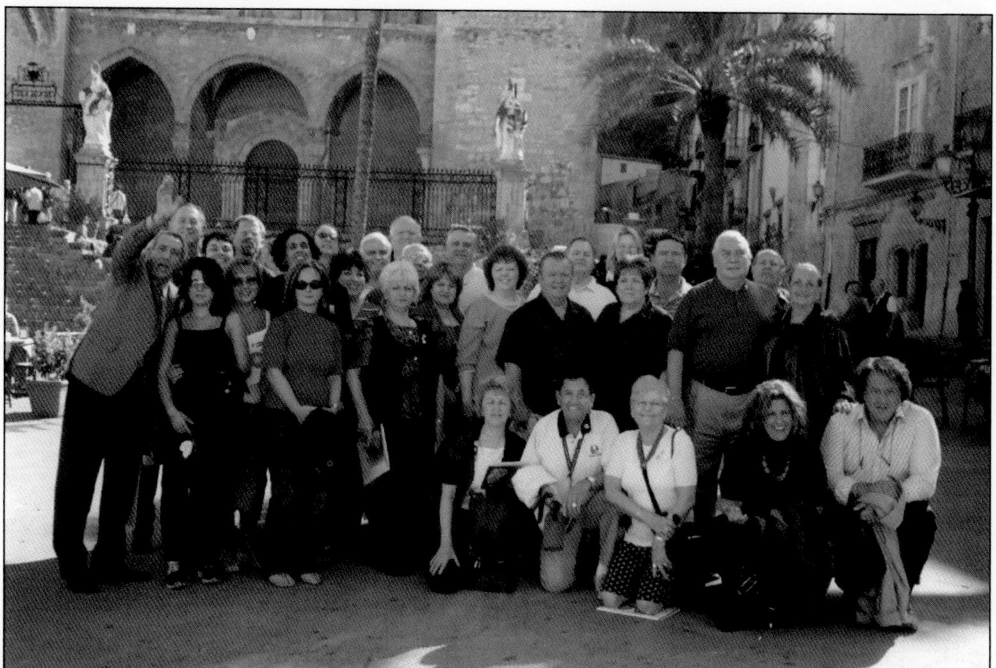

While visiting the city of Cefalù, members from both cities take a moment to reflect their proud heritage. Cefalù was one of the many cities on the historical tour of Sicily. For most of the members of Elk Grove Village Italian Sister Cities, this was their first tour of the ancient land.

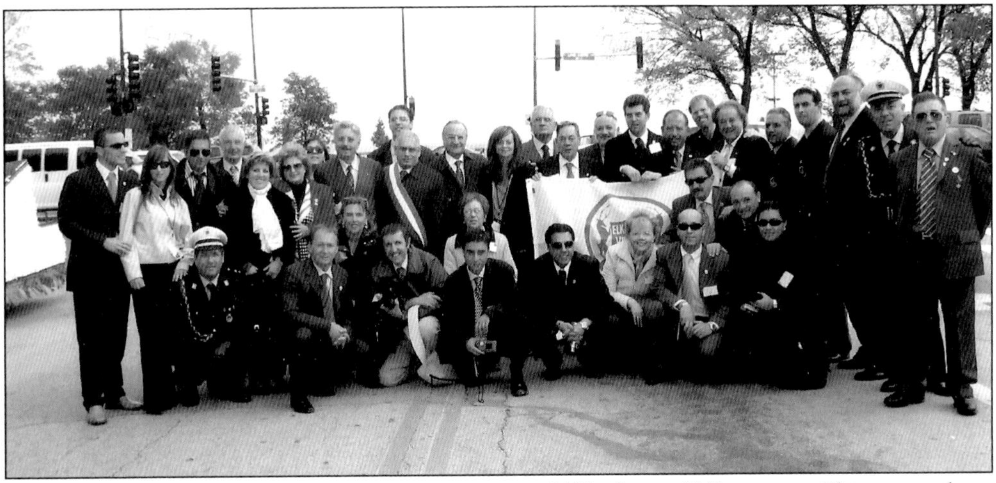

Sister city representatives from Termini Imerese and Elk Grove Village tour Chicago and are amazed with the beautiful skyline. The architectural design of Millennium Park intrigued and sparked many conversations throughout their 2004 visit. Prior to the Columbus Day parade, members gather to remember their special trip to Chicago.

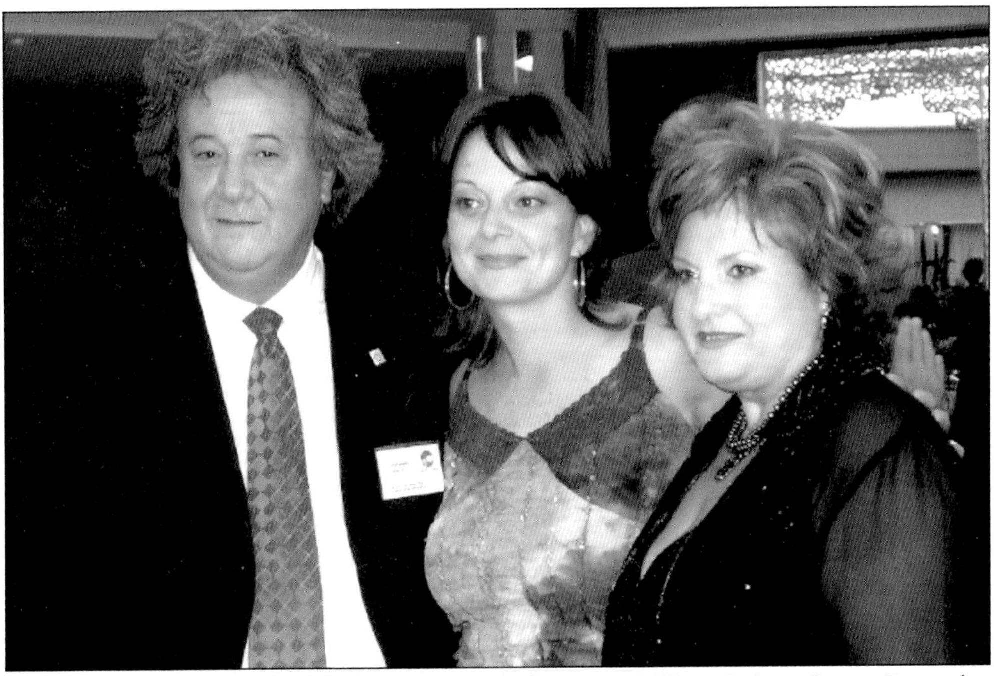

Giovanni Gullo, chairman and cofounder of Elk Grove Village Italian Sister Cities; his daughter Mariann Gullo-Krewenka, treasurer of the organization; and his wife, Maria Gullo, have continuously supported and believed in the importance of the sister city. The ongoing dedication and commitment of this family is greatly appreciated by everyone involved.

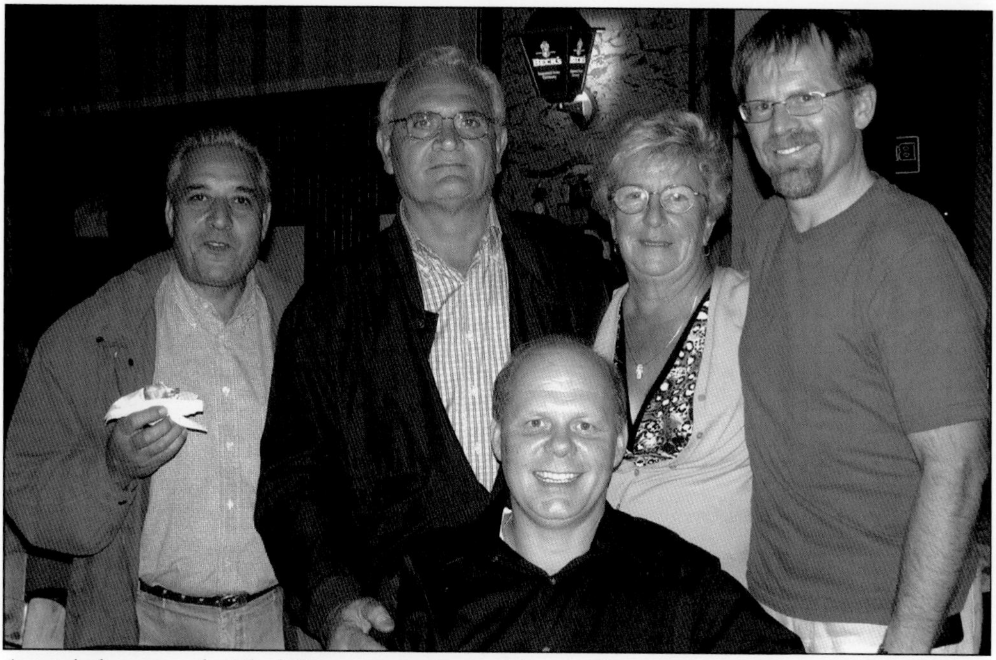

A quick dinner at the Black Forest restaurant in Termini Imerese is a sister city favorite because of the atmosphere and great food. From left to right, friends Giuseppe Coniglio, Andrea Minneci, Ellen Peacock, Rod Pickett, and Bill Marston (sitting), get together for one last celebration before returning home to Elk Grove Village.

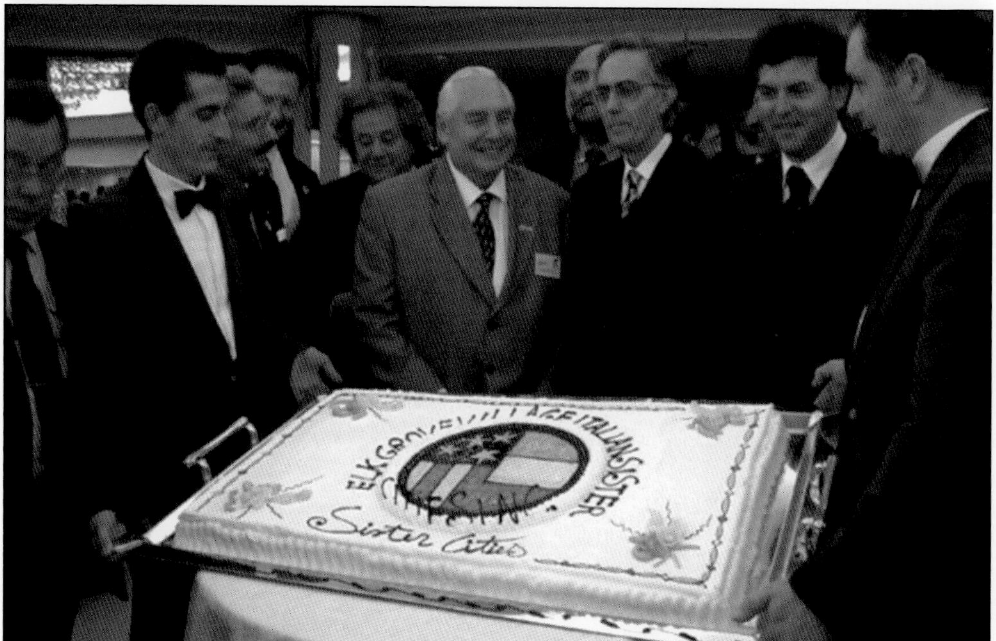

Cake anyone? At a gala celebration in Termini Imerese, Giovanni Gullo, cofounder and chairman of Elk Grove Village Italian Sister Cities; Jim Petri, village trustee and president of Elk Grove Village Italian Sister Cities; Mayor Enzo Giunta of Termini Imerese; and Salvatore Burrafato, president of Termini Imerese Sister Cities, proudly admire the Sister City logo on the cake.

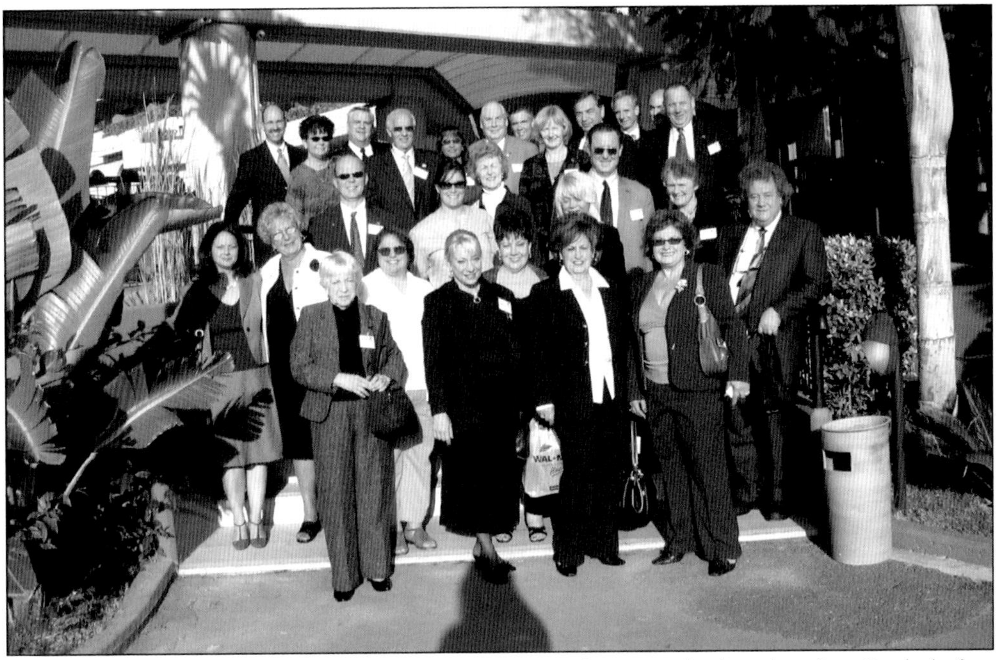

Members of Elk Grove Village Italian Sister Cities gather outside their hotel in Sicily before embarking on their daylong visit with the mayor of Termini Imerese and other officials. The Elk Grove Village members went to Sicily for 10 days in October 2005. This is the second official visit the Sister City members have made to gain a richer understanding of each other's cultures.

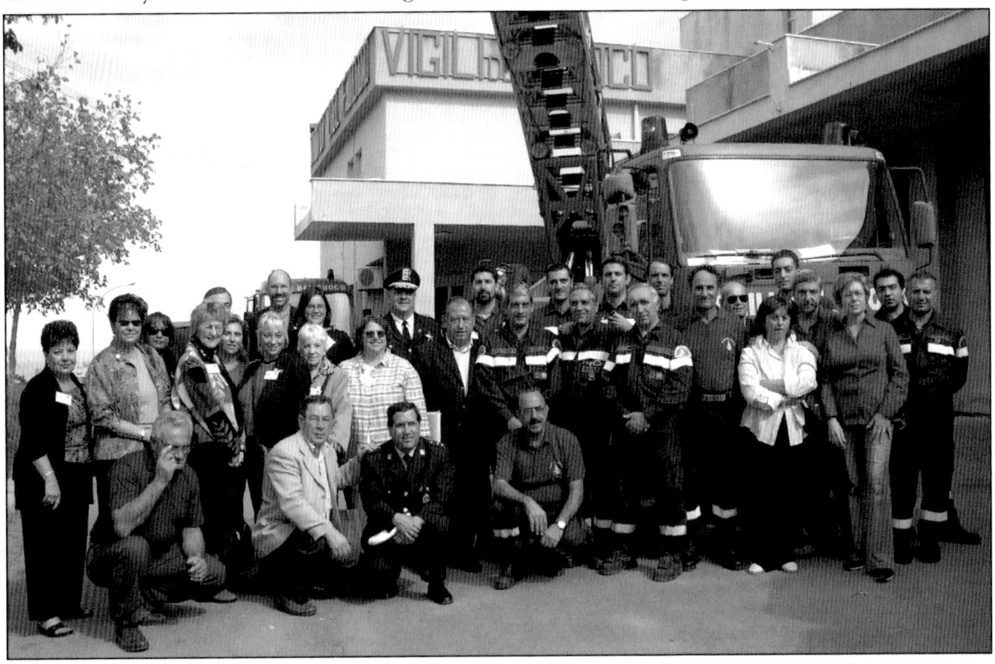

While in Termini Imerese, the group stopped for some tactical demonstrations of fire equipment at the local fire department. Members of the fire department proudly welcome everyone to the station so they can share their lifesaving and safety techniques. The visit to the station was one of many governmental and official meetings during the trip.

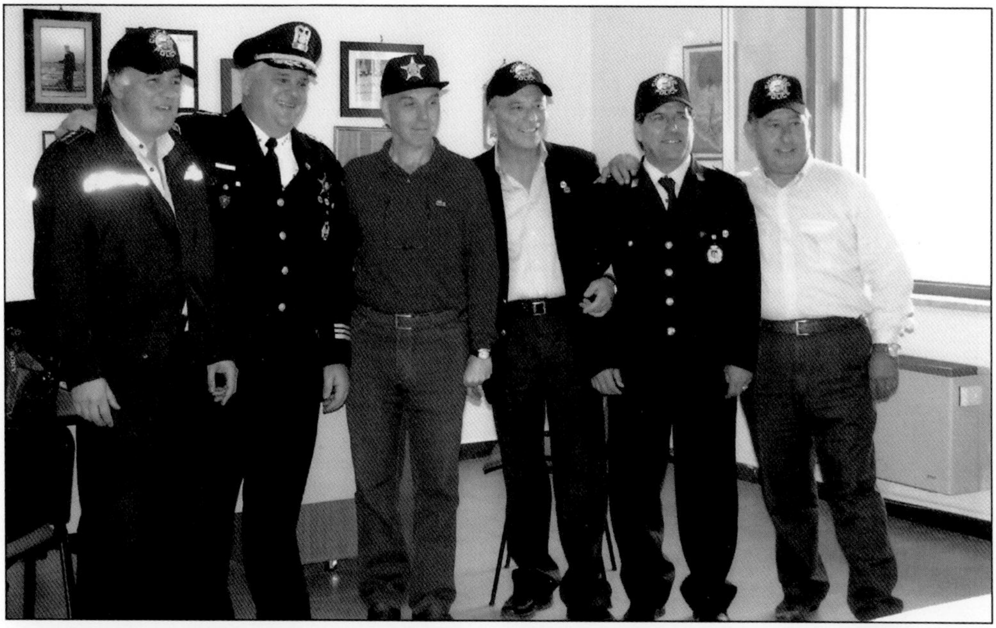

Luigi Candioto eagerly gives a tour and demonstration of his police department. The bond and friendship formed by Chief Steve Schmidt and Candioto cultivated from the very first meeting and continues to thrive today therefore strengthening the cultural exchanges with the ongoing sharing of information and technology. Pictured above from left to right are Paolo Pileri, Schmidt, an unidentified police official, Candioto, Giovanni Aglieri Rinella, and Salvatore Milano.

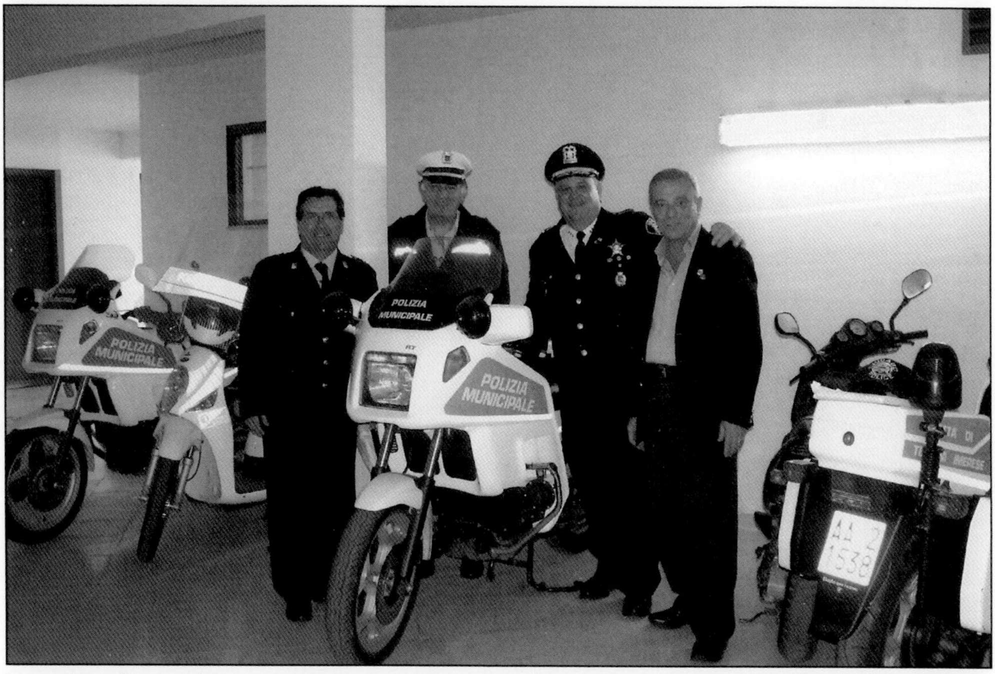

Learning about other communities operations and equipment is very beneficial when helping develop a community's operations and procedures. Schmidt took a tour of the Termini Imerese police department. Pictured from left to right are Rinella, Pileri, Schmidt, and Candioto.

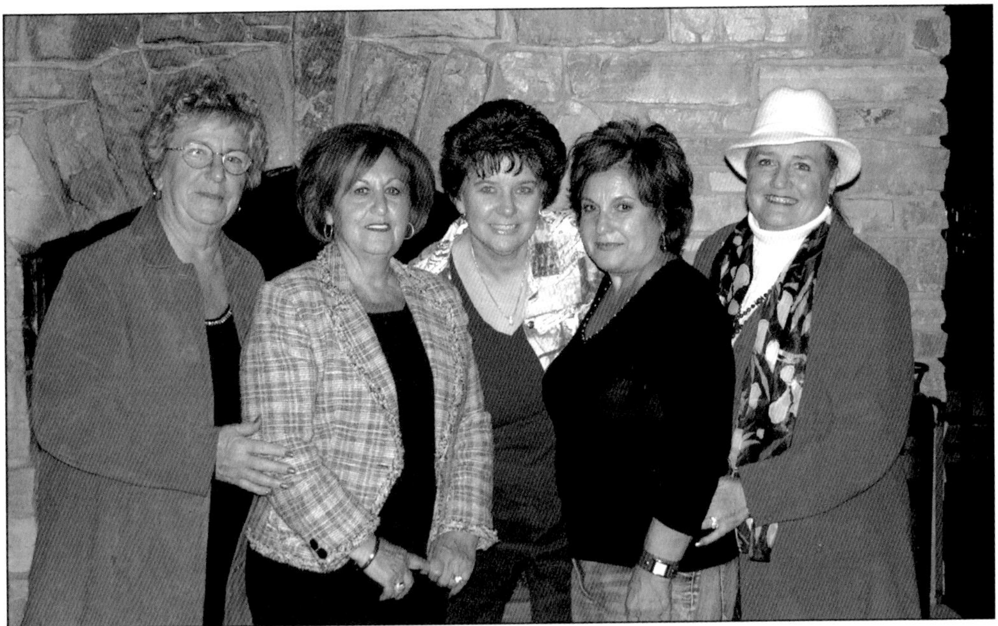

Elk Grove Village Italian Sister Cities members gather for a quick picture after a committee meeting. From left to right are secretary Ellen Peacock; Gina Sclafani; Nancy Colby, historian and public relations; Maria Gullo; and Patti Petri. The committee was finalizing the upcoming visit of six students as part of the first student exchange in the summer of 2007. Committee members not pictured are Cindy Aloiso, Linda Czyz, and Pat Droschak.

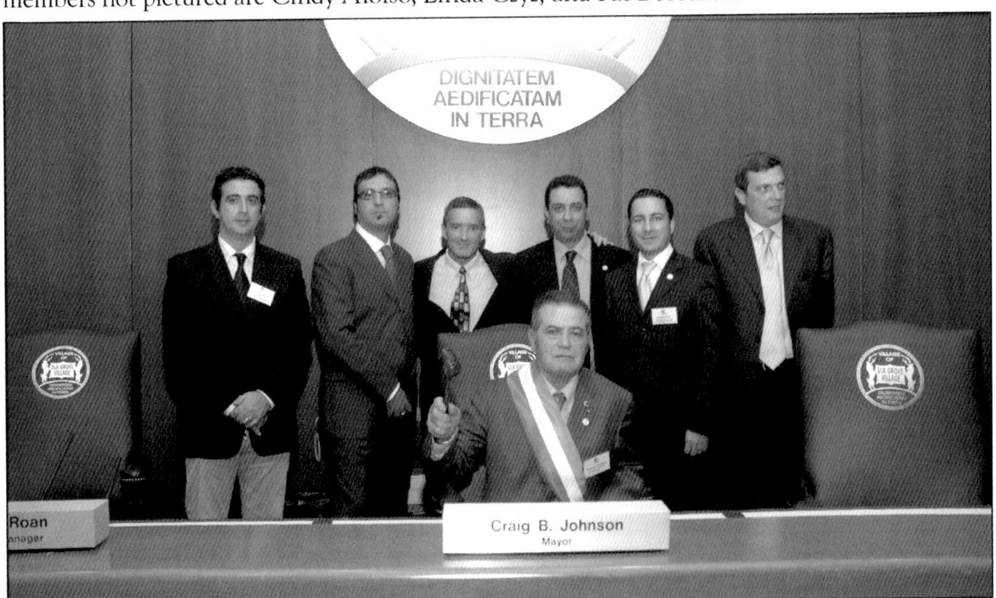

A congregation of mayors and officials in the Elk Grove Village boardroom gather for an official picture. From left to right are Giovanni Battista Caputo, president of the Council of Bagheria; Giorgio Scarsone, mayor of Bagheria; Craig Johnson, mayor of Elk Grove Village; Gianfranco Muscarella, village trustee of Caccamo; Bartolo Vitale, president of the Council of Collesano; Desidero Capitano, mayor of Caccamo; and sitting is Giuseppe Campagna, vice mayor of Trabia.

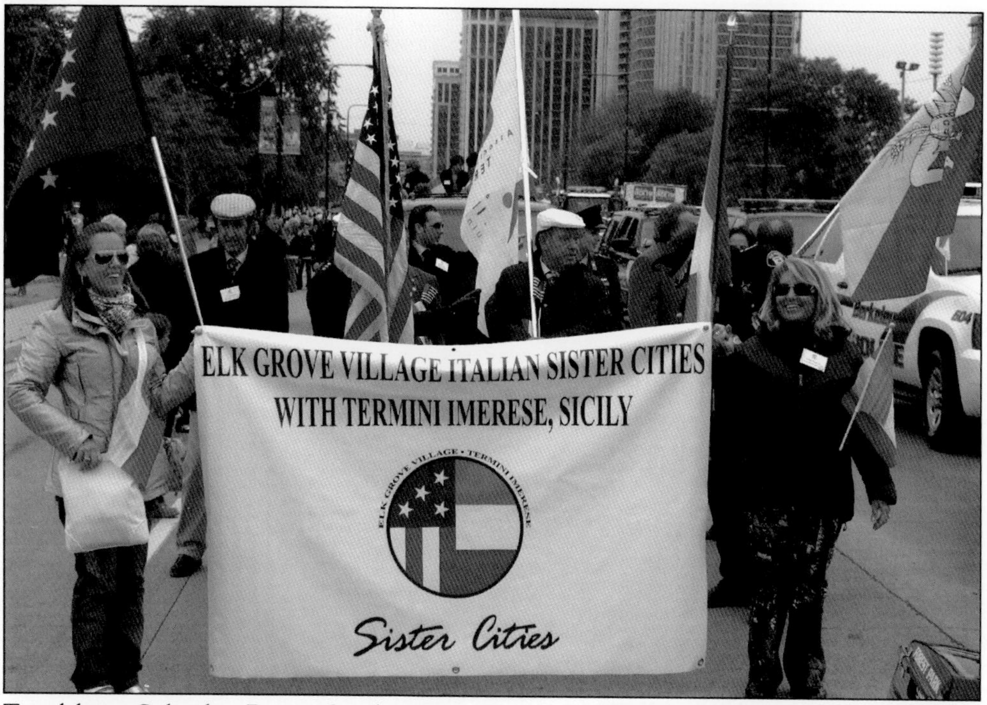

To celebrate Columbus Day in October 2007, Elk Grove Village and Termini Imerese members ride on the float. The parade is a great opportunity for Italian Americans to express pride in their heritage and culture. Above, Termini Imerese Sister City members Claudio Milano (left) and Teresa Pusateri are proudly holding the Sister City banner. Holding the flags behind the banner is Termini Imerese members Ciro Cardinale, Luigi Candioto, Salvatore Milano, Agostino Calderone, and Elk Grove Village Police Chief Steve Schmidt. The Termini Imerese delegates look forward to participating in the annual celebration of Christopher Columbus's discovery of America.

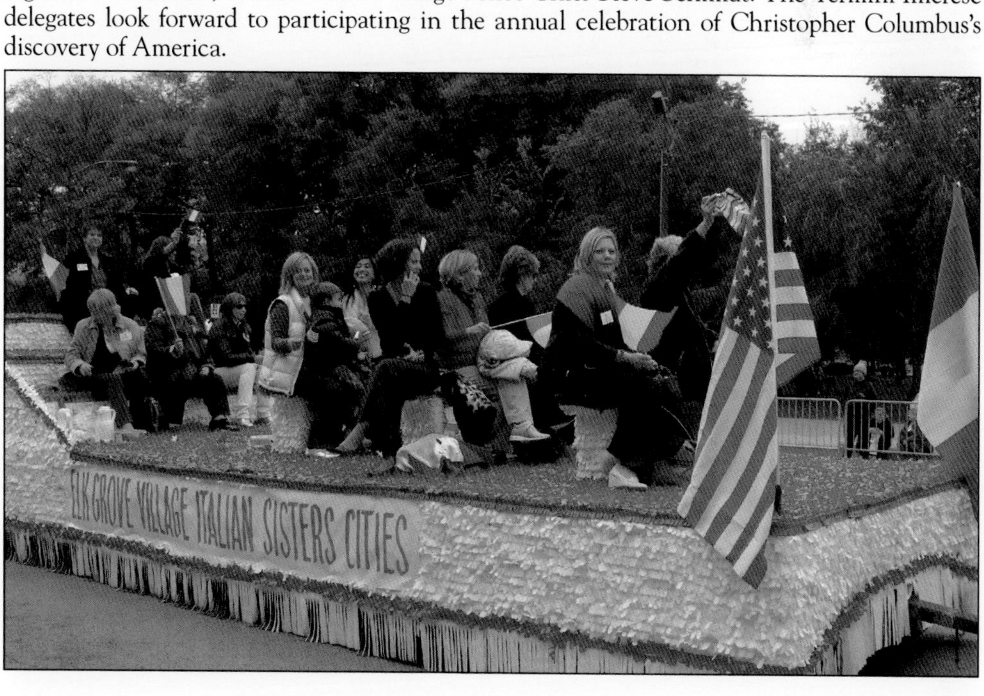

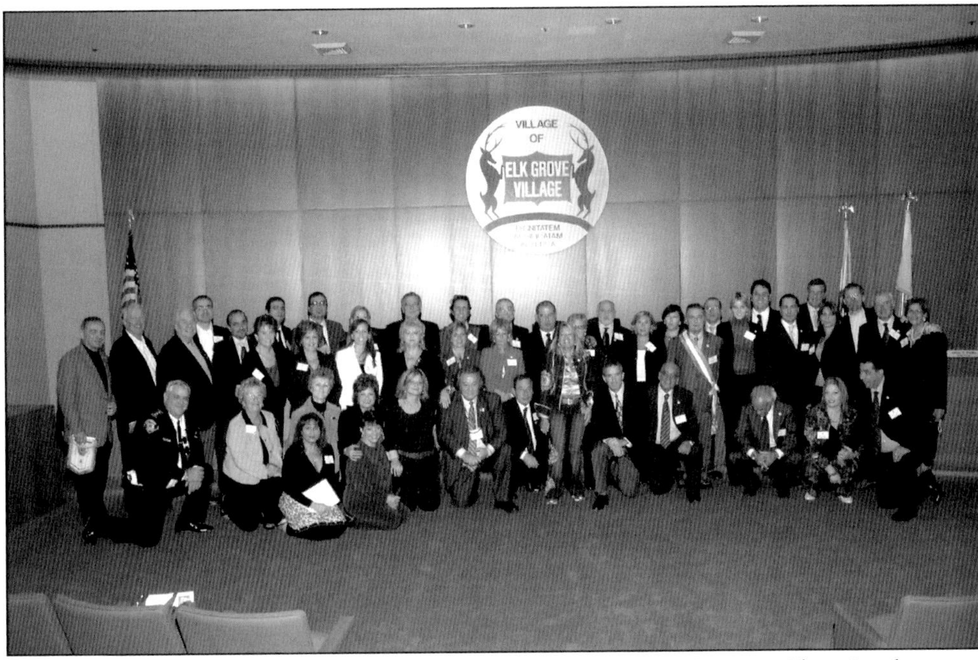

Mayor Craig Johnson and trustees Nancy Czarnik, Jim Petri, Sam Lissner, Chris Prochno, and Pat Feichter kick off the arrival of the Sister Cities delegation on October 12, 2007, in the village boardroom. After the exchange of many wonderful gifts from both sides, everyone paused for a group photograph.

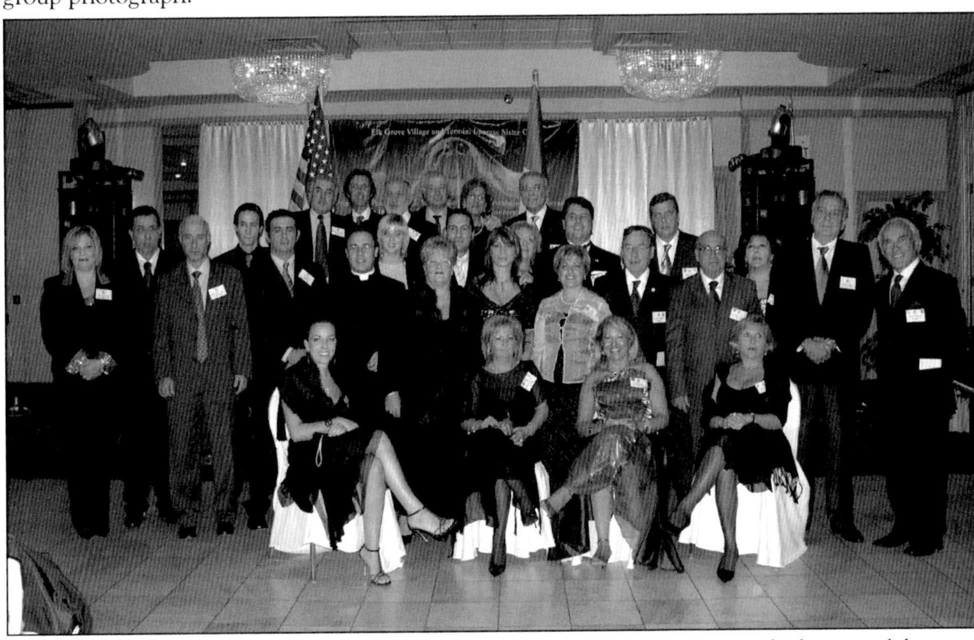

Termini Imerese Sister City members gather for a group picture at the 2007 gala dinner celebration. The gala dinner was the final celebration with the delegates. The theme of the evening was *Il Mondo*, meaning "the world." The vibrations of the taiko drums permeated throughout the room, and the ornate costumes and energetic dance routines absolutely amazed everyone. The evening ended with an incredible tribute to Luciano Pavarotti.

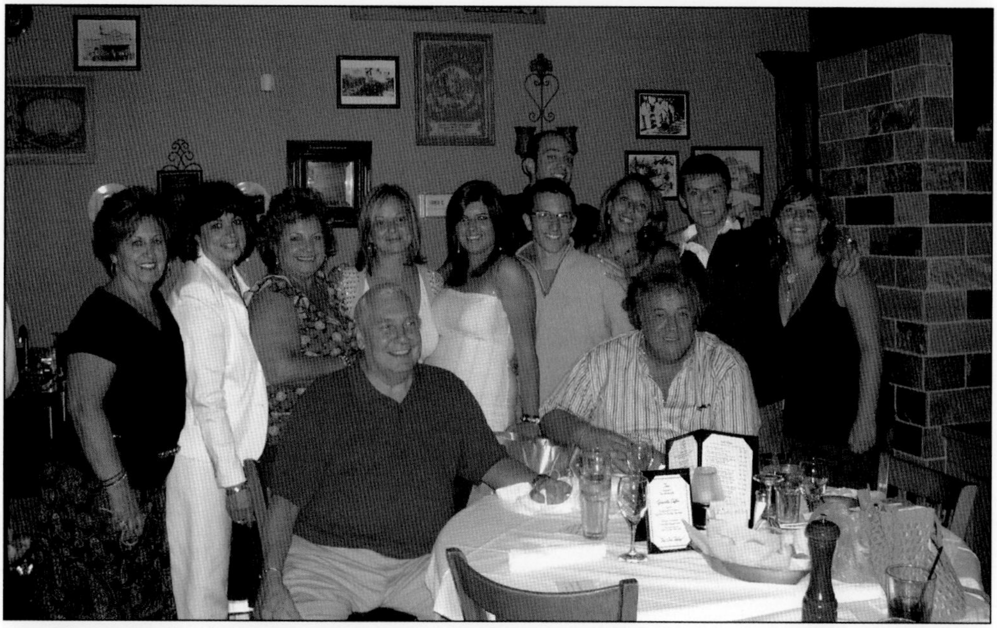

In addition to this life experience in America, part of the program focused on refining their grammar and building their confidence while speaking English. Sister City members from left to right are Gina Sclafani, Elsa Wiegel, Maria Gullo, Mariann Gullo-Krewenka, Eliana Franchina, Paolo Miná, Giuseppe Sorci (behind), Laura Montana, Vito Pialiotta, and Stefania Calderone. Jim Petri (sitting, left) and Giovanni Gullo say farewell to the students.

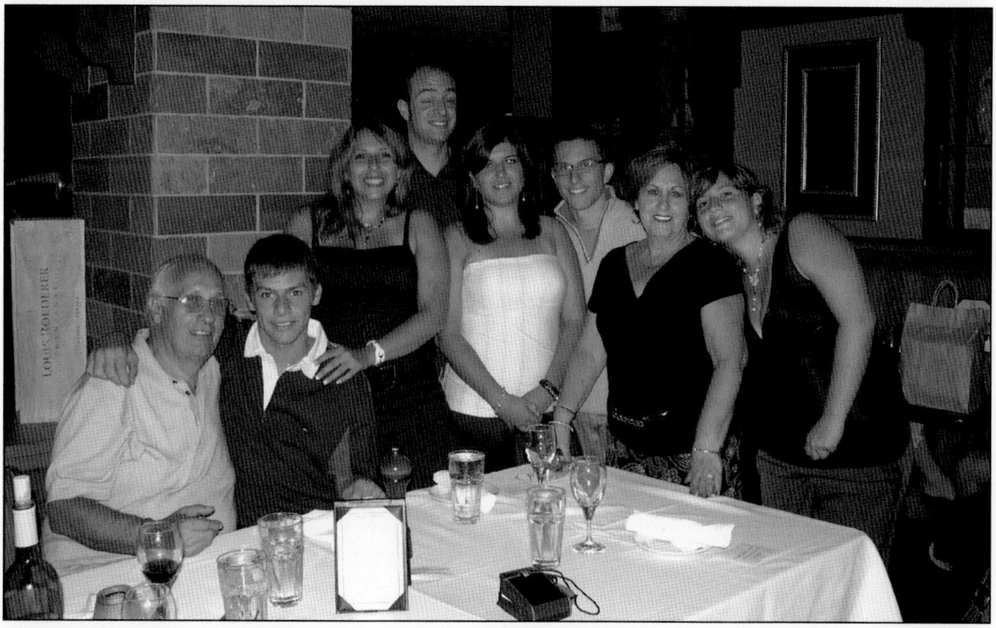

Nat and Gina Sclafani generously hosted the three male exchange students for two of the three weeks. The trip was planned in support of the sister city agreement to participate in exchange of cultures and ideas between the two cities. From left to right, Nat Sclafani, Vito Pialiotta, Laura Montana, Giuseppe Sorci, Eliana Franchina, Paolo Miná, Gina Sclafani, and Stefania Calderone are at the final celebration.

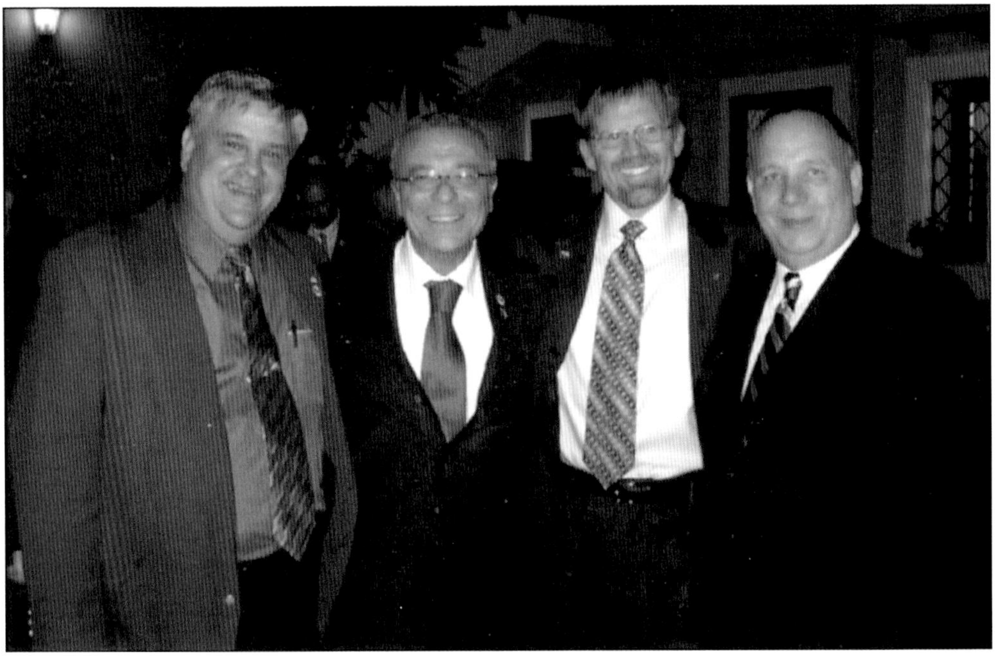

The extended families have touched hearts and lives in many ways. Every trip strengthens the bond of friendship between the two cities. Until the next reunion, memories of these friends will always remain in residents' hearts. Chief Steve Schmidt, Luigi Candioto, Rod Pickett, and Judge Tony Iosco are more like extended family than friends because of the Sister City organization.

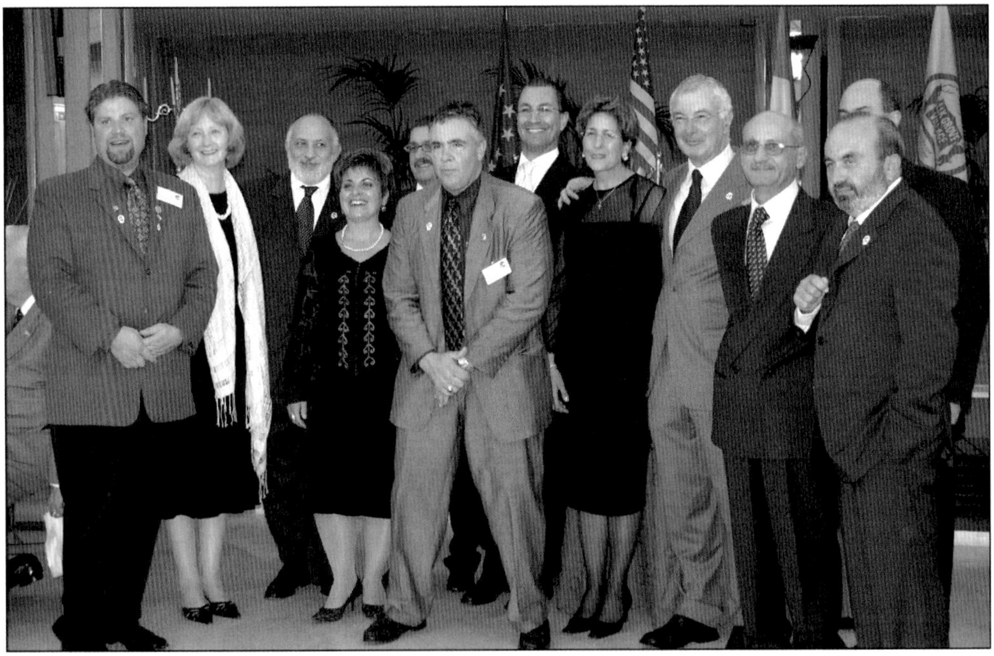

Is there a doctor in the house? Alexian Brothers Medical Center doctors team up with Termini Imerese doctors for one last group picture at the gala dinner celebration in Termini Imerese in October 2005. This exchange has allowed everyone to have a greater appreciation of the many traditions, values, and beliefs inherent in the Italian and American cultures.

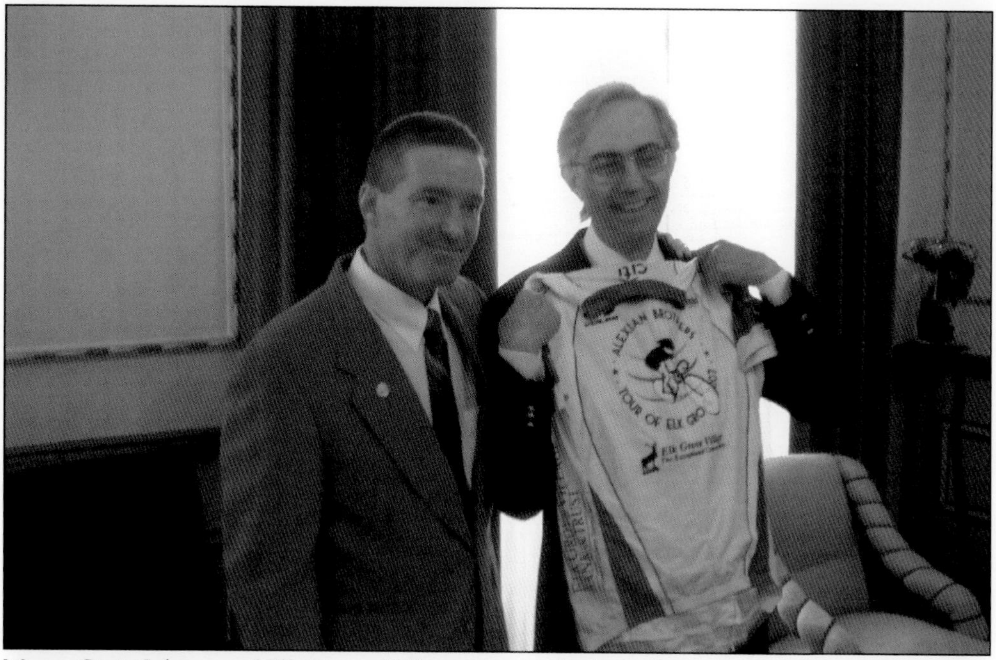

Mayor Craig Johnson of Elk Grove Village presented Mayor Enzo Guinta of Termini Imerese with a 2007 Alexian Brothers Tour of Elk Grove Village winning cycling jersey. The Alexian Brothers Tour of Elk Grove Village, now an annual event, started in the summer of 2006. Johnson is very proud of the largest international cycling event.

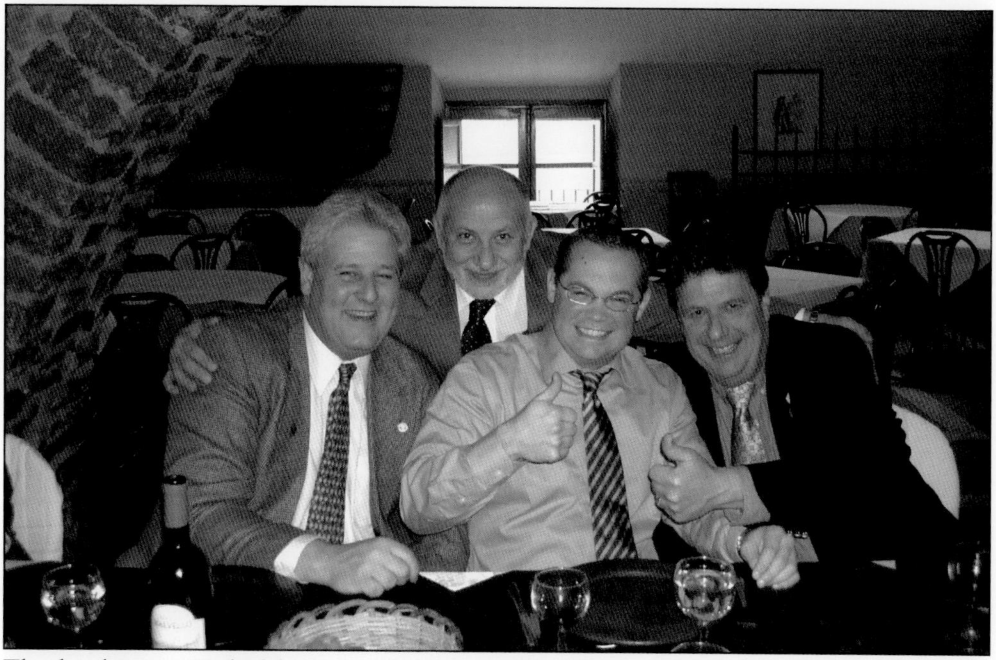

This has been a wonderful trip for Elk Grove Village trustee Jeff Franke, president of Termini Imerese Sister City Mario Montana, deputy village manager Matt Roan, and village attorney George B. Knickerbocker, who have thoroughly enjoyed their taste of Sicily. The five-day whirlwind tour of Termini Imerese and surrounding areas is embedded in their hearts forever.

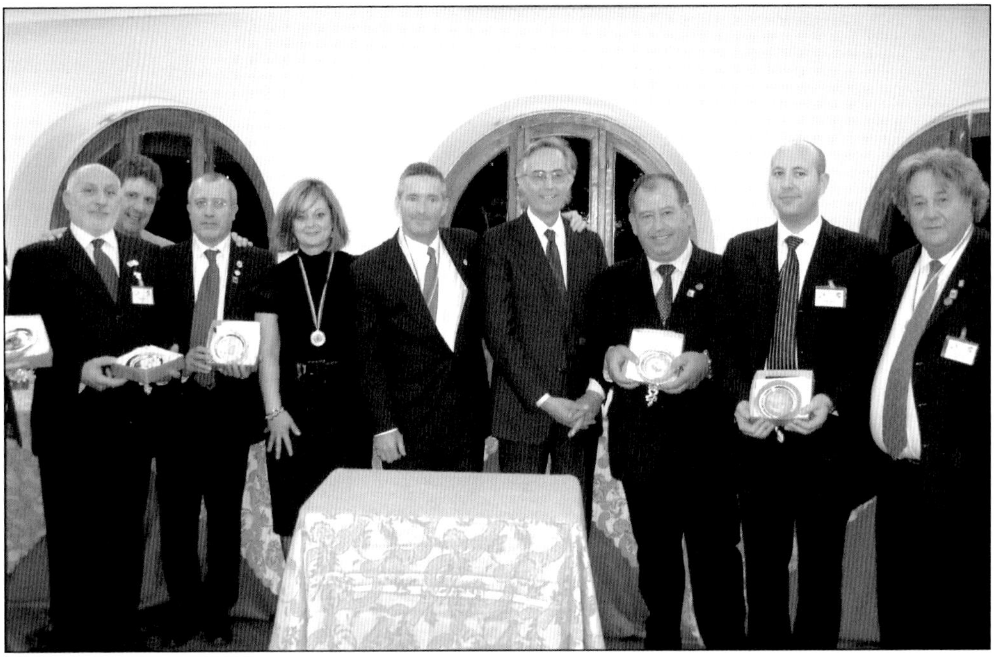

The culmination of the trip was the gala dinner at the beautiful Grand Hotel delle Terme in Termini Imerese. Pictured from left to right are Mario Montana, George B. Knickerbocker (behind Montana), Agostino Calderone, Mariann Gullo-Krewenka, Mayor Craig Johnson, Mayor Enzo Giunta, Salvatore Milano, Daniele Speciale, and Giovanni Gullo.

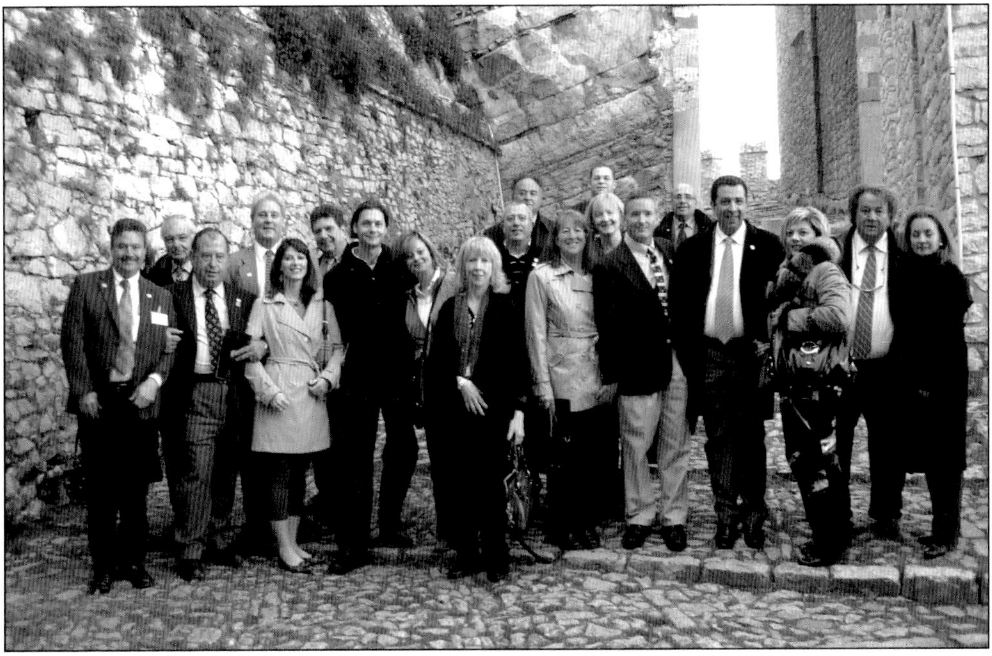

Johnson and his wife, Lorrie; Gullo; Krewenka and her husband, Karl; Knickerbocker; Jeff Franke; Matt Roan; Ronald J. Nunes and his wife, Gina; Susan Breier; and Dr. Debra Susie-Lattner participated in a five-day exchange with sister city Termini Imerese. The group stops to take a quick picture.

Five

SERVICE ABOVE SELF

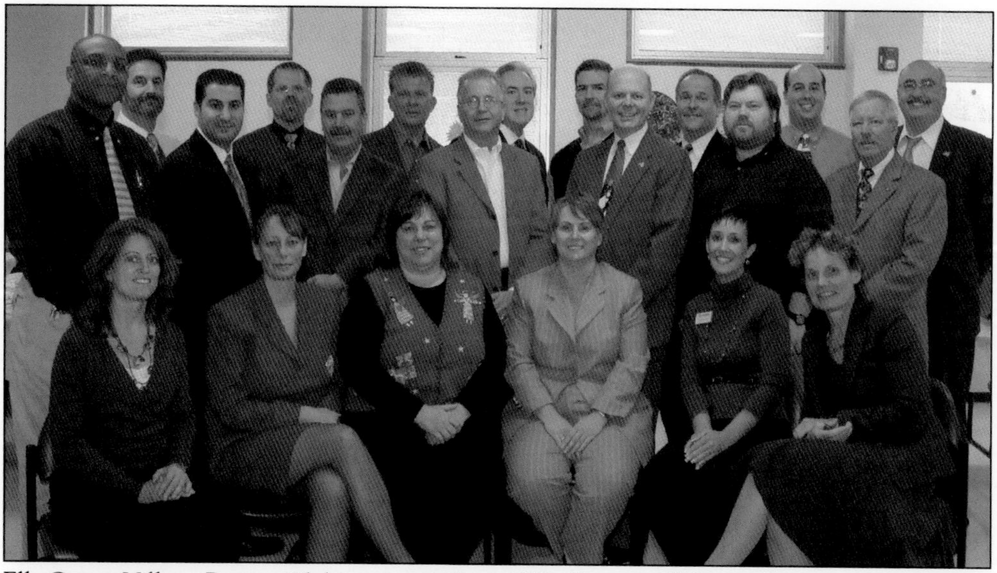

Elk Grove Village Rotary Club was started in 1970. Rotary Club members are business and professional leaders who volunteer in their communities to promote world understanding and peace. The clubs encourage high ethical standards and carry out humanitarian projects to address such issues as poverty, health, hunger, education, and the environment. From left to right are (first row) Dawn Cunningham, Kitty Weiner, Shirlanne Lemm, Sheri Dial, Donna Bartoli, and Nancy Holman; (second row) Raymond Toney, Mike Brottman, Robert Makanoeich, Rod Pickett, Ron Nunes, Frank Ramljak, Rick Gayeski, Ralph Schumann, Kelly Hutchison, Bill Marston, Hank Sobotka Jr., Steve Pickett, Billy Beaupre, Bob Nicholas, and Helmut Gottfert.

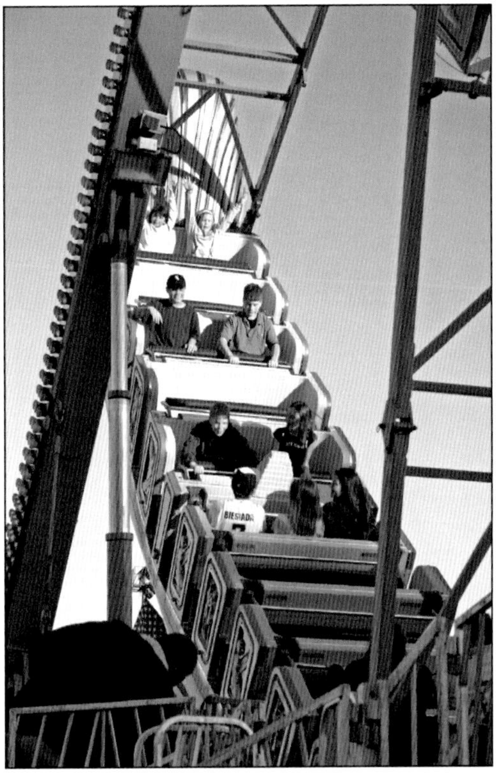

Proceeds from all rides and activities fund scholarships, both educational and vocational, earning the Rotary Club a respected cornerstone of the village. By helping communities to help themselves, the club focuses on sustainable projects. Most of these projects include the areas of education, sanitation, clean water, and recreation. They frequently involve assistance to youth, the aged, the disabled, and others who look to Rotary as a source of hope for a better life.

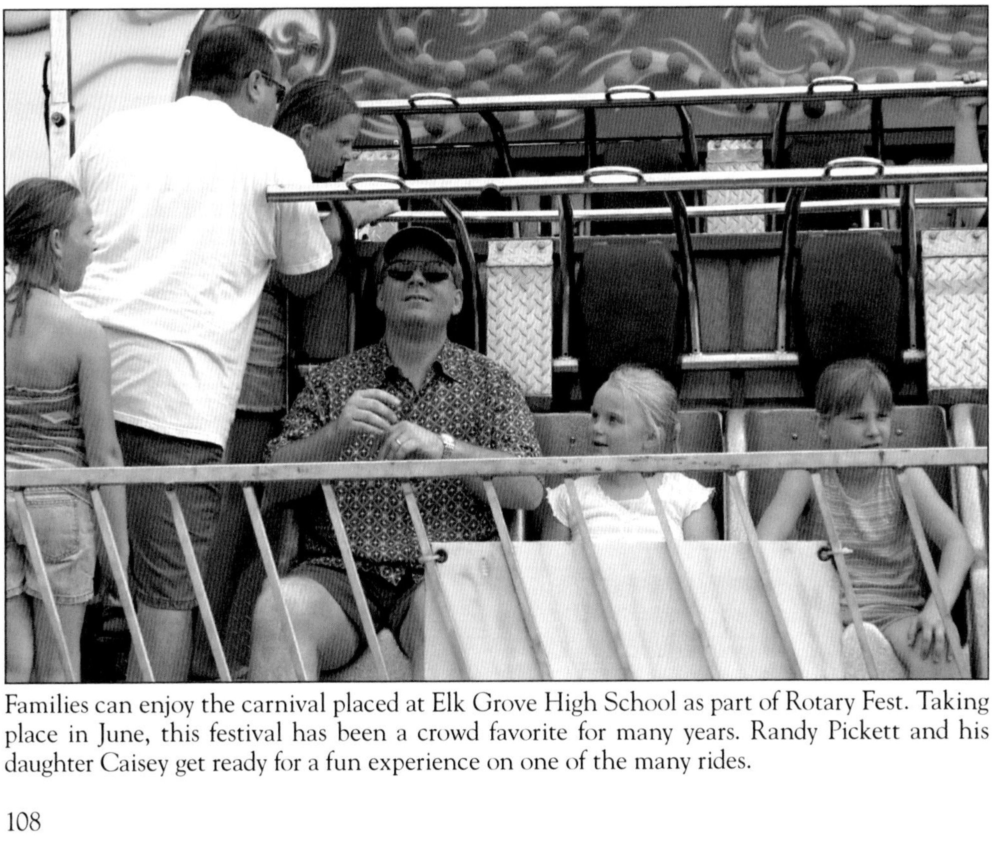

Families can enjoy the carnival placed at Elk Grove High School as part of Rotary Fest. Taking place in June, this festival has been a crowd favorite for many years. Randy Pickett and his daughter Caisey get ready for a fun experience on one of the many rides.

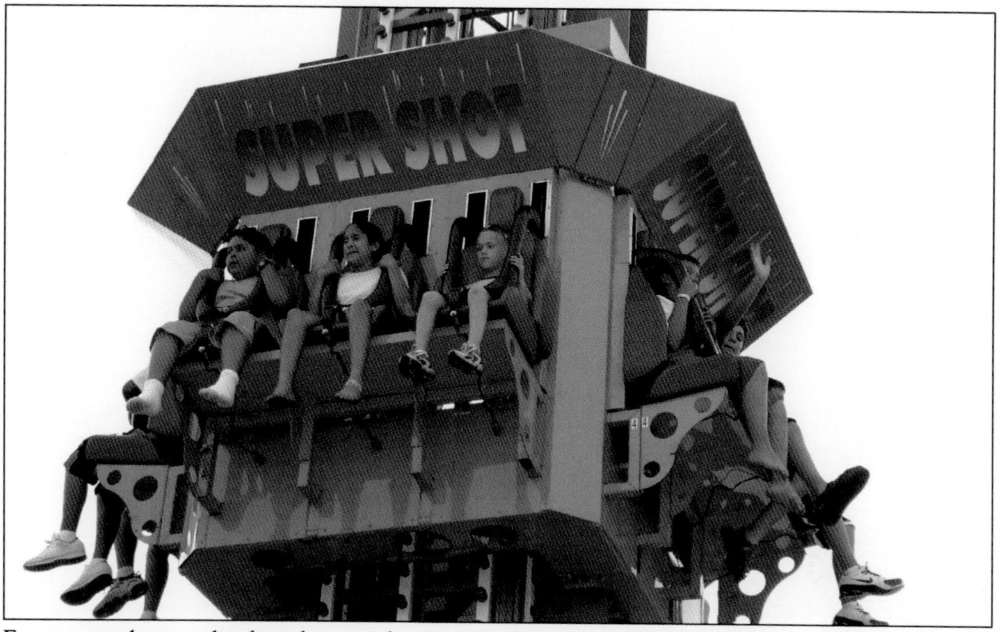

Every year, thousands of residents and visitors look forward to the annual Rotary Fest, sponsored by the Elk Grove Rotary Club. The whole reason for the festival is to raise funds to help the community, with proceeds going back to charities. Live entertainment, food, and a carnival make the park next to Elk Grove High School the place to be. Specials allowing unlimited rides encourage children to experience thrill rides all day long.

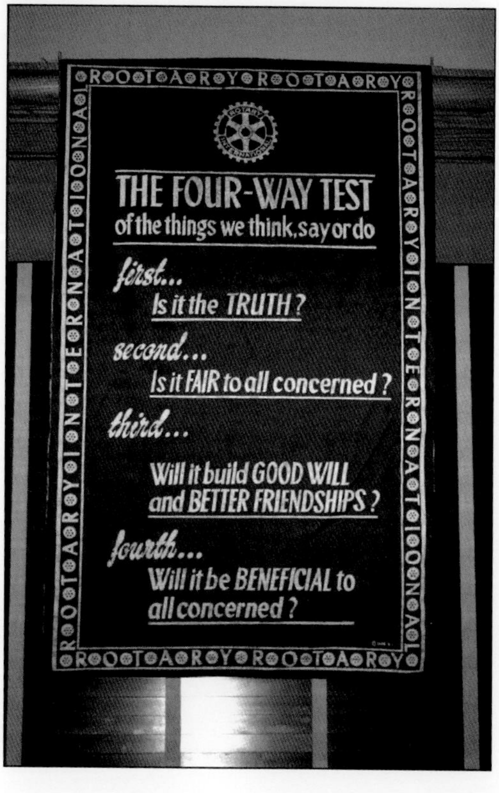

In addition to the motto of "Service above Self," Rotarians are guided in their daily life by a simple test known as the four-way test, created by Rotarian Herbert J. Taylor in 1932 and translated into over 100 languages. Of the things people think, say, or do, is it the truth, is it fair to all concerned, will it build good will and better friendships, and will it be beneficial to all concerned?

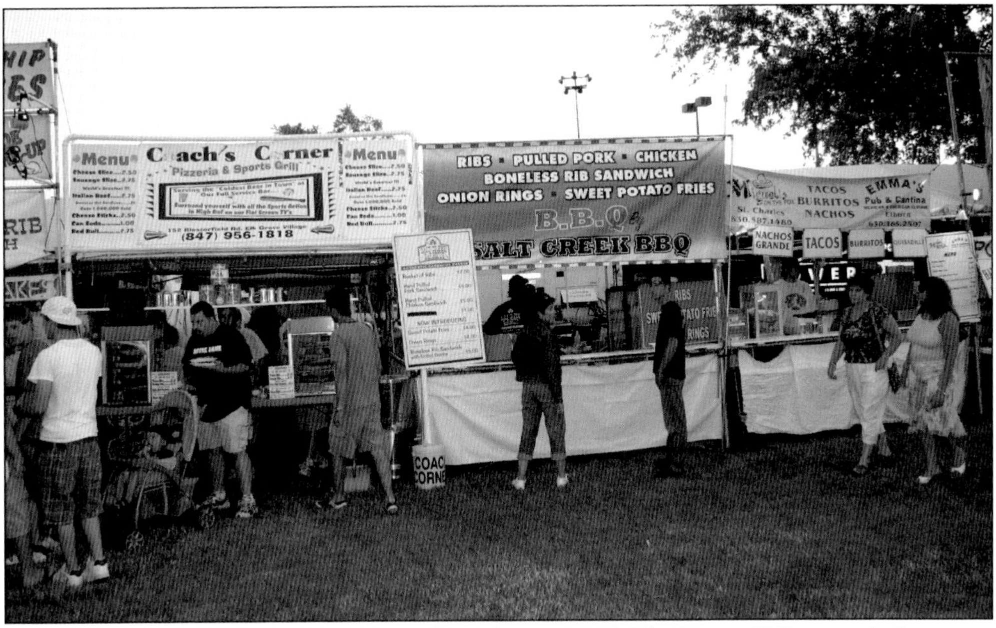

From typical festival food to gourmet fare, the taste of Elk Grove Village includes many vendors selling all kinds of delicious food. The five-day festival allows families to gather and enjoy free entertainment and celebrate the Father's Day weekend. Main stage entertainment plays every night under the big tent. Saturday night includes the village parade and a large fireworks display.

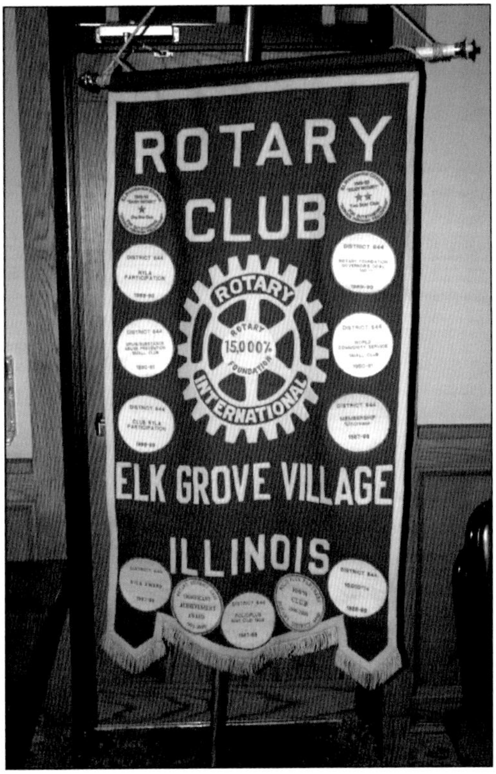

This banner shows some of the awards for the diverse projects, including Rotary Youth Exchange and international contributions. Annually the club supports local and international causes. When members reach goals and complete projects, these and other awards are displayed at the weekly luncheon as a reminder of successes.

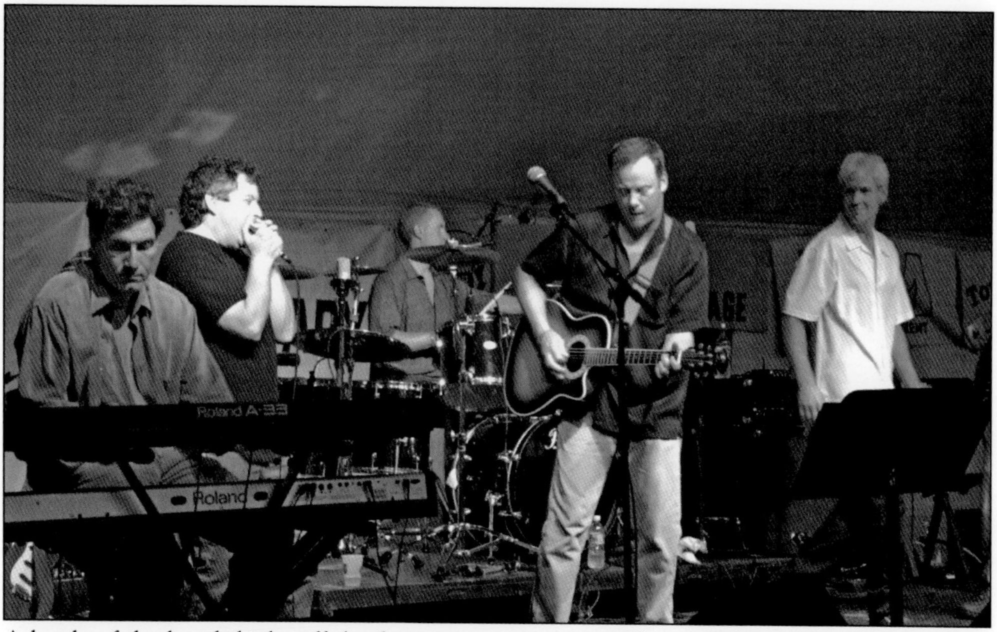

A battle of the bands kicks off the festivities on opening night, with live entertainment every night for five days of the premier festival in the suburbs. Musical acts featuring everyone from local celebrities to national acts are free of charge to Rotary Fest attendees. Pictured above is the band Flyte. They are all Elk Grove High School alumni, including Dave Dopp on keyboard, Joel Peterson on drums, Bill McKenzie on guitar, and lead singer Jim Cunningham.

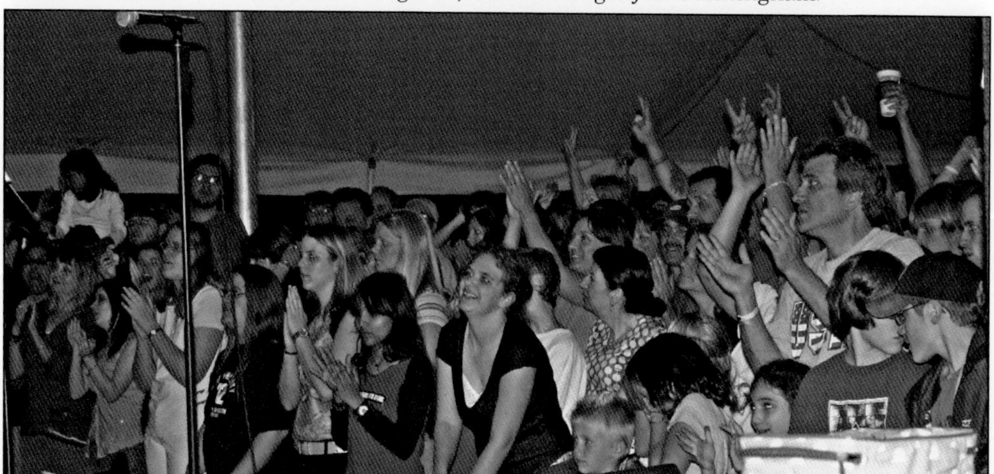

Crowds young and old dance the week away, with music provided by the different groups all while supporting important Rotary programs, including the eradication of polio. Over the history of the festival, car shows, sports competitions, magic shows, reptile demonstrations, dance troops, senior bands, and the world's largest grill have been part of this neighborhood family festival. All proceeds are donated to charity.

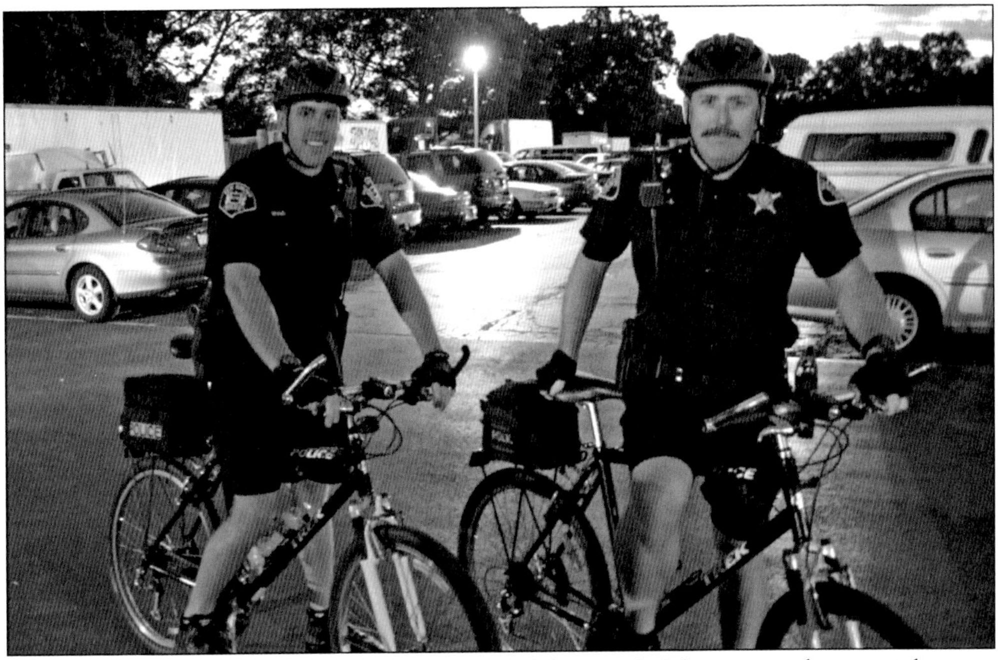

Officers Shaun Berens and Steve O'Neill are on bike patrol. Bikes are used at special events and as needed through warmer months. They allow closer citizen interaction and park patrols. The village support of the Rotary Fest cuts across all lines of government. The festival is only successful because of the cooperative effort of the village.

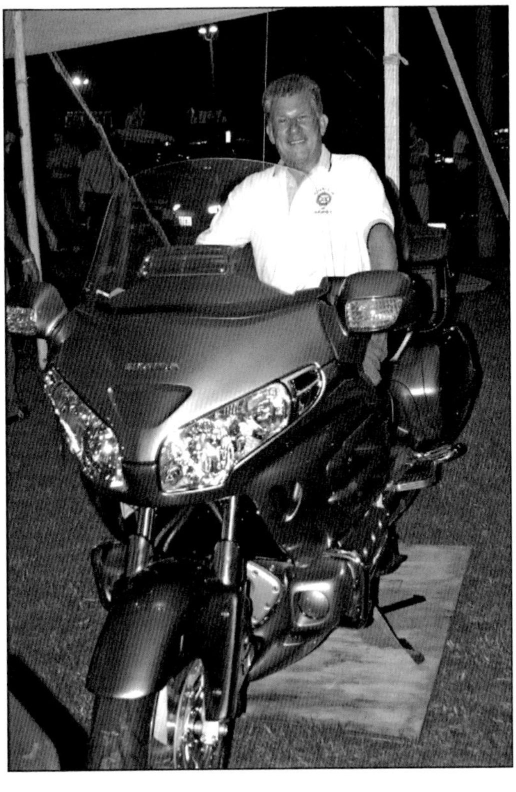

Fund-raising activities allow the Elk Grove Rotary Club to purchase items needed for the community as well as for other important causes. This motorcycle was raffled off to raise money for a multiuse X-ray machine, which was purchased and given to a hospital on the island of St. Lucia.

The Cimino family has been volunteering for the history of the festival, giving their time back to the village that raised their family. From left to right are Jan Cimino, Joe Cimino, and their daughter Mary Jan Cimino. The Rotary Club of Elk Grove Village and the Cimino family, who are members, continue to meet these ideals and make a difference in the community and the world.

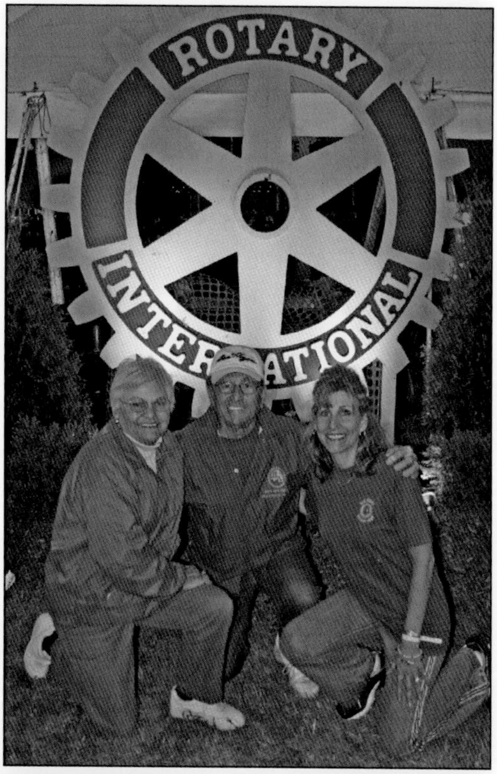

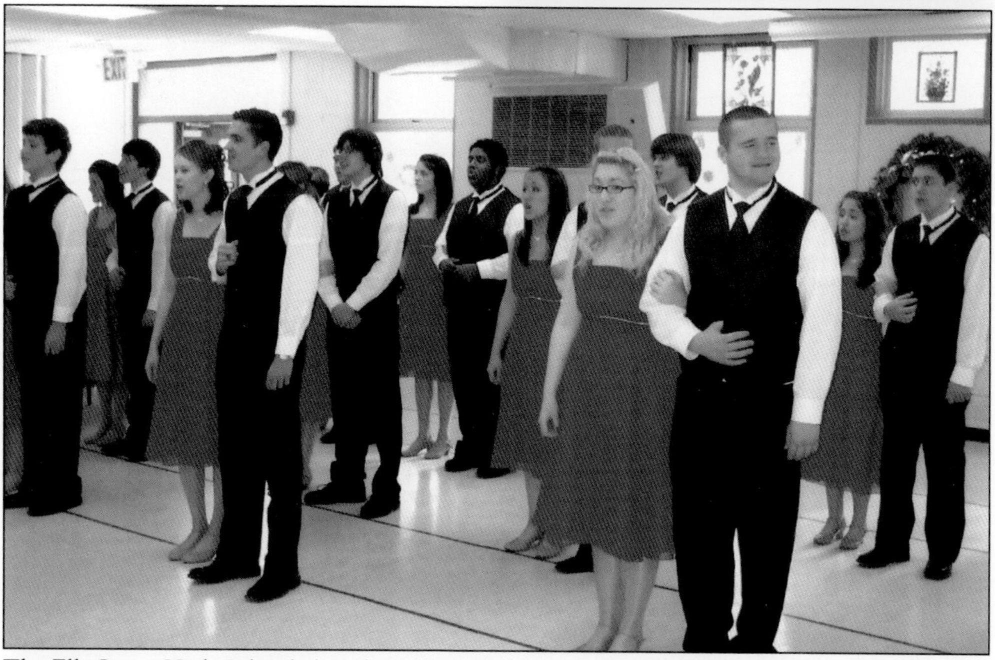

The Elk Grove High School choir has entertained the seniors with a beautiful holiday program for over five years. The performance of Christmas carols was the highlight of the afternoon. The Sheila Ray Adult Center serves as a perfect location to bring the generations together. The seniors look forward to a wonderful afternoon of live entertainment and good food.

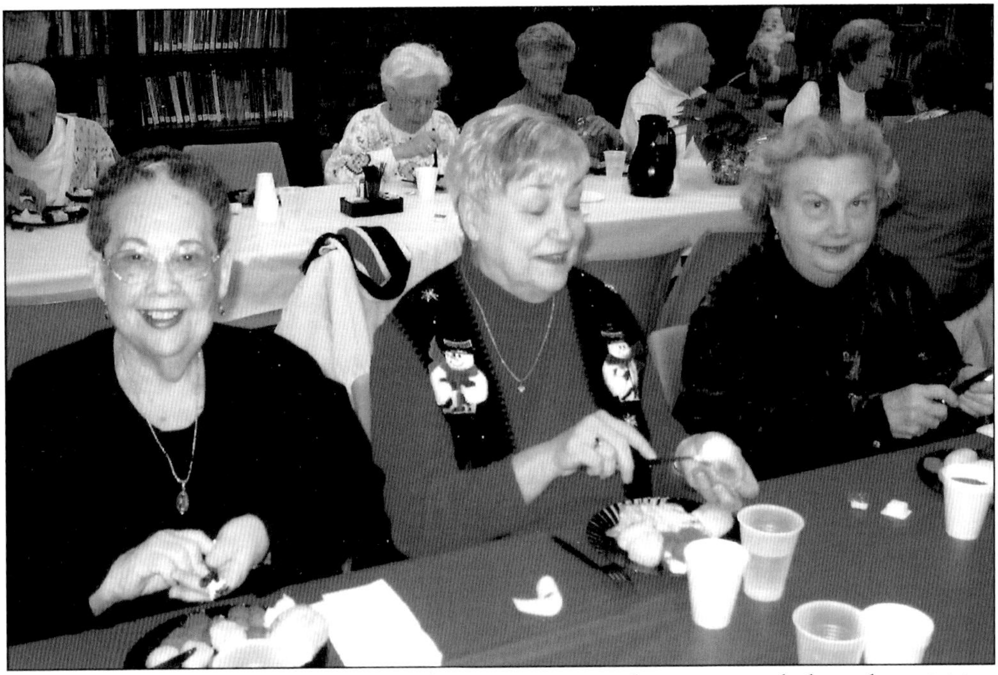

Funds for many projects originate in the community and are returned through activities, including the senior luncheon. Friends, from left to right, Josephine Gaspirano, Clara Fortman, and Gloria Carlson look forward to the time spent with each other every year.

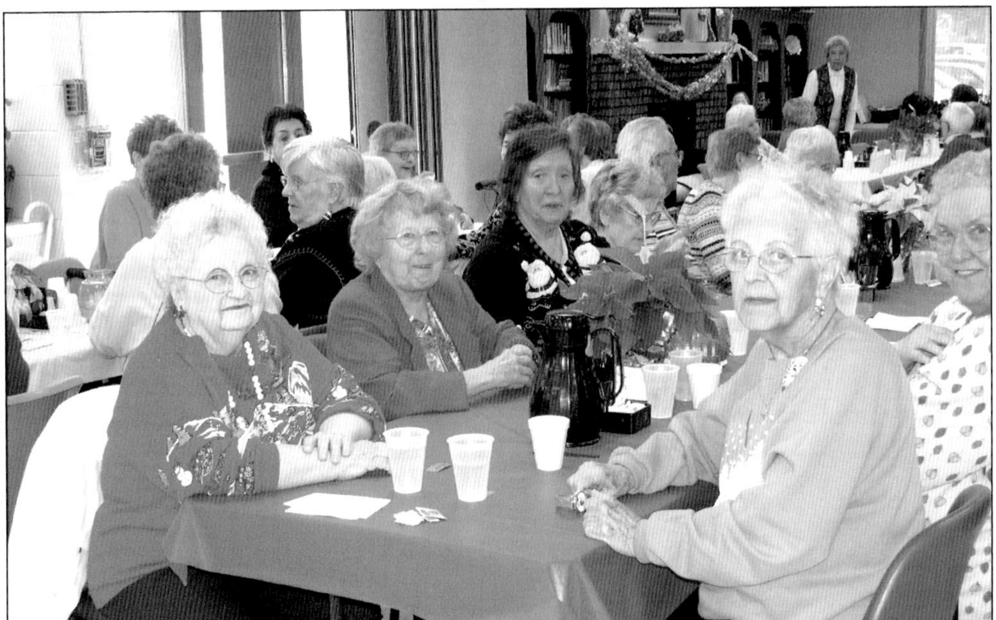

For over five years, Rotarians have worked with a local caterer and Jarosch Bakery, providing fellowship to its members and the community. Every year, Jarosch provides a beautiful holiday cake for everyone to enjoy. Sylvia Panello, Jean Thomas, and Carole McDermott at the far left side of the table, and directly across the table, Francis Smith, look forward to the luncheon every year.

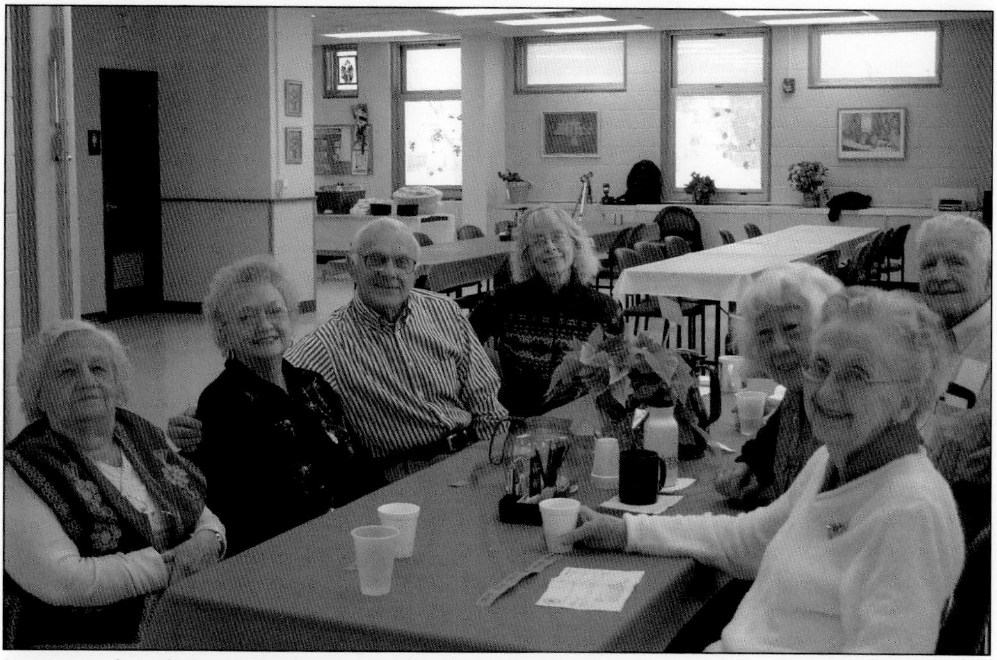

Longtime friends Betty Erickson, Martha Kruse, Ed Zmuda, and Joan Kohlmstedt (from left to right on the far left side of the table) Maria Chrabot, Mary Wa, and Phil Barry, sitting across from them, enjoy spending time together and listening to the concert provided by the Elk Grove High School chorus holiday program.

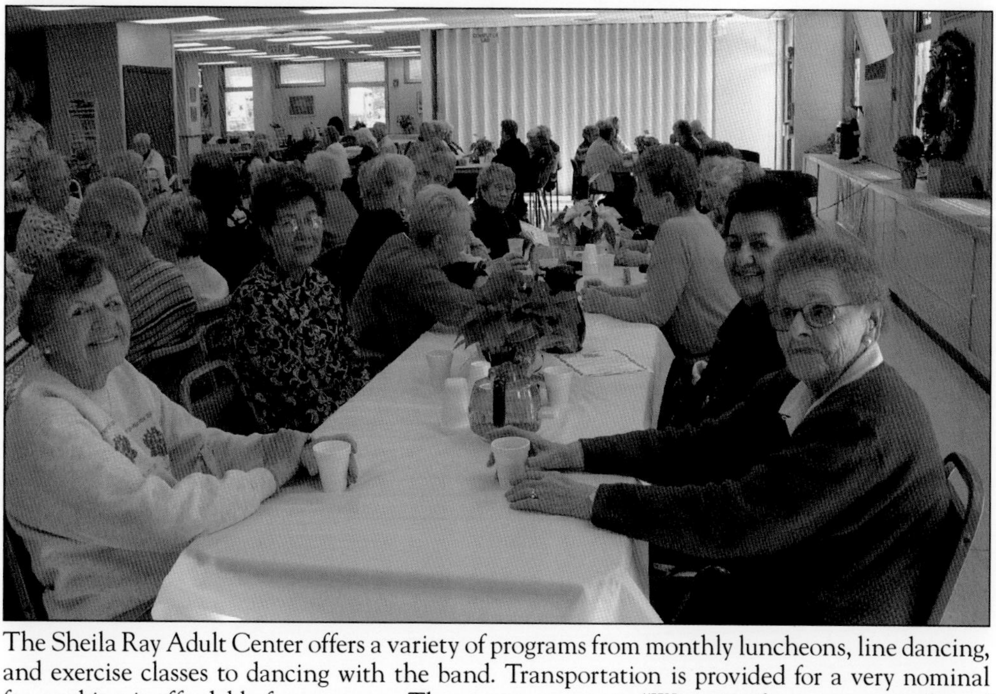

The Sheila Ray Adult Center offers a variety of programs from monthly luncheons, line dancing, and exercise classes to dancing with the band. Transportation is provided for a very nominal fee, making it affordable for everyone. The centers motto is, "We strive for a greater quality of life through recreation and community involvement." From left to right, Cynthia Malinowski, Helen Leski, Betty Cwik, and Virginia Martinez look forward to the celebration of friendship.

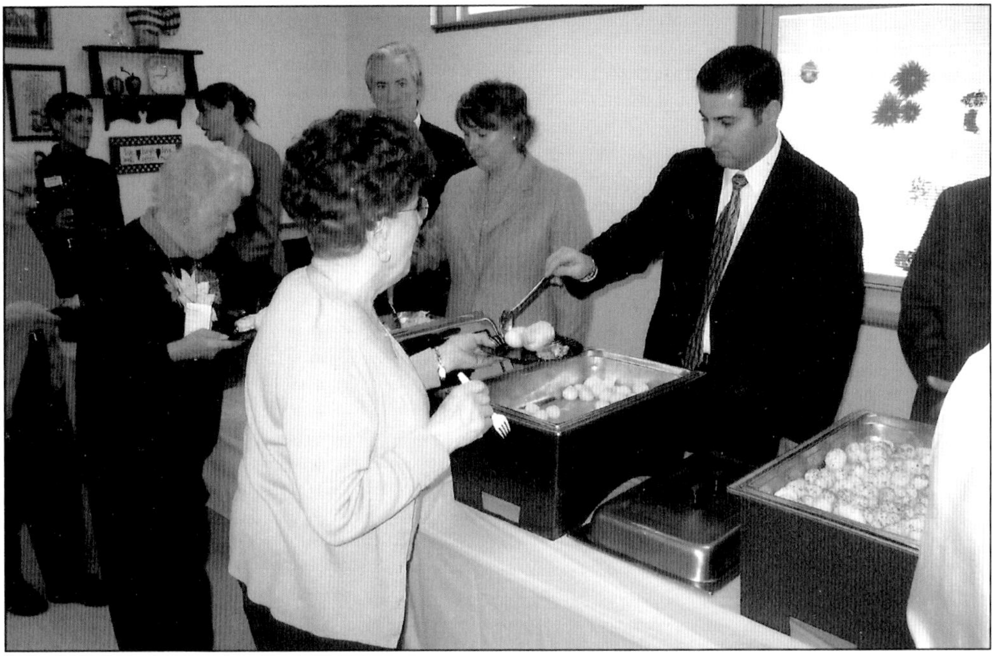

Rotary allows local business leader Robert Makanoeich the opportunity to give back to the community. The object of Rotary is "to encourage and foster the ideal of service as a basis of worthy enterprise." The four areas by which this "ideal of service" is fostered are through the development of acquaintance as the opportunity for service; the promotion of high ethical standards in business and professions; through service in one's personal, business, and community life; and the advancement of international understanding, goodwill, and peace. Rotary has always had the spirit of volunteerism; pictured below are Bill Marston and Bob Nicholas who have served in Rotary for over 40 combined years, building the legacy for the Elk Grove Rotary.

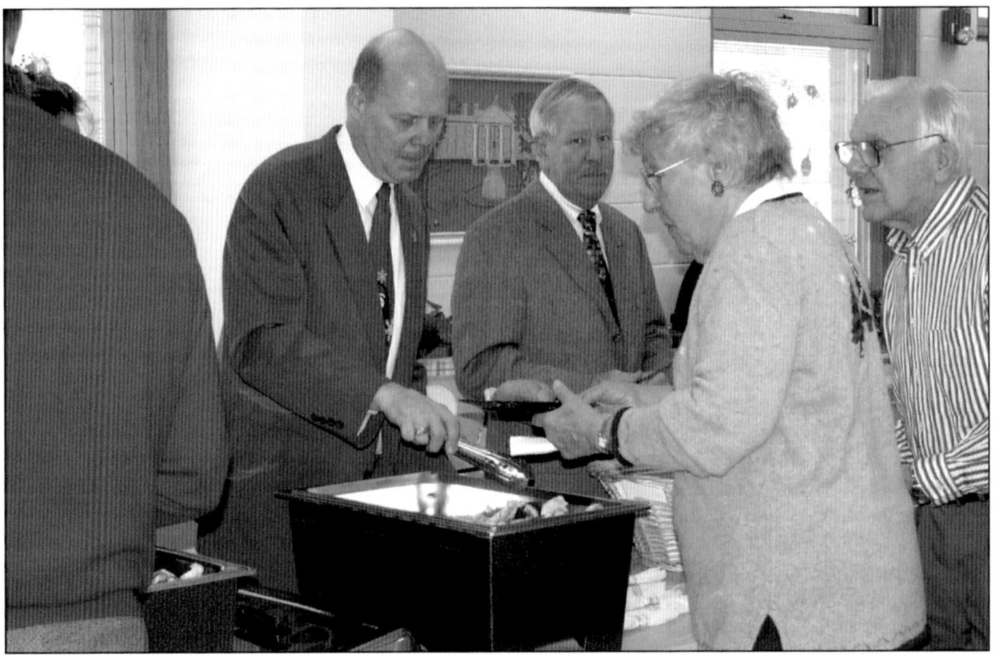

Six

Happy Golden Anniversary

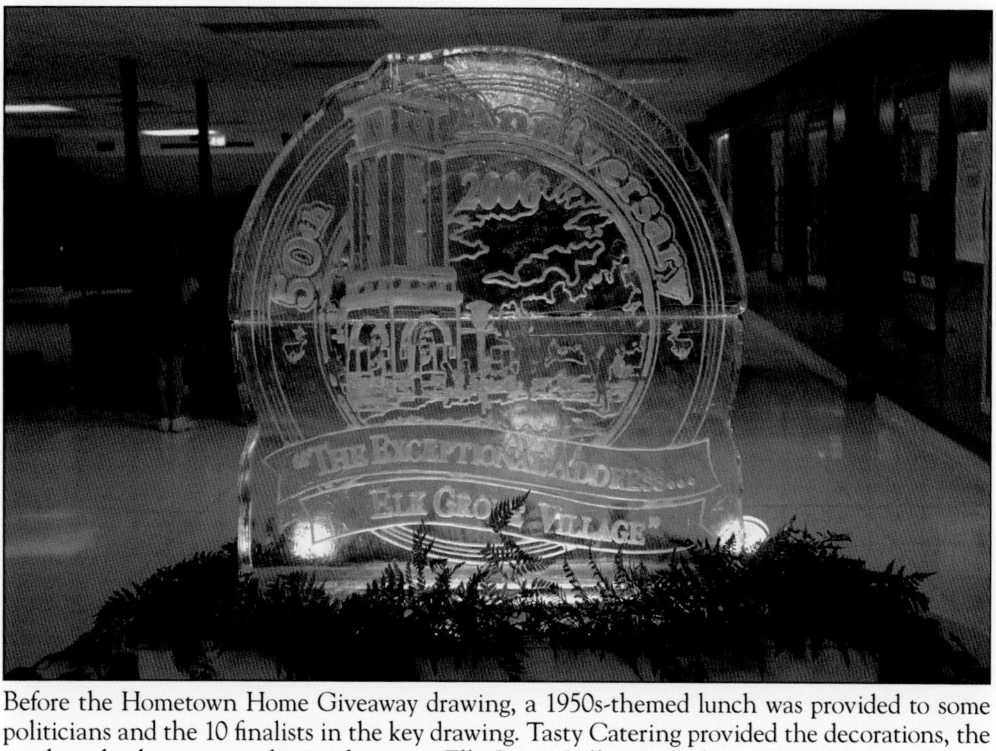

Before the Hometown Home Giveaway drawing, a 1950s-themed lunch was provided to some politicians and the 10 finalists in the key drawing. Tasty Catering provided the decorations, the meal, and a large ice sculpture depicting Elk Grove Village's clock tower. The luncheon was given at Elk Grove High School at 500 West Elk Grove Boulevard.

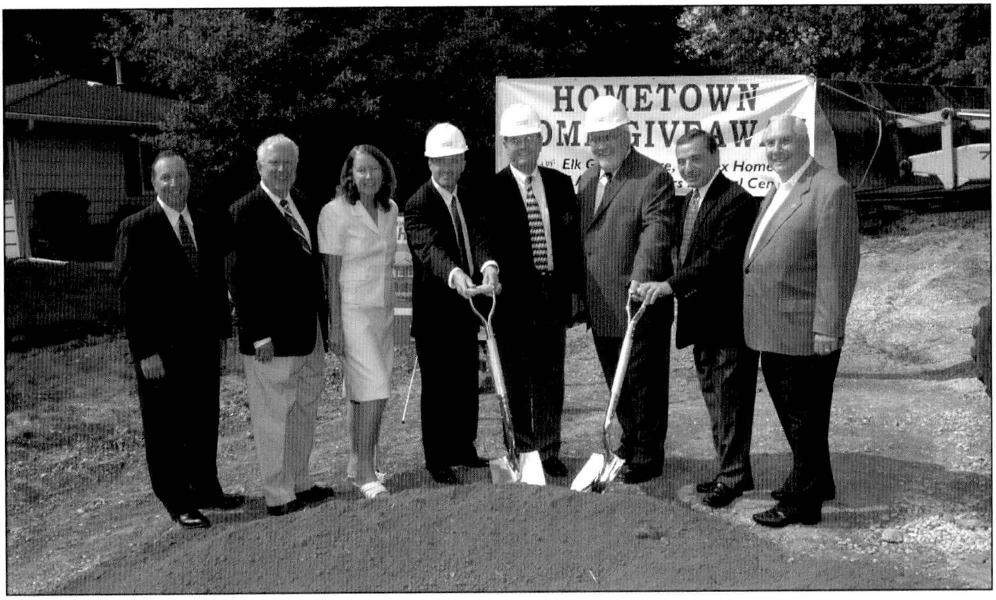

On September 8, 2005, the village hosted the official groundbreaking ceremony for construction of the 50th anniversary Hometown Home Giveaway. From left to right are a Chicago special events unidentified representative, Pat Feichter, Chris Prochno, Mayor Craig Johnson, an unidentified Centex Corporation representative, Alexian Brothers former president Roger Johnson, Sam Lissner, and Jim Petri. Construction of the fully furnished 3,200-square-foot home at 1099 Cheltenham Road began in September 2005.

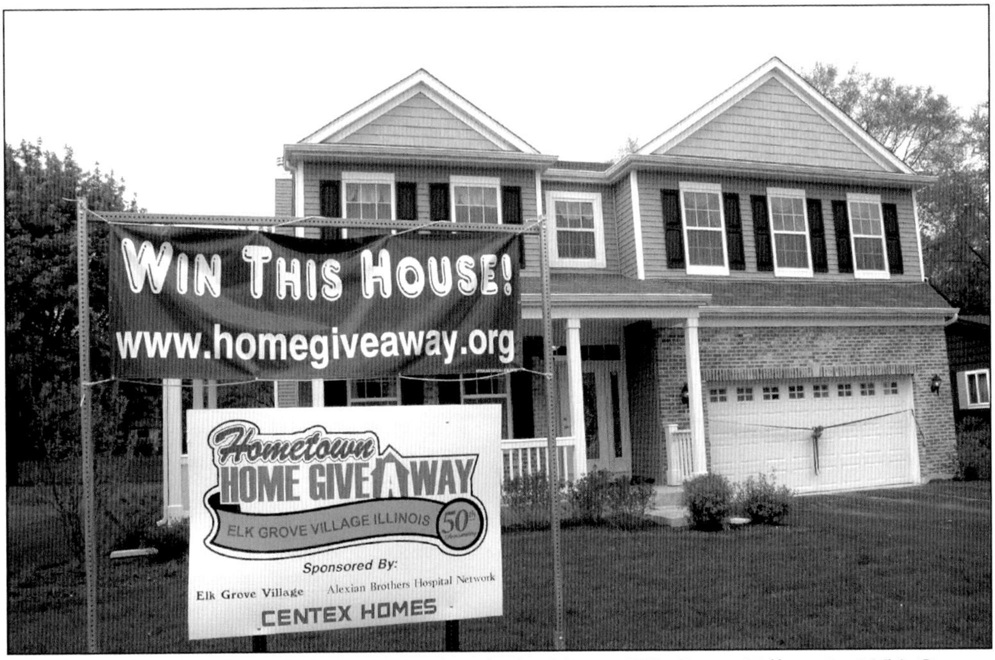

Centex Corporation was very instrumental in the building of Elk Grove Village. In 1956, Centex started building 95 percent of the single-family homes that are in the community today. In 2005, Centex started building the last house that was constructed in Elk Grove. The fully furnished 3,200-square-foot house was valued at $500,000.

The look on her face says it all—their key was the one to unlock the door to their new house. Emil Schiavo picked the key from the fishbowl and handed it to his wife, Barbara, to open the door of possibilities. The Schiavos are longtime residents of Elk Grove Village. Emil is well known for his photography. If there is an event going on, Emil is always there to capture the moment. Mayor Craig Johnson helped officiate the event.

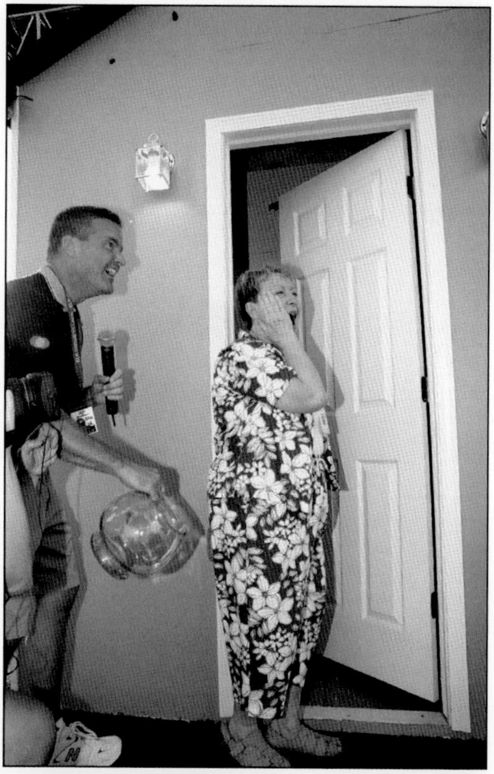

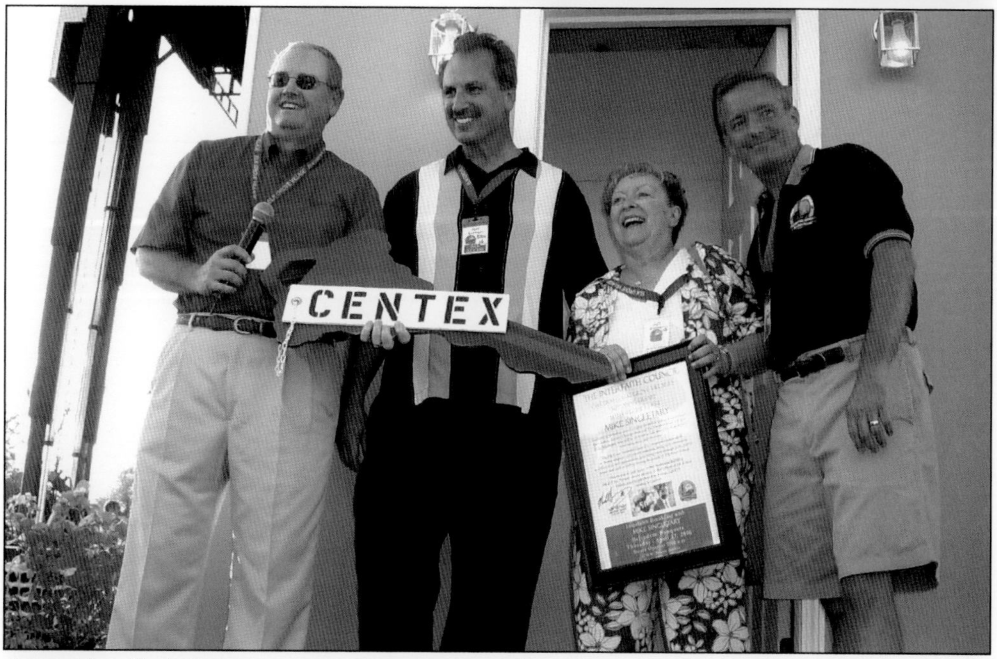

An unidentified Centex representative presents the Schiavos with the key to their new home after Johnson presented a plaque signed by Pro Football Hall of Fame member Michael Singletary. Singletary presented the Interfaith Council plaque to Elk Grove Village in April 2006 at an anniversary event at the Belvedere Banquet Hall on Devon Avenue.

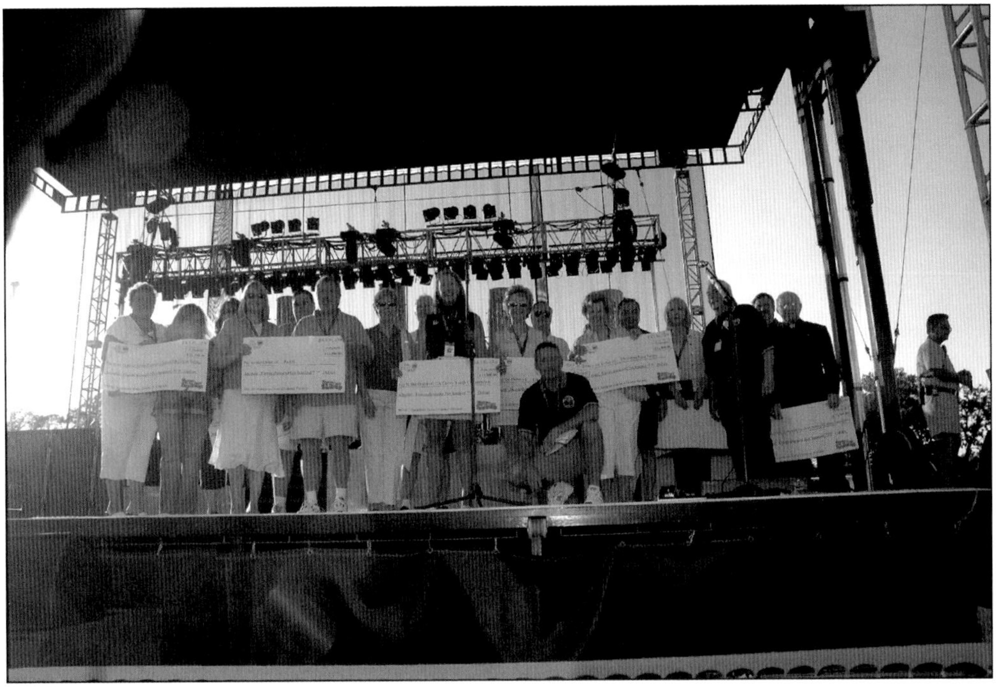

Over a period of eight months, 13,000 raffle tickets were sold for the Hometown Home Giveaway. Tickets were $50 each. Every person who purchased a raffle ticket had his or her name entered into a computer. The computer randomly drew the 10 finalists names that were allowed to pick a key from a fishbowl. Half of the raffle proceeds funded the yearlong activities and the remaining proceeds were given to 11 civic groups. The 10 finalists won $1,000 each and the 11 civic groups received $11,500 each. The checks were presented at the outdoor 50th anniversary celebration.

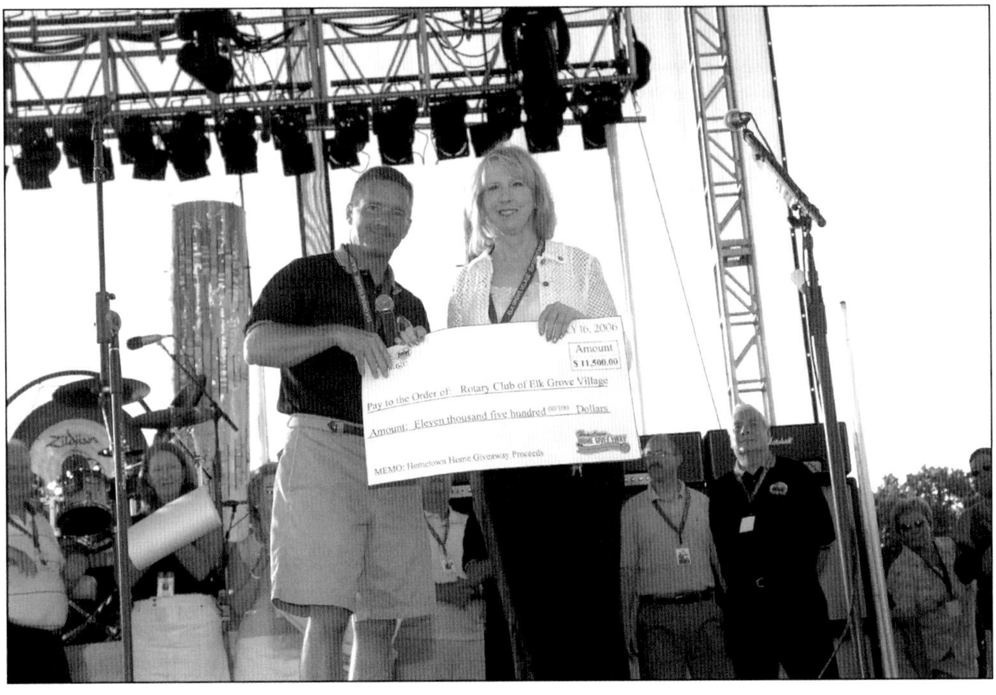

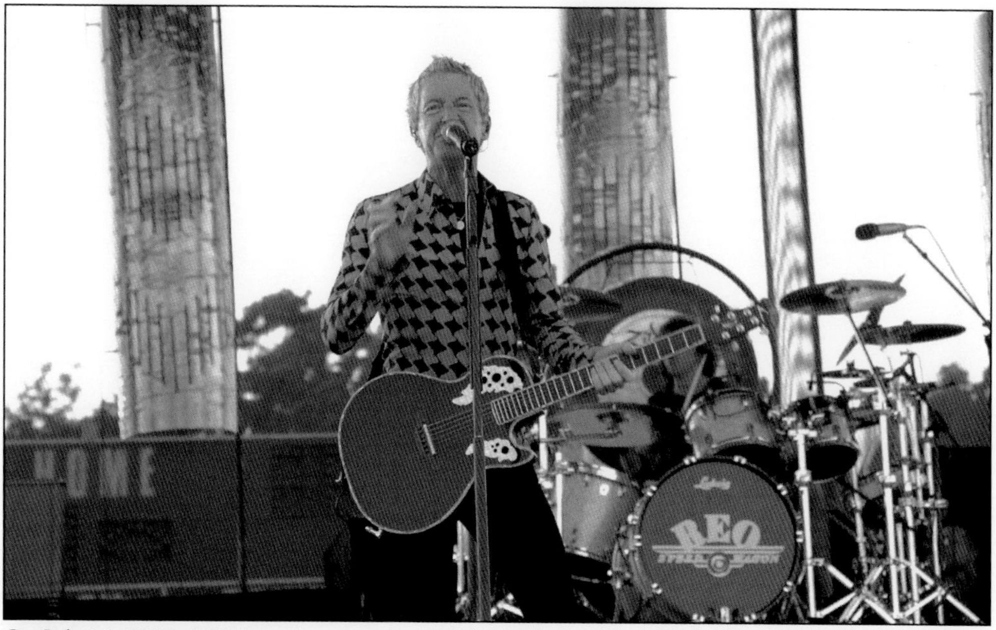

On July 16, 2006, 7,000 residents were treated to a free concert at the Robert Haskell Memorial Stadium at Elk Grove High School. Rock legends REO Speedwagon performed. Residents received free tickets to the concert when they proved their residency in the village. Those in attendance also received free brownies and ice cream. Lead singer Kevin Cronin started the entertainment that lasted for a couple hours.

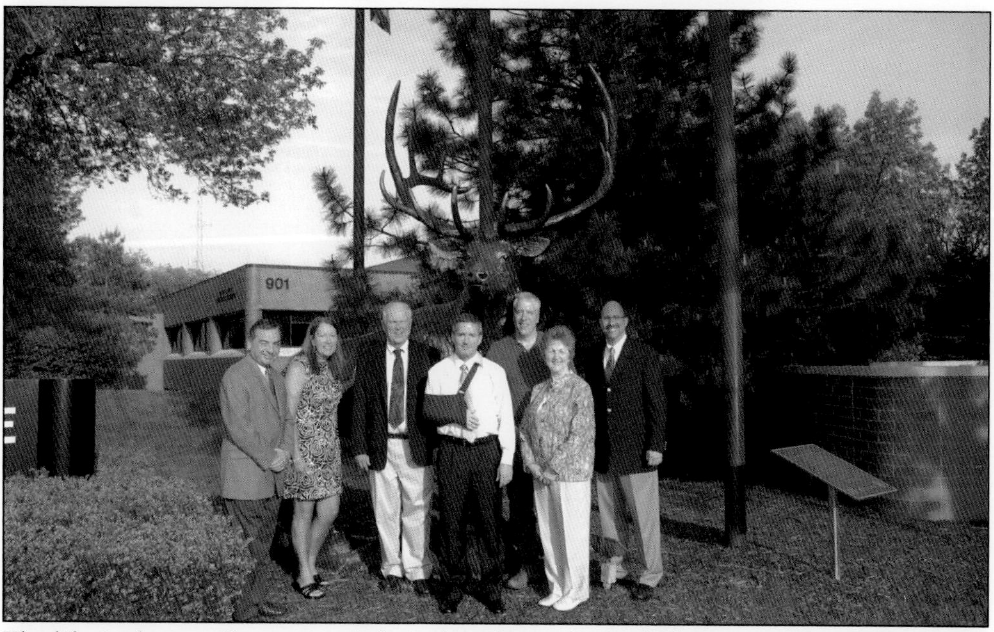

The life-size bronze elk statue is dedicated to the residents of Elk Grove Village following the village's 2006 yearlong 50th anniversary celebration. It resides on the corner of Biesterfield Road and Wellington Avenue in front of the Charles J. Zettek Municipal Building. From left to right, Sam Lissner, Chris Prochno, Pat Feichter, Mayor Craig Johnson, artist Karl Lansing, Nancy Czarnik, and Ray Rummel dedicate the statue on May 8, 2007.

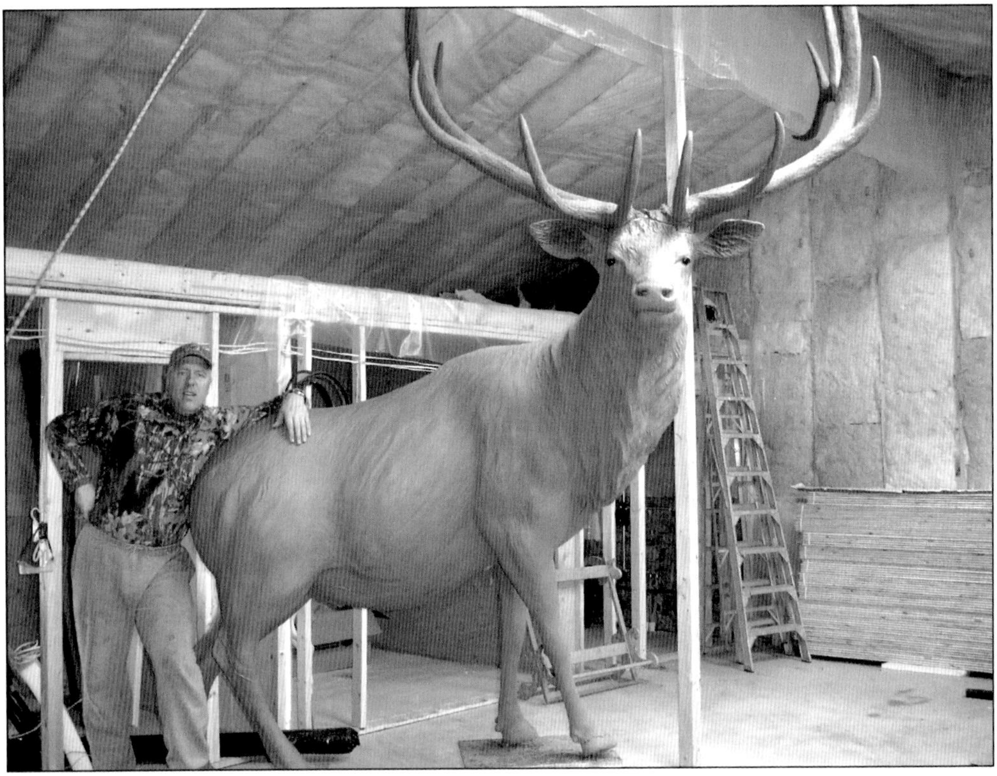

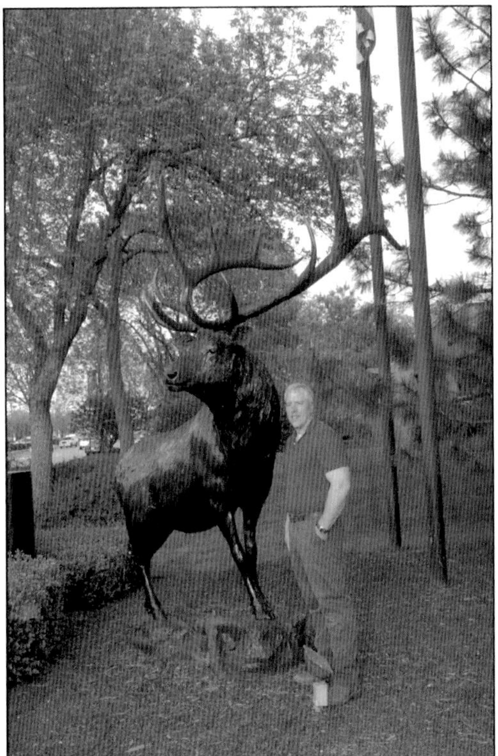

Karl Lansing, a Canadian expert wildlife artist, was hired by the village to create a custom elk sculpture. Specializing in elk pieces, Lansing based his design on a smaller baguette size he created, titled, *Royalty*. He shows his work in progress in his Canadian workshop. "The bronze sculpture is a greater than life-size display, crafted in great detail from many large Elk I see back home in the Rockies. The king of the forest truly comes forth in this display, and I am proud to have been a part of this magnificent work of art in Elk Grove Village."

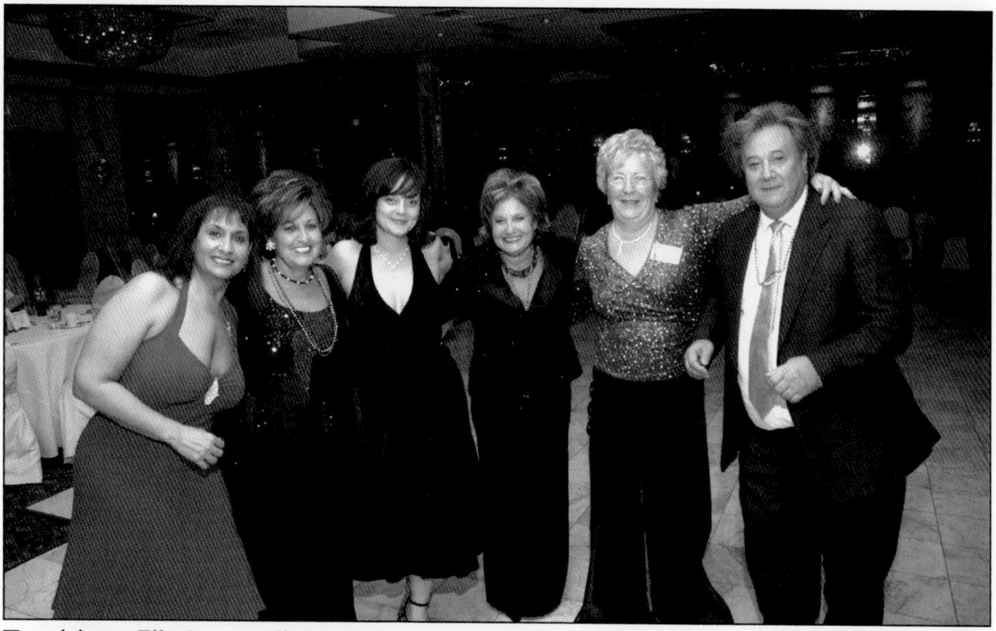

To celebrate Elk Grove Village's 50th anniversary, a formal Mardi Gras dinner dance was held in February 2006. Elk Grove Village Italian Sister Cities members Cindy Aloisio, Gina Sclafani, Mariann Gullo-Krewenka, Maria Gullo, Ellen Peacock, and cofounder and chairman Giovanni Gullo stop their dancing for a quick pose. Members of the Sister Cities organization show their support by attending many Elk Grove Village functions.

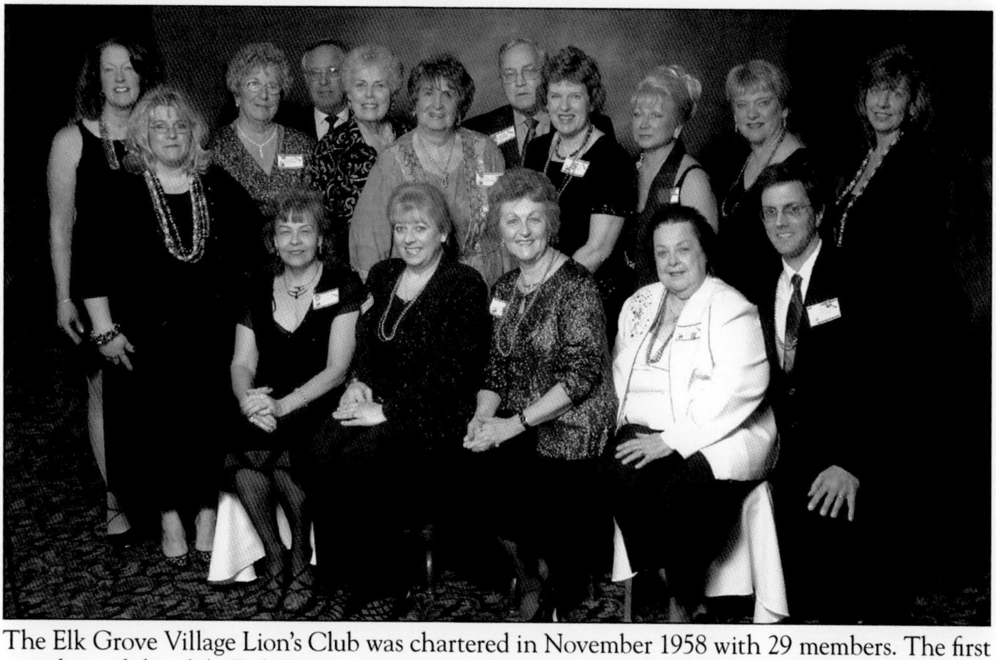

The Elk Grove Village Lion's Club was chartered in November 1958 with 29 members. The first president of the club, Bob Dunn, started the club. The club's contributions include giving the park district Lion's Park, a swimming pool, and a 54-passenger bus. The fire department received two ambulances, and the police department received an evidence van. Members gather at the village's Mardi Gras celebration.

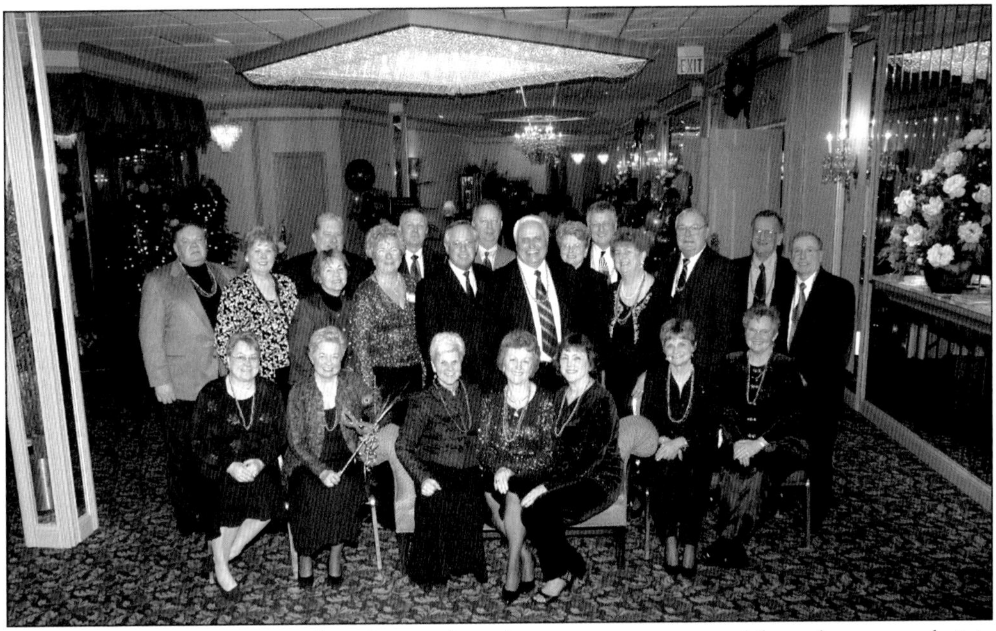

Since 1958, the Elk Grove Village Jaycees have been a training ground for volunteer and civic activities, giving young people between the ages of 18 and 41 the tools they need to build the bridges of success for themselves in the areas of business development, management skills, individual training, community service, and international connections. Once people become 42, they are expected to go and develop their potential in other organizations.

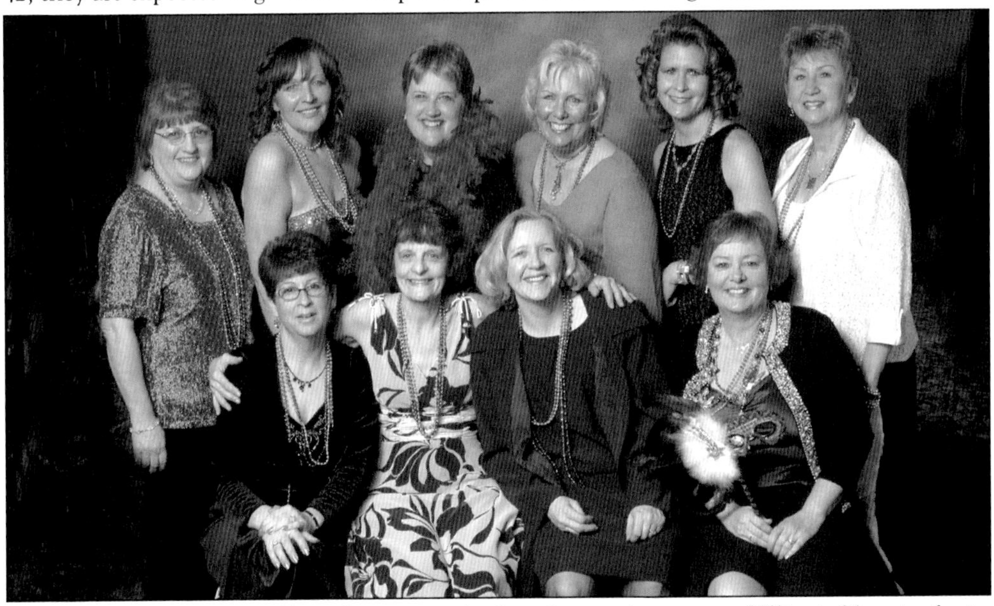

The Elk Grove Village Public Library is ranked in the top 1 percent of Illinois libraries for its services. It takes many dedicated people to keep that ranking. Some of the library representatives take time to celebrate the 50th anniversary at the Mardi Gras dinner in 2006. Pictured from left to right are (first row) Ellen Chromik, Sheryl Dugo, Rose Guban, and Maribeth Devereaux; (second row) Judy Crawley, Jan Chrzan, Donna Mihovilovich, Judy Kennedy, Lisa Malinowski, and Virginia Cavallini.

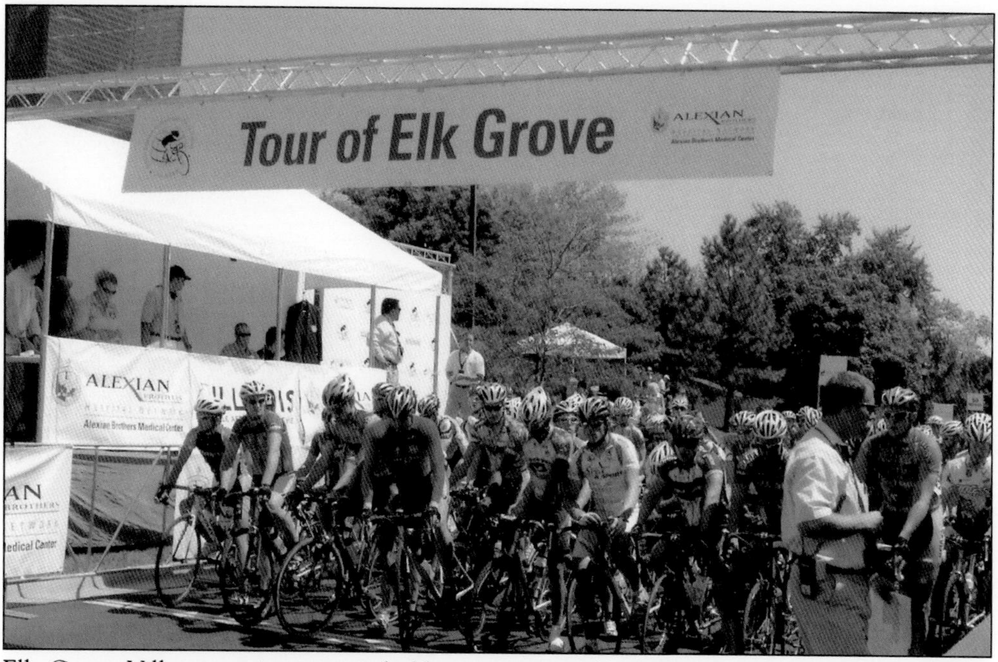

Elk Grove Village continues to uphold its exceptional community title. In 2006, Alexian Brothers Medical Center held the first international cycling classic Tour of Elk Grove in honor of the village's 50th anniversary celebration. This race was held in August on the streets of Elk Grove Village. Professional and amateur athletes from around the world competed for a total cash prize of $153,000 for 14 cycling events. Tour de France cyclist Floyd Landis was one of the acclaimed 68 professional athletes who participated. The overall winner of the first Tour of Elk Grove was Australian Hilton Clarke. Pictured in front of Hilton Clarke holding up his trophy is Giovanni Gullo, owner of Gullo International, who donated $25,000 in prize money.

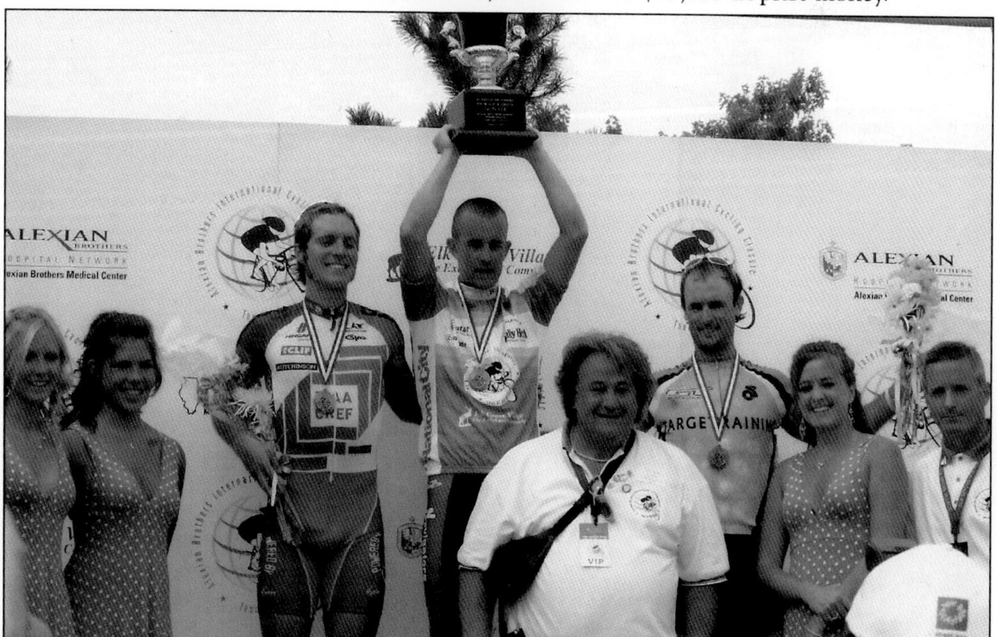

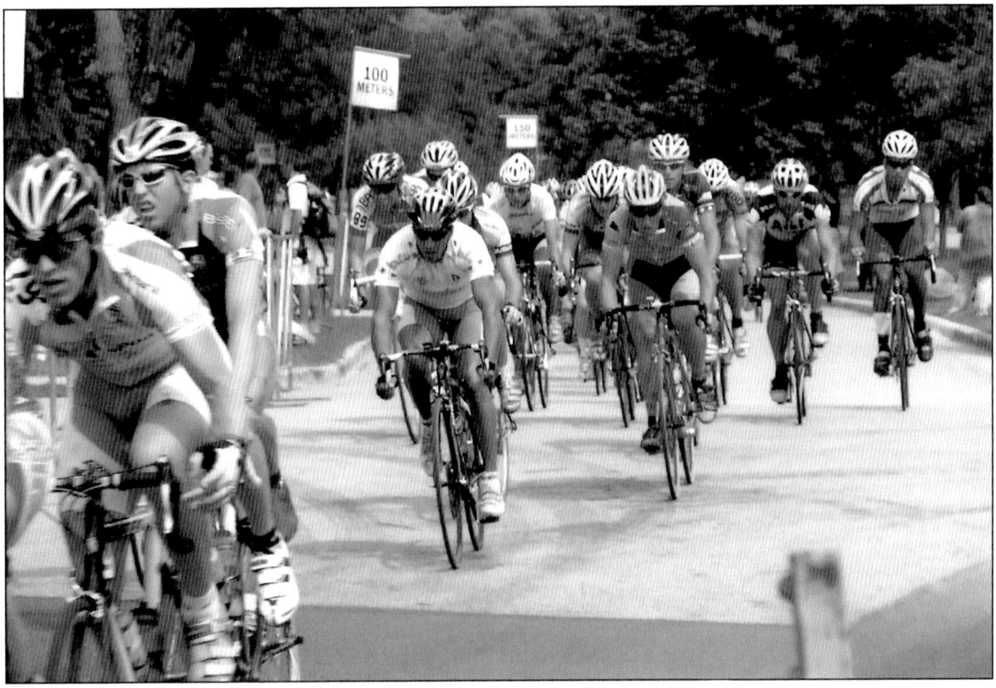

The inaugural, weekend-long Tour of Elk Grove started at Ridge Avenue and Elk Grove Boulevard and took place on the streets of Elk Grove. The prize money made the cycling event one of the largest purses of its kind in the United States. Sixty-eight of the total participants were professional riders. Elk Grove Village Italian Sister Cities were excited to have an Italian rider, Antonio Augetto, from its sister city, Termini Imerese, competing in the race, which is now held annually.

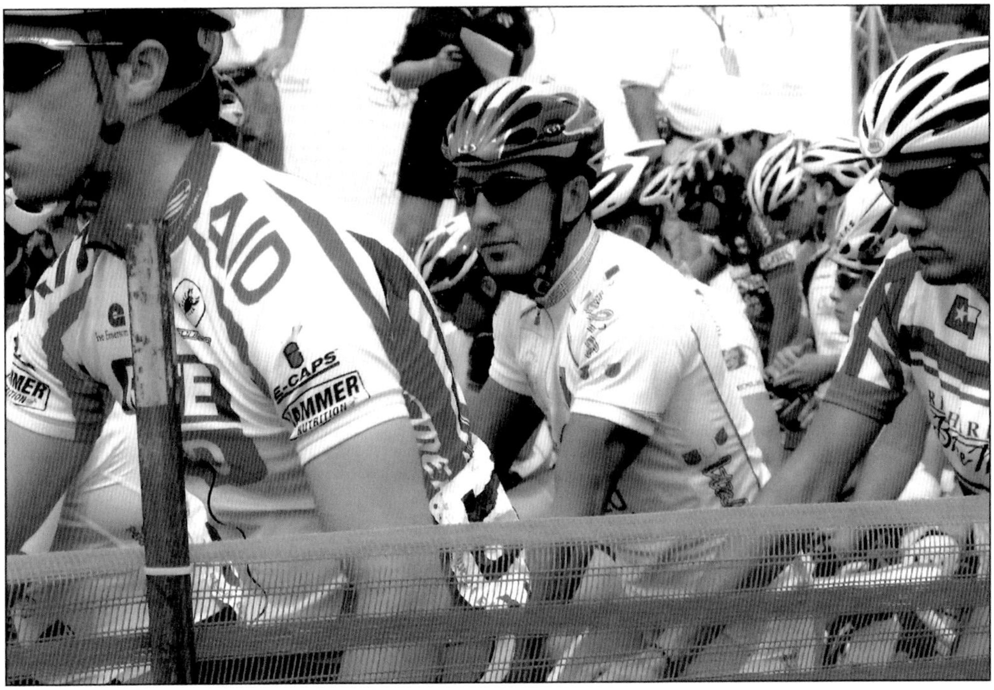

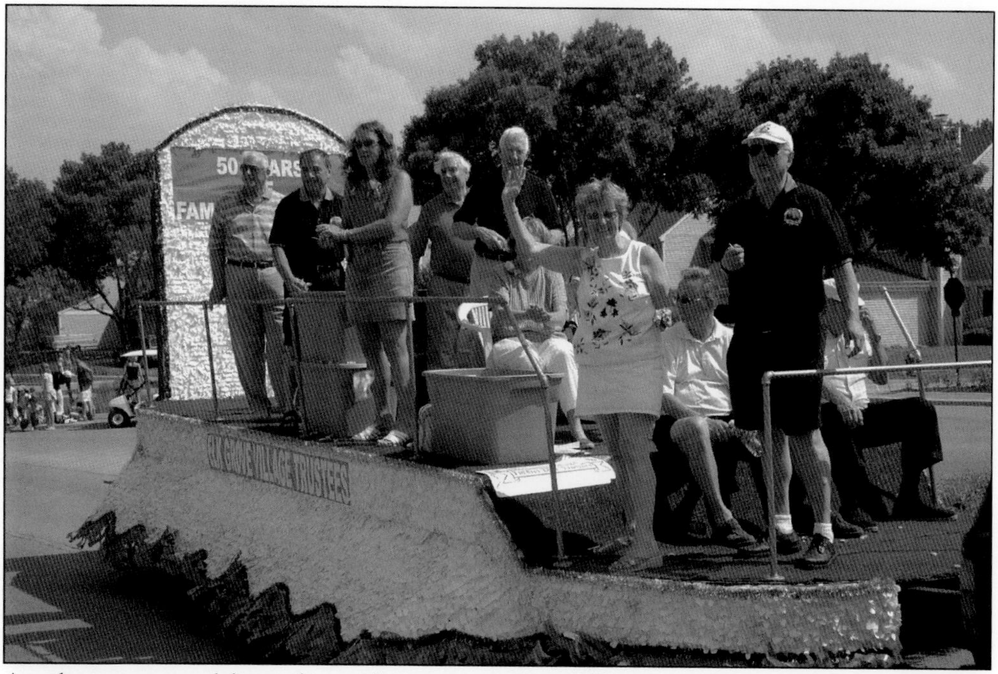

Another event to celebrate the yearlong anniversary of Elk Grove was the 50th Parade. Held in June 2006, residents lined the streets where the parade traveled. One of the floats highlighted the current village trustees and other officials.

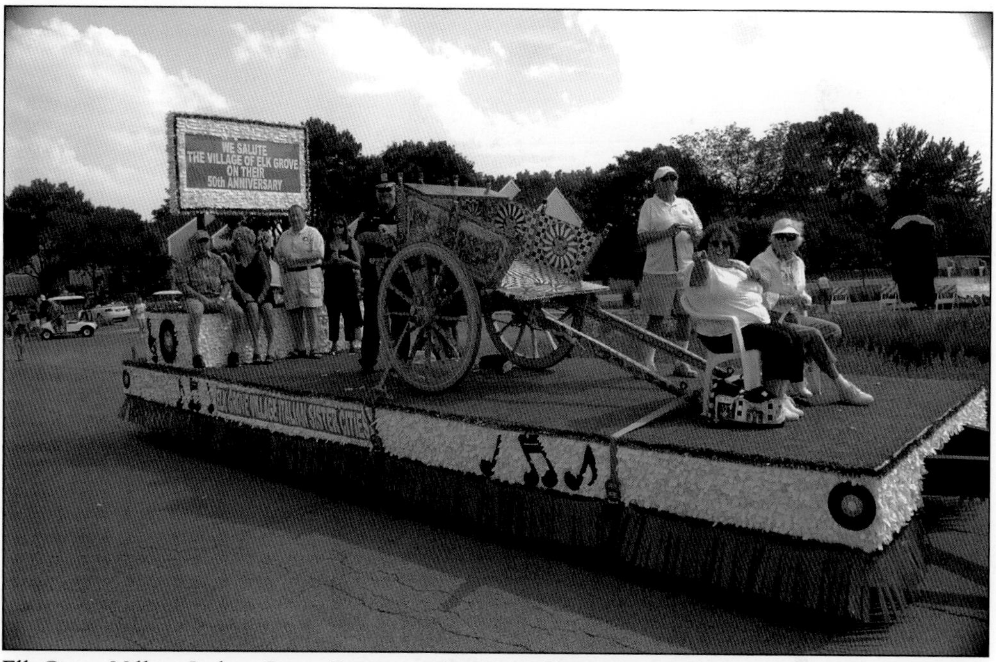

Elk Grove Village Italian Sister Cities members proudly support the hometown parade. Sitting in the back are Sister City members, from left to right, Frank Lateano, Ellen Peacock, Tony Iosco, and Cindy Aloisio. Standing behind the Sicilian cart is Chief Steve Schmidt, and standing in front of the cart is Joe Cimino. Sitting is Linda Czyz and Jan Cimino.

ACROSS AMERICA, PEOPLE ARE DISCOVERING SOMETHING WONDERFUL. *THEIR HERITAGE.*

Arcadia Publishing is the leading local history publisher in the United States. With more than 3,000 titles in print and hundreds of new titles released every year, Arcadia has extensive specialized experience chronicling the history of communities and celebrating America's hidden stories, bringing to life the people, places, and events from the past. To discover the history of other communities across the nation, please visit:

www.arcadiapublishing.com

Customized search tools allow you to find regional history books about the town where you grew up, the cities where your friends and family live, the town where your parents met, or even that retirement spot you've been dreaming about.

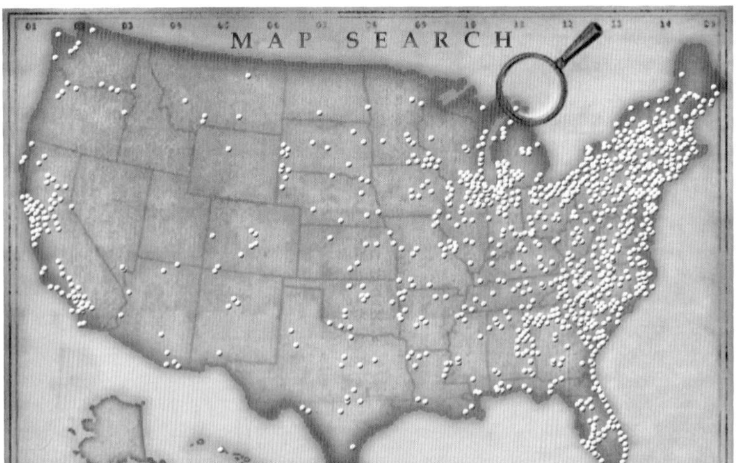